FERRIES

BRITISH ISLES AND NORTHE

C000175608

ISBN 978-1-906608-90-3

Ferry Publications, PO Box 33,
Ramsey, Isle of Man IM99 4LP

Email: ferrypubs@manx.net   Website: www.ferrypubs.co.uk

europe's **leading** guide to the ferry industry

contents...

Condor Liberation (*Kevin Mitchell*)

europe's **leading** guide to the ferry industry
introduction...

This is the twenty-eighth edition of this book, which first appeared in 1983 as the 24-page 'home published' 'Car Ferries from Great Britain and Ireland'. The book aims to list every passenger/vehicle ferry in Great Britain and Ireland, ro-ro freight vessels which operate regular services between Great Britain and Ireland and to nearby Continental destinations and major passenger/vehicle ferries in other parts of Northern Europe. The coverage of Northern Europe is not fully comprehensive (to make it so would probably triple the size of the book) and does not include freight-only operations and vessels - although freight-only vessels have been included where the operators also run passenger services. Ro-ro vessels engaged in 'deep-sea' trade and those operated solely for the carriage of trade cars or paper are also not included.

Each operator is listed alphabetically within sections - major operators, minor operators, freight-only operators, chain, cable and float ferries, passenger-only ferries, other North European passenger operators and vehicle/passenger vessels owned by companies not currently engaged in operating services. After details relating to each company's management, address, telephone numbers, email, website and services, there is a fleet list with technical data and then a potted history of each vessel with previous names and dates.

Each operator was sent the draft text relating to them in March. Where they have not responded, I have attempted to ensure that any telephone, fax and email details match what is quoted on their website but management details may not be 100% accurate.

January 2015 saw the introduction of new emissions regulation in several areas which has resulted in considerable cost for the ferry industry. Some operators have switched to more expensive marine diesel whilst others have installed catalytic scrubbers in order that they can continue to use the cheapest fuel. Stena Line are switching some ships to methanol and new ships using LNG (liquid natural gas) have either been delivered are on order. In the longer term perhaps liquid hydrogen might come into its own. The new rules and the consequent rise in costs led, at the end of September, to the ending of DFDS Seaways' Harwich - Esbjerg service, the UK's last passenger link with Scandinavia.

Whitstable, Kent

Nick Widdows

June 2015

europe's **leading** guide to the ferry industry

foreword...

Having just taken the helm at Irish Ferries, it is a real pleasure to be asked to write the foreword for this important annual publication. Overall, in a recent Oxford Economics study it was calculated that for every €1 million of GDP which the shipping industry generates, another €1.6 million elsewhere is created in the EU economy. Clearly the economic value of the EU ferries industry remains critical and cannot be overestimated. Indeed, Irish Ferries' contribution to the open economy of Ireland is significant and it is estimated that the value of products exported from Ireland on our services is currently over €10 billion on an annual basis. I believe that we are all hugely important for imports and exports in our own individual markets and, as an industry, we must continue to state as much at every opportunity.

Andrew Sheen

I believe it has never been truer to say that we are weathering an environmental regulatory storm. Obviously, there has been an impact with a number of the long sea marginal routes having been forced to close in the last 12 months, although the impact has undoubtedly softened with reduced oil prices (who could have foreseen that one year ago!?) but for how long? There is interesting research and development in various fuel and abatement technologies on-going. However, without serious impact assessments how can regulatory certainty be assured?

As we must, we will recover from this period of adjustment and I know that we will use the opportunity to ensure a more sustainable future for the ferry industry. This will include being vocal about our green credentials, especially when compared with those of the airlines.

It is against this backdrop that we must continue to find ways to engage our younger passengers and show them the many great benefits of ferry travel versus air travel. Maybe, this is something we can all commit towards knowing that our future viability will always rely upon our customers of tomorrow.

With the aforementioned route changes I would hope that you find Ferries 2016 a valuable source of information and would finally sign off by offering my best wishes for the coming year.

Andrew Sheen
Managing Director, Irish Ferries

Isle of Inishmore. (FotoFlite)

a **guide** to using
this book

Sections Listing is in seven sections. *Section 1* - Services from Great Britain and Ireland to the Continent and between Great Britain and Ireland (including services to/from the Isle of Man and Channel Islands), *Section 2* - Domestic services within Great Britain and Ireland, *Section 3* - Freight-only services from Great Britain and Ireland and domestic routes, *Section 4* - Minor vehicle ferries in Great Britain and Ireland (chain and cable ferries etc), *Section 5* - Major passenger-only operators, *Section 6* - Major car ferry operators in Northern Europe, *Section 7* - Companies not operating regular services possessing vehicle ferries which may be chartered or sold to other operators.

Order The company order within each section is alphabetical. Note that the definite article and words meaning 'company' or 'shipping company' (eg. 'AG', 'Reederei') do not count. However, where this is part of a ship's name it does count. Sorting is by normal English convention eg. 'Å' is treated the same as 'A' and comes at the start, not as a separate character which comes at the end of the alphabet as is the Scandinavian convention. Where ships are numbered, order is by number whether the number is expressed in Arabic or Latin digits.

Listing of Ships When a ship owned by a company listed in this book is on charter to another company listed, then she is shown under the company which operates her. When a ship owned by a company listed in this book is on charter to another company not listed, then she is shown under the company which owns her.

IMO Number All ships of 100t or greater (except vessels solely engaged in fishing, ships without mechanical means of propulsion (eg. chain ferries), pleasure yachts, ships engaged on special service (eg. lightships), hopper barges, hydrofoils, air cushion vehicles, floating docks and structures classified in a similar manner, warships and troopships, wooden ships) are required to be registered by the International Maritime Organisation (IMO), an agency of the United Nations. The number is retained by the ship throughout her life, however much the vessel is rebuilt. This number is now required to be displayed on the ship externally and on top so that it can be read from the air. The scheme is administered by Lloyd's Register-Fairplay, who maintain a database of all ships in excess of 100t (with some exceptions), not just those classified through them.

Company Information This section gives general information regarding the status of the company. That is, nationality, whether it is public or private sector and whether it is part of a larger group.

Management The Managing Director and Marketing Director or Manager of each company are listed. Where these posts do not exist, other equivalent people are listed. Where only initials are given, that person is, as far as is known, male.

Address This is the address of the company's administrative headquarters. In the case of some international companies, British and overseas addresses are given.

Telephone and Fax Numbers are expressed as follows: + [*number*] (this is the international dialling code which is dialled in combination with the number dialled for international calls (00 in the UK, Ireland and most other European countries); it is not used for calling within the country), ([*number*]) (this is the number which precedes area codes when making long-distance domestic calls - it is not dialled when calling from another country or making local calls (not all countries have this)), [*number*] (this is the rest of the number including, where appropriate, the area dialling code). UK '08' numbers are sometimes not available from overseas and the full number must be dialled in all circumstances.

Internet Email addresses and **Website** URLs are given where these are available; the language(s) used is shown. The language listed first is that which appears on the home page when accessed from a UK based computer; the others follow in alphabetical order. In a few cases Email facility is only available through the Website. To avoid confusion, there is no other punctuation on the Internet line.

Routes operated After each route there are, in brackets, details of 1 normal journey time, 2 regular vessel(s) used on the route (number as in list of vessels) and 3 frequencies (where a number per day is given, this relates to return sailings). In the case of freight-only sailings which operate to a regular schedule, departure times are given where they have been supplied. Please note that times are subject to quite frequent change and cancellation.

Winter and Summer In this book, Winter generally means the period between October and Easter while Summer means Easter to October. The peak Summer period is generally June, July and August. In Scandinavia, the Summer peak ends in mid-August whilst in the UK it starts rather later and generally stretches into the first or second week of September. Dates vary according to operator.

Spelling The convention is used in respect of town and country names is that English names are used for towns and areas of countries where such names exist (eg. Gothenburg rather than Göteborg) and English names for countries (eg. Germany rather than Deutschland). Otherwise local names are used, accented as appropriate. In a few cases, English names have slipped out of common usage and the local name is more commonly used in Britain, ie Dunkerque not Dunkirk, Helsingør not Elsinore and Vlissingen not Flushing. Many towns in Finland have both Finnish and Swedish names; we have used the Finnish name except in the case of Åland which is a Swedish-speaking area. In the case of Danish towns, the alternative use of 'å' or 'aa' follows local convention. The following towns, islands and territories are expressed using their English names - the local name is shown following: Antwerp - Antwerpen/Anvers, Fyn - Funen, Genoa - Génova, Ghent - Gent, Gothenburg - Göteborg, Hook of Holland - Hoek van Holland, Jutland - Jylland, Copenhagen - København, Ostend - Oostende, Oporto - Porto, Seville - Sevilla, Sealand - Sjælland and Venice - Venezia.

Terms The following words mean *'shipping company'* in various languages: Redereja (Latvian), Rederi (Danish, Norwegian, Swedish), Rederij (Dutch), Reederei (German) and Zegluga (Polish). The following words mean *'limited company'*: AB - Aktiebolaget (Swedish) (Finnish companies who use both the Finnish and Swedish terms sometimes express it as Ab), AG - Aktiengesellschaft (German), AS - Aksjeselskap (Norwegian), A/S - Aktie Selskabet (Danish), BV - Besloten Vennootschap (Dutch), GmbH - Gesellschaft mit beschränkter Haftung (German), NV - Naamloze Vennootschap (Dutch), Oy - (Finnish), Oyj - (Finnish (plc)) and SA - Société Anonyme (French).

Types of Ferry

These distinctions are necessarily general and many ships will have features of more than one category.

Car Ferry Until about 1970, most vehicle ferries were primarily designed for the conveyance of cars and their passengers and foot passengers. Little regard was paid to the conveyance of lorries and trailers, since this sort of traffic had not begun to develop. Few vessels of this type are still in service.

Multi-purpose Ferry From about 1970 onwards vehicle ferries began to make more provision for freight traffic, sharing the same ship with passengers and cars. Features usually include higher vehicle decks, often with retractable mezzanine decks, enabling two levels of cars or one level of freight and coaches, and separate facilities (including cabins on quite short crossings) for freight drivers.

Cruise Ferry In the 1980s the idea of travelling on a ferry, not just to get from A to B but for the pleasure of the travel experience, became more and more popular and ferries were built with increasingly luxurious and varied passenger accommodation. Such vessels also convey cars and freight but the emphasis is on passenger accommodation with a high level of berths (sometimes providing berths for all passengers).

Ro-pax Ferry A vessel designed primarily for the carriage of freight traffic but which also carries a limited number of ordinary passengers. Features generally include a moderate passenger capacity - up to about 500 passengers - and a partly open upper vehicle deck. Modern ro-pax vessels are becoming increasingly luxurious with facilities approaching those of a cruise ferry.

Ro-ro Ferry A vessel designed for the conveyance of road freight, unaccompanied trailers and containers on low trailers (known as 'Mafis' although often made by other manufacturers). Some such vessels have no passenger accommodation but the majority can accommodate up to 12 passengers - the maximum allowed without a passenger certificate. On routes where there is a low level of driver-accompanied traffic (mainly the longer ones), ordinary passengers, with or without cars, can sometimes be conveyed. On routes with a high level of driver-accompanied traffic, passenger capacity will sometimes be higher but facilities tend to be geared to the needs of freight drivers eg. lounge with video, high level of cabins on routes of three hours or more. Technically such vessels are passenger ferries (having a passenger certificate).

Con-ro Many ro-ro vessels are capable of having ISO (International Standards Organisation) containers crane-loaded on the upper 'weather' deck. In this book the term con-ro applies only to vessels whose upper deck can only take containers and has no vehicle access.

Fast Ferry Streamlined vessel of catamaran or monohull construction, speed in excess of 30 knots, water jet propulsion, generally aluminium-built but some have steel hulls, little or no freight capacity and no cabins.

Timescale Although the book goes to press in June 2015, I have sought to reflect the situation as it will exist in early Summer 2015 with regard to the introduction of new ships or other known changes. Vessels due to enter service after July 2015 are shown as '**Under Construction**'. The book is updated at all stages of the production process where this is feasible, although major changes once the text has been paginated are not possible; there is also a 'Late News' section on page 216 for changes which cannot be incorporated into the text.

List of vessels

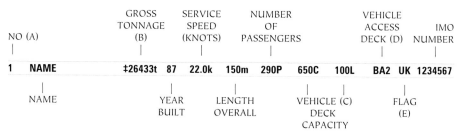

NO (A)	GROSS TONNAGE (B)	SERVICE SPEED (KNOTS)	NUMBER OF PASSENGERS		VEHICLE ACCESS DECK (D)	IMO NUMBER
1 NAME	‡26433t 87	22.0k	150m 290P	650C 100L	BA2 UK	1234567
	NAME	YEAR BUILT	LENGTH OVERALL	VEHICLE (C) DECK CAPACITY	FLAG (E)	

(A) » = fast ferry, • = vessel laid up, F = freight-only vessel (max 12 passengers), F‡ = freight-only vessel (with passenger certificate), p = passenger-only vessel

(B) C = Cars, L = Lorries (**15m**), T = Trailers (**13.5m**), r = can also take rail wagons, - = No figure quoted.

(C) B = Bow, A = Aft, S = Side, Q = Quarterdeck, R = Slewing ramp, 2 = Two decks can be loaded at the same time, C = Vehicles must be crane-loaded aboard, t = turntable ferry.

AG = Antigua and Barbuda	DK = Denmark	IR = Irish Republic	PT = Portugal
AL = Åland Islands	EE = Estonia	LU = Luxembourg	PL = Poland
BB = Barbados	ES = Spain	LT = Lithuania	RU = Russia
BE = Belgium	FO = Faroes	LV = Latvia	SG = Singapore
BM = Bermuda	FI = Finland	MD = Madeira	SE = Sweden
BS = Bahamas	FR = France	MT = Malta	UK = United Kingdom
CY = Cyprus	GI = Gibraltar	NL = Netherlands	
DE = Germany	IM = Isle of Man	NO = Norway	
	IT = Italy	PA = Panama	

(D) The following abbreviations are used:

In the notes ships are in CAPITAL LETTERS, shipping lines and other institutions are in *italics*.

Capacity In this book, capacities shown are the maxima. Sometimes vessels operate at less than their maximum passenger capacity due to reduced crewing or to operating on a route on which they are not permitted to operate above a certain level. Car and lorry/trailer capacities are the maximum for either type. The two figures are not directly comparable. Some parts of a vessel may allow cars on two levels to occupy the space that a trailer or lorry occupies on one level, some may not; some parts of a vessel with low headroom may only be accessible to cars. All figures have to be approximate.

Ownership The ownership of many vessels is very complicated. Some are actually owned by finance companies and banks, some by subsidiary companies of the shipping lines, some by subsidiary companies of a holding company of which the shipping company is also a subsidiary and some by companies which are jointly owned by the shipping company and other interests like a bank, set up specifically to own one ship or a group of ships. In all these cases the vessel is technically chartered to the shipping company. However, in this book, only those vessels chartered from one shipping company to another or from a ship-owning company unconnected with the shipping line are recorded as being on charter. Vessels are listed under the current operator rather than the owner. Charter is 'bareboat' (without crew) unless otherwise stated. If chartered with crew, vessels are 'time-chartered'.

Gross Tonnage This is a measure of enclosed capacity rather than weight, based on a formula of one gross ton = 100 cubic feet. Even small alterations can alter the gross tonnage. Under old measurement systems, the capacity of enclosed car decks was not included but, under the 1969 Convention, all vessels laid down after 1982 have been measured by a new system which includes enclosed vehicle decks as enclosed space, thereby considerably increasing the tonnage of vehicle ferries. Under this Convention, from 1st January 1995 all vessels were due to be re-measured under this system. Tonnages quoted here are, where possible, those given by the shipping companies themselves.

The following people are gratefully thanked for their assistance with this publication, many of them in ferry companies in the UK and abroad: Gary Andrews, John Bryant, Cees de Bijl, Andrew Cooke, Matthew Davies, Matthew Punter, Ian Hall, Peter Thirkildsen, Ian Smith (The Camrose Organisation), and Gomer Press.

Whilst every effort has been made to ensure that the facts contained here are correct, neither the publishers nor the writer can accept any responsibility for errors contained herein. We would, however, appreciate comments from readers, which we will endeavour to reflect in the next edition which we plan to publish in summer 2016.

IRISH FERRIES – THE STORY SO FAR

The Irish Continental Group story goes back to 17th May 1968 when the first direct Rosslare-Le Havre car ferry sailing took place. This first venture, of one round trip sailing per week using the Dragon and Leopard, was a joint Anglo-French operation provided by Normandy Ferries, part of the P&O group, in partnership with French shipping line SAGA, owned by the Rothschild family. In its first season, the new service carried 31,000 passengers.

The following year sailings were increased to two per week between mid-June and mid-August. Public reaction was enthusiastic with the result that 1969 passenger carryings more than doubled to 68,000, and the Dragon and Leopard continued to operate during the 1970 and 1971 seasons with two sailings per week during the summer peak. Just as the service was maturing, it came to an abrupt end. In planning their 1972 schedules, Normandy Ferries found that they required both the vessels exclusively on their English Channel services in order to retain their competitive position. Given the short notice, it was impossible to charter suitable replacement ships for the route with the result there was no Ireland-France service.

Behind the scenes, frantic efforts were being made to re-establish the service on a sounder footing, one that would have its commercial roots in Ireland. Consequently, in 1972, the then Government requested B&I Line and Irish Shipping to consider the possibility of re-opening the service; the request was answered by Irish Shipping.

Irish Shipping had a fascinating history in its own right. In 1940, the first full year of World War II, the Irish Government led by Taoiseach Eamonn De Valera was experiencing difficulty chartering ships to bring essential supplies to Ireland. A decision was taken to establish Irish Shipping as the national shipping line. Operations began in March 1941 and by the end of that year they had performed heroic service transporting essential supplies into Ireland, utilising ships that had been chartered for this purpose. After the War in 1945, the company began to return its chartered vessels and, by 1948, had begun to acquire its own, newly-built fleet. By 1972, when the decision was made to restart the Rosslare-Le Havre service, Irish Shipping was a substantial shipping company with 31 years' service.

IRISH CONTINENTAL LINE FORMED

In order to implement their plan, Irish Shipping established a new company, Irish Continental Line, in partnership with other Irish and Scandinavian interests. Irish Shipping held a 30% shareholding, Lion Ferry of Sweden and the Norwegian shipping company Fearnley & Egar held 25% each while Aerlod Teo, a subsidiary of Coras Iompair Eireann (CIE), held the remaining 20%. A ferry with 547 berths and space for 210 cars which was then under construction for Lion Ferry was duly purchased for the Rosslare-Le Havre service and on 17th January 1972 the *Saint Patrick* was launched at the shipyard of Schichau Unterweser in Bremerhaven, Germany.

On 31st May1973 the *Saint Patrick* arrived at Rosslare for the first time, flying the Irish flag. Immediately, she began regular scheduled sailings to France, beginning with three round trips per week increasing to every second day in each direction during July and August. The new service operated until the end of December 1973. Thereafter, it became an all-year-round operation.

Three years after the new service was started, the Scandinavian involvement in Irish Continental Line was to draw to a close. In 1977 Irish Shipping bought out the Lion Ferry and Fearnley & Egar shareholdings to become 80% owners of the company while CIE continued to hold the balance. In the same year Irish control was further consolidated when ownership of the *Saint Patrick* transferred from Irish Shipping to Irish Continental Line. This was a far-sighted move that was to prove itself during the liquidation of Irish Shipping in the mid-1980s.

SAINT KILLIAN ENTERS SERVICE

After the transfer of the *Saint Patrick* to Irish Continental Line ownership, a decision was made to purchase a second vessel for the link; built in 1973 in Yugoslavia for Stena Line, she was purchased and came into service between Ireland and France in 1978 as the *Saint Killian*. She offered a substantial increase in capacity on the route with over 1,400 berths and 490 car spaces. Now, for the first time, Irish Continental Line could offer during the summer of 1978 a daily service between Rosslare and France.

In 1964 B & I introduced the first of their new multi-purpose car ferries the *Munster* on the Liverpool-Dublin service. *(FotoFlite)*

In 1973 the *Saint Patrick* open regular sailings between Ireland and France. *(FotoFlite)*

The *Saint Killian* also enabled the company to open a second route from Rosslare to Cherbourg with a sailing time of 17 hours, four hours shorter than the run to Le Havre. This service was aimed at holidaymakers heading for Brittany and Western France. Despite the successes, it was not always plain sailing and, by the winter of 1978, Irish Continental Line had suffered a decline in trade due to the state of the international economy. Traffic fell and costs rose. In the early days of the route, facilities at Rosslare were not as finely developed as they are today; ships had to be refuelled in France where prices rose by 20%, amounting to a £10,000 a day fuel bill for the two ships, increases which then proved a heavy burden for the company.

BELFAST-LIVERPOOL SERVICE

Once the company surmounted the difficulties of the late 1970s, it was able to plan ahead. Two fundamental decisions were made: to start a Belfast-Liverpool car ferry service and to 'jumboize' the *Saint Killian*.

The Belfast-Liverpool service had been in operation for over 100 years. After the withdrawal of P&O from the service, Irish Continental Line decided to take over the route, restarting it as Belfast Car Ferries on 1st May 1982. The *Saint Patrick*, which started the Rosslare-Le Havre run in 1973, was transferred to the Belfast-Liverpool service and renamed *Saint Colum I*. In the early years, the outlook for the Belfast-Liverpool service was promising. In 1984, for instance, the *Saint Colum I* made 350 voyages, carried 208,000 passengers, 46,056 cars and 7,108 freight units with a total of 19,000 trade cars also being carried, a quarter of all the trade cars imported into Northern Ireland that year, but gradually the economics of the service became worse. In the face of competition from other routes, and with no hope of improvement, the service was finally closed down in October 1990 and the ship sold to Greek owners.

SAINT KILLIAN JUMBOISED

A Dutch shipyard was appointed to 'jumboize' the *Saint Killian* by cutting her in two and adding a new 32-metre mid-section at a cost of IR£7.5 million. The contract, which took just three months to complete, added enormously to the overall carrying capacity of the vessel. Berths were increased from 800 to 1,400 and car spaces from 200 to 300. Following this work she was renamed the *Saint Killian II* and returned to the Ireland-France services.

To replace the *Saint Patrick* on the Ireland-France route, Irish Continental Line purchased the Viking Line vessel *Aurella* at a cost of 16.5 million. She was refitted in Amsterdam and renamed *Saint Patrick II* prior to joining *Saint Killian II* on the Ireland-France service.

In 1983, a third summer service came into operation from Ireland to France on the Cork-Le Havre route, with sailings from the end of June to the end of August. This new route proved popular with Irish holidaymakers and with French and other Continental visitors wishing to arrive closer to their holiday destinations in Counties Cork and Kerry.

While Irish Continental Line was growing the market year-on-year with improvements in traffic, the other part of the Group was not doing so well. In 1979 and 1980 a series of charter deals for Irish Shipping vessels was arranged in Hong Kong, commitments that were considered financially ruinous for the company. Irish Shipping was trading against a dismal world economic background which made freight carrying an unprofitable proposition. When the then Government decided to place Irish Shipping into liquidation towards the end of 1984, there was a public outcry with calls that Ireland was being deprived of a strategically important deep sea fleet, one that had proved its worth for over 40 years in conditions of war and peace. Despite these calls, the Government proceeded with the liquidation of Irish Shipping that became effective in November 1984.

This immediately placed Irish Continental Line management in a quandary: their company had enjoyed a successful, profitable trading record, but it was largely owned by Irish Shipping and had now become part of the liquidation process. Despite this, the company continued to trade as a going concern with the Irish Shipping liquidation having little practical effect. For two-and-a-half years, Irish Continental Line carried on in a state of uncertainty in an interregnum between ownership.

Finding a buyer for what was a financially sound operation proved slow and frustrating with legalities over title and other matters having to be resolved. It was not until Christmas 1985 that advertisements appeared in the national press inviting purchase offers. The scramble to settle the ownership of the company was only just beginning. In January 1986 B&I Line placed a valuation of £7 million on Irish Continental Line and led the bidding. In all, 24 potential bidders emerged, including a consortium of freight companies. During the course of 1986 two bids materialized from groups within the management of Irish Continental Line itself.

Complex taxation matters concerning the ownership of the two vessels used on the Rosslare-France routes were another complication that had to be resolved. In November 1986 sole ownership of the two Irish Continental Line vessels was acquired, a move which cleared the way for the completion of the sale which took place in March 1987 when a consortium of institutional investors was successful in its bid for the company.

For the Irish Continental Group, as the new holding company was now known, 1987 was to be one of the most exciting in the 19-year history of the Ireland-France ferry service. Under new ownership, a big revamp began. Irish Ferries and Belfast Ferries (then in operation) were the new operating divisions. The Board of Directors was restructured, a new Managing Director was recruited and steps were taken to revitalise the company. APEX fares and other incentives were introduced to give customers the benefit of discounts for early bookings. Freight customers were given a new, more competitive tariff structure. New quality standards were introduced throughout the company and the ships were refurbished to become 'floating hotels'. Much organisational change took place internally and outwardly there came a change of image. A new corporate identity and logotype were introduced with strong new colour themes and a shamrock motif which featured prominently. This new design style was carried through in all the company's promotional literature and advertising.

The Group enjoyed slightly belated success with its Stock Exchange debut. Originally it had been planned to launch the company's shares on the Smaller Companies' Market of the Stock Exchange in Autumn 1987 but the timing was hardly propitious. On 19th October 1987, world stock markets plummeted, in what became known as 'Black Monday'. The Irish Continental Group share launch was deferred until 9th February 1988 when a total of IR£2.7 million was raised. The first day of dealings was 6th April 1988. About 80% of the company's staff subscribed to the issue with the result that the employees now hold a significant proportion of the Group's shares.

Trading improved with 1988 turnover up to IR£34 million and pre-tax profits at IR£823,000. With the new structure in place, the Line was moving in the right direction. Two shore-based changes reflected this direction. The sales headquarters of the company was moved to Merrion Row in Dublin while reservations procedures were fully computerised with on-line connections to travel agents and sales offices abroad.

Within a short period, the fruits of re-organisation were being felt. For the year to 31st October 1989, its first as a publicly-quoted company, Irish Continental Group reported a turnover of IR£35.63 million and a pre-tax profit of IR£1.5 million, a 31% increase on the previous year.

A NEW DECADE OF GROWTH BEGINS

During 1990, Irish Continental Group recorded turnover up 12% to just over £40 million, with pre-tax profits up 60% to £2.4 million. Passenger numbers also increased by 13% over the previous year, from 285,000 to 324,000 with the strongest growth coming from mainland Europe where traffic increased by 22%.

From November to March each year, freight is the important source of revenue with 90% of loads accounted for by roll-on/roll-off freight vehicles, the remaining 10% coming from trade car imports from France and other mainland European countries. To ensure that hauliers received a year-round freight service, a freight-only vessel was chartered during the summer to support the passenger fleet.

In early 1991, Irish Continental Group reached conditional heads of agreement to purchase the share capital of the B&I Line and in early 1992 a major milestone was passed when it was formally announced that the Irish Continental Group had acquired outright ownership of B&I Line, following almost two years of talks with the Irish Government. The acquisition immediately enhanced the status of the Irish Continental Group and positioned the company as Ireland's leading passenger car ferry and freight shipping enterprise with an extensive range of services to France, the United Kingdom, Belgium and Holland. A new Managing Director joined Irish Continental Group and a new management structure was set in place at B&I Line.

During 1992, following the acquisition of B&I Line, the enlarged Irish Continental Group was restructured into three divisions: Ferry Services, European Container Service and Dublin Ferryport Terminals. Frank Carey was appointed as Group Marketing Director, Alex Mullin as Group Operations Director and along with Managing Director Eamonn Rothwell and Finance Director Gearoid O'Dea they formed the senior management team. Major investment was made by acquiring the *Isle of Innisfree* to replace the *Munster* on B&I Line's Rosslare - Pembroke Dock route, while a winter charter was secured for the Irish Ferries vessel *Saint Patrick II* sailing in the Baltic between Finland and Estonia. In 1992, B&I Line joined with Dublin Port to mount a campaign arguing the merits of having a new multi-user ferry terminal sited in Dublin Port.

In 1993, the Irish Continental Group continued on the investment trail, first by acquiring a 25% shareholding in Bell Lines and later by purchasing the ferry vessel *Pride of Bilbao* – the fifth largest night ferry in the world. At the time of her purchase, the *Pride of Bilbao* was under charter to P&O operating between the UK and Spain.

NEW SHIP FOR DUBLIN-HOLYHEAD LINK

In April 1994 a £46 million order was placed with Dutch shipbuilders Van der Giessen-de Noord for the construction of a new 23,000 gross tons ro-pax vessel for the Dublin-Holyhead route. The new vessel would enter service in June 1995 replacing the existing chartered vessel the *Isle of Innisfree*.

Meanwhile, in August 1994, Irish Ferries announced their intention to establish a service between Ireland and the Brittany port of Brest. However, because of the failure of the French Government to give their approval for the construction of the necessary linkspan at Brest, the company were forced to shelve their plan to sail there in 1995. The failure by the French Government was the subject of a complaint by Irish Ferries under European Union (EU) competition laws. As an alternative measure, agreement was reached with the port of Roscoff for the introduction of a 1995 summer service between Rosslare, Cork and Roscoff. Similarly, local opposition in the Roscoff region against the introduction of the Irish Ferries service to Roscoff also gave rise to a complaint by Irish Ferries to the EU.

On 27th January 1995 the new *Isle of Innisfree* was launched at the Rotterdam yard of Van der Giessen-de Noord. The new ferry was at the time the largest capacity multi-purpose passenger/ro-ro ferry operating between Ireland and the UK with capacity for 600 passenger cars, 108 accompanied freight trucks (or 142 trailers/coaches) and a passenger/crew complement of 1,760. In size, the new vessel had an overall length of 600 feet (181.6 m), a beam of 80 feet (23.4 m) and a distance of 124 feet (37.8 m) from keel to mast head. Mrs Clodagh Rothwell, wife of Irish Continental Group Managing Director Eamonn Rothwell, performed the naming ceremony.

1995 marked the beginning of a new era on the Irish Sea when the name and identity of Ireland - UK ferry operators B&I Line changed to that of its sister company Irish Ferries, operators of the Ireland-France ferry services. The name change to Irish Ferries saw B&I Line adopt the familiar Irish Ferries green/blue flag motif and white shamrock with vessels being repainted in white with the name Irish Ferries and a new colourful design on each hull.

The *Isle of Innisfree* made her maiden voyage on 23rd May on the Dublin - Holyhead route, signalling a new era in passenger ferry travel on the Irish Sea. The following year a contract for the design and construction of a second new superferry at a cost of approximately IR£60 million was placed with Dutch shipbuilders Van der Giessen-de Noord. When introduced in January 1997 the new 33,000 ton ferry would be the largest car-carrying ferry operating in North Western Europe with a passenger / freight capacity substantially larger than either of Irish Ferries' existing Irish Sea vessels.

In 1996, due to falling summer revenues on the French services brought about by various competitive factors, it was decided to discontinue loss-making winter services to France. Having operated year-round since 1973, services ended in September to be recommenced in March 1997. Meanwhile, the *Saint Patrick II* was offered for sale.

The new IR£60million *Isle of Inishmore* was launched in Rotterdam in October 1996. The ceremony was performed by Mrs. Sandra Carey, wife of Irish Continental Group Marketing Director Frank Carey. With space for 2,200 passengers, a car capacity of 855 units and truck capacity of 122 units, the *Isle of*

Following the takeover of B & I by ICL and the rebranding of the company as Irish Ferries, the *Isle of Innisfree* was ordered and introduced on the Dublin-Holyhead route in 1995. *(FotoFlite)*

Inishmore arrived at Dublin from Rotterdam on 17th February 1997, entering service on the Dublin-Holyhead route on 2nd March following sea trials and crew training. With the arrival of the *Isle of Inishmore*, the *Isle of Innisfree* was released from the Dublin-Holyhead route and transferred to the Rosslare-Pembroke Dock route.

The *Saint Killian II* was withdrawn from service after fourteen years sailing under the Irish flag, making her final departure from Ringaskiddy, Cork to Le Havre on 27th September 1997. During 1998 the vessel was sold to Cap Enterprises (Marintas) of Piraeus and re-named *Medina Star* before entering service on a new Black Sea rail/ferry route between Poti in Georgia and Odessa in the Ukraine.

In April 1997 the chartered Swedish-owned *Normandy* entered service on the Ireland - France routes. Meanwhile the *Saint Patrick II* was chartered for four-and- a-half years to Hellenic Mediterranean Lines of Greece. Under the charter agreement, Hellenic would obtain title to the vessel on completion of the charter.

FASTEST AND BIGGEST FERRIES

In June 1998, agreement was reached with Austal Ships of Australia for the construction of a new £29 million high-speed ferry to be introduced on to the Dublin - Holyhead route in Summer 1999. The twin-hulled aluminum-built vessel with a capacity for 800 passengers and 200 cars would complete the voyage from Dublin to Holyhead in just 110 minutes. She would operate up to four return sailings daily and though named *Jonathan Swift* would be marketed under the name 'Dublin Swift'. The fast craft would operate alongside the *Isle of Inishmore* providing a total of six return sailings daily.

Meanwhile, in July 1999, Irish Continental Group contracted with Aker Finnyards, Finland to build a 50,000 gross ton vessel – the world's largest car ferry ever – at a cost of 100 million Euro. The new vessel would be large enough to double Irish Ferries' freight-carrying capacity on their premier Dublin-Holyhead route when in service by Spring 2001. In January 2000 the giant keel section of the *Ulysses* was laid at a ceremony at Aker Finnyards.

The following January the *Normandy* was sent for a IR£4 million refit. Two months later the *Ulysses* arrived at Dublin Port on Sunday 4th March after her four-day voyage from Finland. Swimmer Mairead Berry – Ireland's 25-year-old Paralympic Games gold medallist – was named the 'golden godmother' to *Ulysses* at a special naming ceremony held in Dublin and attended by the Taoiseach, Bertie Aherne TD, some two weeks later in advance of her maiden voyage to Holyhead on Sunday 25th March 2001.

In 2005 the *Normandy* was transferred to the Bahamas flag and the bulk of her Irish staff replaced with staff from the new EU countries. This was followed in 2006 by the decision to switch the rest of the fleet to Cypriot registry, with mainly eastern European crews. This provoked a lengthy strike by both officers and crew which, once eventually settled, then allowed the company to introduce its new manning arrangements in an effort to save costs and to allow them to meet the now increased competition from the airlines. The new crews soon established themselves with a reputation for excellent customer service.

The next priority was the replacement of the now ageing *Normandy*. Whilst a new build could still not be justified, the Color Line vessel *Kronprins Harald* was due to become available in 2007 and was eagerly snapped up by Irish Ferries at an overall cost of some 60 million Euro. She was sent for an extensive refit prior to entering full commercial service early in 2008 between Ireland and France. The former Norwegian vessel was renamed the *Oscar Wilde*, continuing the literary theme of the Group.

With three modern vessels and one fast craft, Irish Ferries have placed themselves in a strong position on the Irish Sea, not only to compete with their shipping rivals but also with the cheap airlines between Ireland and the UK. Already passengers are showing signs of returning to Irish Ferries, with their competitive fares and luxurious and reliable ships. Passengers are now re-discovering the ease of ferry travel compared with airline travel and all that this style of travel entails today.

In 2014 with the improving world of economy and that of Ireland as well, Irish Ferries introduced the chartered Italian vessel *Cartour Epsilon* (later renamed *Epsilon*) on the Dublin-Holyhead service and at weekends between Dublin and Cherbourg. When the vessel was introduced it was expected that she would be a short-term measure until new tonnage came onstream on the Central Corridor.

Miles Cowsill

The *Epsilon* is seen here leaving Dublin for Holyhead in her first season on the Central Corridor. *(Gordon Hislip)*

The *Ulysses*, introduced in 2002, still remains the largest car ferry on the Irish Sea between the UK and Ireland. *(Irish Ferries)*

THE IRISH SEA'S CENTRAL CORRIDOR : AN IRISH FERRIES PERSPECTIVE

CENTRAL CORRIDOR 2015

Whether considering Ireland's ferry industry from an all-island or Republic of Ireland only perspective, it is clear that the so called middle or central corridor is the largest and most important channel for today's passenger and freight trades.

The Central Corridor comprises Dublin Bay on the Irish side and the triumvirate of UK ports in the North West – Holyhead, Liverpool and Heysham. From 2015, the Dublin Bay side can be more easily defined as Dublin Port as the Dun Laoghaire connection with Holyhead, which had been in existence for nearly 200 years, was declared closed.

Today, the three routes of the Central Corridor are Holyhead - Dublin, Liverpool - Dublin and Heysham - Dublin. In 2014, just over 2 million passengers sailed to and from Holyhead whilst nearly 127,000 opted for Liverpool and Heysham.

The split between the routes for freight was somewhat more even with half of the Dublin bound traffic sailing from Holyhead and the other half using the longer sea crossings via Liverpool and Heysham. Over 700,000 truck movements took place during 2014.

Crossing times on the corridor vary but typically crossings from Liverpool and Heysham take about 8 hours whilst Holyhead / Dublin is just over 3 hours, with fastcraft sailings taking just under 2 hours.

IRISH FERRIES - AND THE B&I LINE CONNECTION

When looking at the Irish Ferries connection with the Central Corridor it is necessary to first go back in time to examine the origin of the company's entry into the Irish Sea marketplace and, more specifically, the decision to develop its interests in the Dublin / Holyhead route prior to becoming the market leading operator that it has become in 2015.

In the debate that sometimes rages concerning the merits or otherwise of state versus private ownership, the history of Irish Ferries and of its parent company, the publicly-quoted Irish Continental Group Plc, provides a case study from which corporate planners and academics might gain inspiration.

Over decades - prior to its acquisition by Irish Continental Group in the early 1990s and its merger with former Ireland – France ferry operator, Irish Continental Line - B&I Line had been Ireland's flag bearer on the prime central and southern corridor routes to the UK.

Like many companies that operate under state ownership, B&I enjoyed all of the advantages and disadvantages that derive from being a taxpayers' asset. In the case of B&I, the advantages were few, one of which was freedom from the obligation always to return a profit to its shareholders.

Being a business underwritten and guaranteed by Government gave the company latitude that privately-owned businesses seldom ever enjoy. Consequently, across a span of almost 30 years between 1965 and 1991 records show that B&I inevitably lost money or returned insignificant profits on just a few occasions. But it was not just the lack of profits that took the biggest toll. The situation that bedeviled B&I was reflected in various ways, all of which combined to undermine its viability.

There was the problem of over-manning. As a state company, directors knew they had a part to play in maintaining job numbers, however strong the contra arguments might have been. More problematic was the fact that workers could see this Achilles heel and were wont to kick it with increasing regularity. Away from the problems of staffing, difficulties existed in other key areas. Major amongst them was the need for investment in new fleet and facilities.

B&I Line was creaking at the seams and, while management was expert enough to know the route that they should take to put the business on a solid footing, every good commercial decision had to be evaluated in political terms.

Following the takeover of B & I Line by ICL Group, the chartered vessel *Stena Nautica* was placed on the Dublin-Holyhead route. She was renamed *Isle of Innisfree*. *(Miles Cowsill)*

The *Isle of Innisfree* is seen here prior to her launch at the yard of Van der Giessen du Nord. *(Irish Ferries)*

The *Isle of Inishmore* and *Jonathan Swift* pass each other off Dublin. *(Irish Ferries)*

An impressive view of the main freight deck on the *Ulysses*. The vessel can accommodate up to 300 trucks or 1,342 cars. *(Irish Ferries)*

This all changed in the early-1990s when Government decided to rid itself of their troublesome, loss-making, investment-starved shipping line by putting it up for sale to the highest bidder, it being the winning package put forward by Irish Continental Group.

At a stroke, B&I Line was free of state control and had moved into the uncertain world of private ownership – a place where proposals would be approved on merit alone.

Though few believed it at the time, this was a pivotal development, a 'win-win' situation that was to prove highly advantageous to all concerned, even those who were opposed to it at the time.

IRISH CONTINENTAL GROUP - A VERY COMMITTED OWNER

Stripped to its fundamentals, two key elements made up the ICG bid – one was a cash offer significantly higher than the next highest offer that the Government had received and, two, an undertaking by ICG to undertake a fleet modernisation programme sufficient to prepare B&I for the future.

As history shows, ICG's offer was accepted and soon after the work of remoulding B&I got underway.

What was notable in the decade or so that followed was that the investment pledge that ICG had made was, to use an apt pun, blown 'right out of the water' as the company embarked on a ship building programme that, over a very few years, was to equip it with one of the world's most modern ferry fleets – a succession of new builds that included a new fast ferry and the world's largest car ferry.

In very short measure, it had become clear that Government's decision to divest itself of B&I was the correct one and that ICG's promise to invest had been delivered – not just at sea but in its dockside and freight handling facilities.

THE "QUIET REVOLUTION" ON THE IRISH SEA

When ICG took over the B&I Line routes in 1992, the seascape, so to speak, was very different from today.

At that time, just 30% of the island of Ireland's ro-ro freight traffic was being shipped via Republic of Ireland ports with 70% going via the Northern Ireland ports of Larne, Belfast and Warrenpoint.

Notwithstanding the increasing demand for access via Dublin, the island's primary conurbation and the Republic of Ireland's capital city, the limitations of the ferry capacity on offer via Dublin Bay at that time effectively forced the daily freight traffic via Northern Ireland – with all of the consequent cost impacts of the additional road haulage involved.

ICG did not take long to figure out a solution and after a brief increase in capacity being implemented through the use of chartered tonnage, the company embarked on an investment program in 1994 which would last nearly a decade and which would surpass the wildest dreams of users, staff and political interests who had wrestled with the Central Corridor ferry conundrum for the previous thirty years.

What is often referred to as the "quiet revolution", ICG set about implementing the most ambitious fleet renewal and development plan ever seen in Irish waters which would cost nearly half a billion Euros and would see a transformation of both the capacity and the standards of ferry travel from the Republic of Ireland and, in particular, the Dublin - Holyhead route.

THE CHANGING OF A FLEET – A TRUE GAME CHANGER

First of the new vessels to roll down the slipway of Van der Giessen-de Noord, Rotterdam in Irish Ferries livery was the *Isle of Innisfree* in 1995.

Introduced to service the Dublin – Holyhead route, it transformed the company's ability to compete and attract new passenger and freight traffic, both attracted by its greater capacity and more luxurious on-board features. It could carry 600 cars or 85 trucks and 1,650 passengers.

So successful has it been, it was not long before market demand led to its transfer to the Rosslare - Pembroke Dock service in order to make way for a second new build, the larger *Isle of Inishmore* – provided by the same yard in Rotterdam as the *Isle of Innisfree*.

Taking over services on the busy Dublin - Holyhead route in 1997, the *Isle of Inishmore*, the largest ferry in North West Europe at the time, lifted the barrier yet another few notches by offering yet more freight and car carrying capacity whilst raising even further the standard of comfort and luxury that passengers could enjoy.

The *Isle of Inishmore* can carry 710 cars or 120 trucks and 2,000 passengers.

With these two vessels, a point had then been reached at which Irish Ferries was seen to have transformed its services on both the central and southern corridors.

A GROWING ECONOMY – AND A DESIRE TO GO FASTER

As Ireland's economy continued to grow into the late 90s, Irish Ferries business on its key Central Corridor service via Dublin - Holyhead was enjoying further success, particularly from freight customers who had now opted to move away from Northern Ireland ports in favour of the more direct access from and to Dublin and its hinterland.

Evident was the growing demand for a vessel that could deliver a faster service, one that would attract a wider cross-section of passengers, including business users keen to use time more efficiently.

This resulted in Irish Ferries decision to build a new fast ferry – the Australian-built, aluminium bodied, twin-hulled *Jonathan Swift* - and to introduce it as an alternative travel option on the Dublin – Holyhead route where she continues to operate alongside conventional services.

Marketed as the Irish Ferries Swift Service, the 1999 built vessel quickly became a success as she provided a real advantage in crossing times, being able to complete the berth to berth journey in 1 hour 49 minutes versus the conventional vessel time of 3 hours 15 minutes – with capacity for 200 cars, coaches and 700 passengers.

ULYSSES – A GIANT STEP FORWARD

By the end of 1999, it was clear that Irish Ferries had a terrific combination in its two Dublin - Holyhead vessels, the *Isle of Inishmore* and the *Jonathan Swift*.

With continued growth in the Irish economy , and notwithstanding the improvements in tonnage and frequency being provided by Irish Ferries' key competitors on the Central Corridor - Stena Line, P&O Ferries and Merchant Ferries – it was clear that the massive increase in capacity provided since 1995 was simply not going to sufficiently meet demand for the company's services.

The choices were simple enough – maintain the existing service and maximize the returns from the two vessels, add a third vessel with all of the extra costs and potential inefficiencies that that would bring or to build an even larger vessel that would provide even more capacity but with improved economies of scale and the potential to meet demand for many years to come.

In 2001, Irish Ferries delivered what was then the largest ferry in the world – *Ulysses*.

Built in Turku, Finland by Aker Finnyards, with over 4km of vehicle decks, *Ulysses* has become synonymous with reliability and predictability as her performance surpassed all expectations with a fourteen year unblemished record of never having missed a sailing because of weather.

Apart from the vessel's success in operating terms, it also raised the bar in lots of other ways with unrivalled quality of onboard facilities and a genuine claim to being the hardest working ship in Northern Europe in terms of daily carryings across all categories of traffic.

The arrival of *Ulysses* resulted in the transfer of the *Isle of Inishmore* to Irish Ferries' Rosslare - Pembroke route where she still provides a first class service today.

The *Isle of Innisfree* ultimately moved to New Zealand where she still trades today as the *Kaitaki* – on charter and still in the ownership of Irish Continental Group.

In order for Irish Ferries to meet the demand for fast ferry operations on the Irish Sea, the company ordered from Austal Shipping in Australia the *Jonathan Swift*. The vessel has operated on the route for 16 years and remains a popular and important feature of the company's operations today. *(Gordon Hislip)*

Oscar Wilde. (Miles Cowsill)

EPSILON - FILLING THE GAPS

In 2013, Irish Ferries recognized that the time had come to plug the only remaining gaps in its Dublin - Holyhead schedules where the company was unable to compete, particularly for freight traffic.

By chartering the ropax vessel *Cartour Epsilon* (later renamed *Epsilon*), the company was able to provide an additional two round trips per day on Dublin - Holyhead.

Built in 2011 by Visentini, Italy, the 2,900 lane metres vessel provided added flexibility to Irish Ferries on its Central Corridor services. The *Epsilon*'s PC of 500 provided the additional cover for the fastcraft *Jonathan Swift* during weather disruption whilst also offering the added bonus of facilitating the start of a new Irish Ferries route between Dublin and Cherbourg in Northern France.

In January 2014, the new service from Dublin to France commenced with a once weekly call at weekends. This proved to be an instant success, pushing the Irish Ferries plans along the road of further development as the Irish economy was at last showing good signs of recovery after the devastation of the crash during one of the worst recessions of recent times hit the country between 2008 and 2012.

Despite Ireland's post-'Celtic Tiger' slump, and the economic downturn that has hit world economies generally for most of the past decade, the investment programme undertaken by Irish Ferries has had an overarching beneficial impact on the business. In addition, it has enhanced Irish Ferries position as a key service provider in the context of Ireland's trade and tourism sectors.

According to former ICG director, Tony Kelly (now retired following a career-long life of service to the Company) 'the investments we made - all privately financed without recourse to state grants or other forms of public funding - have seen us deliver on the promises we made to Government at the outset.'

'More importantly, over the period and in the longer term, it has raised the status of the company and transformed the position that we enjoy in the broader economic context' Mr. Kelly said.

Looking to the future, if past performance can ever be an indicator of future trends, it is clear that Ireland's status as an open island economy, heavily dependant on trade and tourism, is one that will continue to place focus on the ferry sector.

On a wider canvas, the battle to secure market share as the Ireland and UK economies continue to emerge from recession will see growth in the freight-only sector with larger vessels and the development of routes likely to form part of this bigger picture.

Changes likely to affect the Ireland/UK air sector will also have an impact as competition heats up between the major players. As ever, the ferry sector has proven itself capable of meeting these challenges head-on.

Of course, few skies are ever clear of some cloud. Up and down fluctuations in the cost of fuel is one factor that injects an element of uncertainty. However, any broad analysis of the ferry sector can only lead to one conclusion: that the outlook remains broadly positive and that ferry operators generally have adapted to meet market demands and placed themselves in a pretty good place.

The *Ulysses*, which can operate up to two round sailings a day, 50 weeks of the year.
(Irish Ferries)

A night time view of the *Condor Liberation* at St Peter Port, Guernsey. *(Condor Ferries)*

The *Condor Liberation* berthed at St Helier, Jersey. *(Matt Davies)*

CONDOR LIBERATION –THE NEXT GENERATION OF FAST FERRY

In the current economic climate the introduction of new build ferry tonnage is something of a rarity and a new fast ferry with vehicle capability even more so. The *Condor Liberation* is the first new ferry to enter service on the English Channel in three years and with a total absence of new build orders is likely to remain the newest vessel for some time. The vessel is one of only three fast ferries to be delivered in Europe since 2010 – the others being Mols-Linien's 112 metre Incat HSC *Cat Express 2* in 2013 and Færgen's 113 metre Austal catamaran *Leonora Christina* in 2011. Although to all intents new, the *Condor Liberation* was in fact launched in January 2010 at Henderson, Australia as *Hull 270* by Australian fast craft specialist Austal and built on a speculative basis. However she failed to find a buyer and following completion of sea trials was placed into a maintained state of lay-up, initially in Australia and later at Austal's yard at Balamban, Cebu, Philippines. Although actually five years old, the unused vessel was extensively modified internally and had new technical equipment fitted before entering service with Condor and with the only mileage on the clock being sea trials the *Condor Liberation* can rightly be described as new.

Condor Ferries, which has been owned by the European Infrastructure Fund of Australian Company Macquarie since 2008 and whose origins as Channel Islands fast ferry operator go back to 1964, initially negotiated a purchase option with Austal on *Hull 270* in January 2014. A 61.5 million Australian dollar (£32.8 million/€43.7 million) deal to purchase was subsequently concluded in August 2014. In addition a $6 million modification contract was placed with Austal to undertake a number of modifications prior to delivery, including fitting a stern ramp and wings to the central bridge console. Condor closed the deal after successfully negotiating new 8 and 10 year licences with the States of Guernsey and Jersey to operate ferry services between the Islands and the UK without which the financial investment in *Hull 270* could not have been justified. A new vessel was needed as two of Condor's existing 86 metre Incats, the *Condor Express* (1996) and *Condor Vittesse* (1997) were starting to age and becoming less reliable. The licence is not exclusive but ensures that another ferry operator would have to provide the same level of service and frequency as Condor, who carry 1 million passengers and 200,000 vehicles per year.

With a much greater vehicle capacity of 245 cars compared to 160 of the Incats and an ability to operate in rougher weather, the *Condor Liberation* has been able to replace both craft, considerably improving Condor's operational efficiency and sailing reliability and justifying the investment in the vessel which the Company reports as being £50 million after purchase and modification. In consequence peak fast craft sailing frequency to/from the UK has been reduced from three crossings each way to two per day and all sailings consolidated on Poole, thus ending the port of Weymouth's 190 year old link with the Channel Islands. Meanwhile both Incat vessels were sold to Seajets for domestic service in Greece.

The *Condor Liberation* is a 102 metre long "next generation trimaran" design evolved from Austal's 127 metre trimaran *Benchijigua Express* built in 2005 for Fred. Olsen Express for service between the Canary Islands of Tenerife and La Gomera. Following detailed learning analysis, the design was reconfigured to improve payload, fuel efficiency and sea-keeping quality. With great interest in a more efficient vessel which is able to operate more comfortably in challenging sea conditions, Austal hoped the new design would open up new markets beyond existing ferry designs, particularly in developing areas such as the China - Taiwan Strait. After determining that a slightly smaller 102 metre vessel with capacity for 1,165 passengers and 254 cars was the optimum size for the market Austal built *Hull 207* on a speculative basis. Consequently the design of the interior and vehicle deck was pitched to easily permit modifications to suit the requirements of the operator. With relations between China and Taiwan remaining unstable, fuel prices rising and the world in recession, a buyer for the vessel was not forthcoming despite interest from Fred. Olsen Express, Viking Line, Hellenic Seaways and proposed new Channel start up operator Euroferries. The latter whose repeated attempts to start a 75 minute crossing between Ramsgate and Boulogne have come to nothing entered into a four-year charter agreement and made a down payment for preparatory work to take place. Although a handover was scheduled for January 2013 with a service launch advertised for the following month Euroferries failed to complete the deal.

A trimaran hull facilitates greater cargo weight for the same speed without requiring extra power and offers better sea-keeping ability than a catamaran. It also provides inherent stability in comparison to catamarans which roll quickly and uncomfortably when pitching resulting in unpleasant corkscrew motions. The side hulls of the trimaran are small meaning that the craft is essentially a mono-hull with small stabilisers. It acts like a child's bicycle does when fitted with stabilisers and prevents roll accelerations. With less slamming from water hitting the hull, resultant bangs and vibration throughout the structure have been virtually eliminated in all but the heaviest seas and motion is estimated to be 30% lower than on a catamaran. The real evidence of this is that Fred. Olsen's stores supply their trimaran with just a tenth of the sick bags supplied to their catamarans.

Experience of the *Benchijigua Express* led to further refinements in ride quality and efficiency in *Hull 207*. The vessel was given a straight stem bow to maximise water length for speed and fitted with three T-foil fin stabilisers. They are like horizontal wings; a 10 sq metre fin is located at the bow on the centre hull and a 2.5 sq metre fins is located on each hull at the stern. The foils, which can be removed and serviced without dry-docking, help control pitching. They have sensors which sense when a foil is moving upwards and send a signal to the other foils to provide a counteractive force. Sea trial data suggests the ride quality of *Condor Liberation* is superior to the *Benchijigua Express* and motion is 56% lower than on a 100 metre catamaran when operating in head seas. Once sufficient experience is gained operating the *Condor Liberation* and heavy weather trials have been undertaken Condor intends to apply the MCA to have the 3.5 metre wave height restriction currently applying to fast craft operating in UK waters increased.

Typically similar sized fast ferries including the *Benchijigua Express* have four engines but the *Condor Liberation* is fitted with just three MTU 20V 8000 diesel engines which have the world's highest power-to weight ratio providing greater efficiency, lower fuel consumption, less emissions and reduced maintenance. Her 127 metre big sister can carry 750 tons with 36mW at 39 knots whereas she can carry 700 tons with 27mW at 39 knots - some ¾ of the power. At 39 knots (45 mph) the *Condor Liberation* has a range of 630 nautical miles and consumes 4,000 litres of marine grade diesel per hour, comparing very favourably to the 5,000 litres of the Incats which have a much smaller capacity. On trials she achieved 39 knots using 90% of power when laden with 45 knots being achieved lightship. Operating for the Condor the crafts normal service speed is 35 knots. Propulsion is from three Wartsila LJX 1300 water jets each driven through its own ZF 53800 reduction gearbox with manoeuvrability in port from one of two retractable bow thrusters with one being required and the other acting as a spare. Maintenance downtime has been designed to be minimised with easy access to the thrusters, water jets and the main engine room provided by hatches from the vehicle deck.

The principal dimensions of the *Condor Liberation* are a length of 102 metres, breadth of 26.8 metres, draught of 4.2 metres and a gross tonnage of 6,307. The craft comprises four decks and has a main vehicle deck, a mezzanine vehicle deck with fixed decks at the side and a hoistable centre section to allow carriage of freight, a passenger accommodation deck and the bridge deck which includes a large outside area complete with seating and which is one of the more generous outside areas available on a fast craft. Vehicle deck capacity is 245 cars or 190 lane metres for freight plus 145 cars with dangerous goods carried at the aft open end. With the additional vehicle deck capacity and increased headroom Condor no longer charges a higher fare for SUVs and 4 x 4s.

To isolate noise and vibration, the entire passenger superstructure is resiliently mounted on the hull with the reduced exposure to vibration and stress facilitating the use large panoramic windows throughout. These undoubtedly add to the internal appeal of the *Condor Liberation* and provide a quieter and more comfortable travelling environment. In a first for large high speed craft, the passenger accommodation is fitted with high efficiency LED lighting, requiring less electrical power and reducing running cost and emissions.

Prior to entering service on 27th March 2015, substantial modifications to *Hull 270* were carried out in Poole during a two month preparatory refit and she was formally renamed the *Condor Liberation* following a public competition which received 7,000 entries to choose her name. The winning choice recognises the 70th anniversary in 2015 of the liberation of the Channel Islands from German occupation. She arrived in Poole on Boxing Day 2014 following a 10,500 nautical mile journey from the Philippines from where she departed on 4th December. The interior of the *Condor Liberation* was

The view forwards from the Horizon Lounge with the open bow section of the upper car deck in the foreground. *(Matt Davies)*

The vehicle deck has an upper deck with fixed sections on either side and a centre hoistable mezzanine which can be lifted allowing coaches or freight to be carried. *(Matt Davies)*

The forward Horizon Lounge has been reconfigured from the original build specification. (*Matt Davies*)

The starboard side premium Ocean Club Lounge has 70 seats and complimentary drinks, snacks, Wi-Fi and at seat waiter service are provided. (*Matt Davies*)

rebuilt by Southampton based marine outfitting specialist company Trimline and engineering work which included repainting the vessel into a new Condor livery and the fitting new navigation equipment and control gear to the bridge was undertaken by Burgess Marine.

The original specification for *Hull 270* saw her fitted out with 1,165 seats with 248 business class seats in the forward saloon comprising a mixture of airline style reclining and at table leather seats. 414 tourist class airline style seats were provided mid-ships with a further 503 tourist class seats aft in open saloons. Following modifications the passenger certificate of the *Condor Liberation* has been reduced to 873 and three classes of passenger seat provided. The forward lounge essentially remains as built but with seating layout slightly reconfigured and is now the Horizon Lounge where seating is classed as "Ocean Traveller" and available for a £7.50 upgrade. A mix of 270 luxury airline-style or at table leather seats with power points and panoramic view forward is offered and the lounge has its own Café Bar which has been branded as the Horizon Bar.

The remainder of the *Condor Liberation* comprises 533 of original "Tourist" class seats now branded as "Ocean Tourist". Aft of the Horizon Lounge and centre mid-ships, splitting the seating lounges to either side is a facilities block containing a small kiosk that has become the Information desk, a Purser's office, crew mess facility, toilets and stairwell for the bridge. As built the craft had a lack of food outlets having just two small Café Bars. The facilities block has therefore been extended aft replacing centre seating in the previously open full width lounge and splitting it in two. The extended block now accommodates a galley, a Self Service Restaurant counter "Le Casquet's Bistro" and a colourful "Kid's Zone" where children can watch movies. The existing Café Bar which previously stood alone is now located at the aft end of the facilities block. It has been branded as the Island Bar and fitted out to serve soft and alcoholic drinks, Costa Coffee and a range of cakes, pastries and panini.

Mid-ships on the starboard side opposite the extended facilities block the previously open "Tourist" class seating area has been replaced by an enclosed "Ocean Club Lounge" containing 70 luxury reclining leather seats some at tables, power sockets and at seat complimentary refreshments. An upgrade to Ocean Club costs £29.00 per person. Aft of the facilities block further centre seating was removed to accommodate the large "Adore" Duty Free Shop. The extended facilities block and new shop split the entire mid-ship and aft sections of the vessel into entirely separate port and starboard side lounges joined only by a centre passageway in between the Island Bar and Duty Free Shop.

With the introduction of the *Condor Liberation*, Condor Ferries has introduced a new look and refreshed brand with three new colours of dark blue, pink and gold to represent more of a leisure and holiday outlook. The new identity which includes Condor's strap line of "Good Times" is gradually being rolled out across vessels, terminals, staff uniforms, marketing materials and Company website. For Condor, the *Condor Liberation* represents a considerable and significant long term investment and undoubtedly she represents a step change in capacity and efficiency for the Company and in ride quality and onboard facilities for the Customer hopefully bringing "Good Times" to both the Company and the Channel Islands.

Matt Davies

REVIEW 2014/15

The following is a review of passenger and freight ferry activities during 2014 and the first half of 2015. Some events occurring in the first half of 2014 will have also been mentioned in 'Ferries 2015'.

EAST COAST & THAMES

On DFDS Seaways' Rosyth - Zeebrugge, the chartered *Longstone* was replaced in May 2014 by the *Finlandia Seaways*. With the future of this route in doubt in the light of increased costs brought about by the new sulphur emissions rules, in November DFDS Seaways, the Scottish Government and Forth Ports signed a Memorandum of Understanding in which they agreed to continue the Rosyth-Zeebrugge service.

The Newcastle - IJmuiden service was disrupted in September by a cabin fire on the *King Seaways* caused by a passenger deliberately setting fire to his bedding. The passenger responsible was later jailed for 11 years for what was described by the judge as a "spectacular piece of recklessness".

P&O's Middlesbrough - Rotterdam service was, for most of the year, in the hands of the *Wilhelmine*, chartered from Cobelfret Ferries. In November, the charter ended and, as Cobelfret needed the ship following the launch of their new Zeebrugge - Gothenburg service, it could not be renewed. A replacement in the form of the *Estraden* was arranged with owners Bore Shipowners, but this would not be available until January 2015. However an additional ro-ro vessel in the form of the *Mistral* had been chartered in October. Although acquired to operate as a second vessel on the Zeebrugge - Middlesbrough service, she was initially deployed on the Tilbury run, enabling the *Norsky* to operate on the Rotterdam - Middlesbrough service. Similar juggling of ships - including a short re-charter of the *Wilhelmine* - continued until the end of the refit period in February 2015.

In April 2014 DFDS finally ran out of patience with the P + S Werften Shipyard at Stralsund, Germany and took delivery of their two new ro-ros, the *Ark Germania* and *Ark Dania* in 'as is' condition. The *Ark Germania* was almost complete and moved to Esbjerg, where she took over the Immingham service from the *Fionia Seaways*. Sister vessel, the *Ark Dania*, was less finished and was moved by tugs to the Fayard Shipyard at Odense, Denmark for fitting out. Although she looked almost complete, it was not until November that she entered service on the same route.

Booming traffic on Vlaardingen - Immingham led DFDS Seaways to switch the *Anglia Seaways* to the route in September as third vessel. This lasted until March 2015 when the company redeployed the *Ficaria Seaways*, one of the lengthened 'flower class' vessels, from Gothenburg - Immingham to the Vlaardingen - Immingham route. Other switches enabled capacity to be more evenly matched to traffic and the *Anglia Seaways* to be placed on the charter market. She served with P&O from March until May and then returned to her original route, covering for the *Britannia Seaways*.

In late August, Stena Line also increased capacity on the Maas - Humber corridor. They chartered the *Stena Scotia*, from sister company Stena RoRo and started a Rotterdam - Killingholme service to supplement their Hook of Holland - Killingholme route.

The most significant change on the North Sea was undoubtedly the ending, after nearly 135 years, of DFDS Seaways' Harwich - Esbjerg service, with the last voyage taking place on 29th September. The increase in costs which the introduction of new sulphur emissions rules in the North Sea from 1st January 2015 would generate was blamed for the route's final end. The last remaining passenger service between the UK and Scandinavia, the route's demise was followed at the end of October by the cessation of the twice weekly Gothenburg - Tilbury freight service, following the end of the contract with the Stora Enso paper group. In May 2015 the *Flandria Seaways*, a regular on the Vlaardingen - Felixstowe service, was sold to Mexican owners.

Stora Enso also ended their arrangement with CLdN /Cobelfret on the Zeebrugge - Gothenburg route whereby Cobelfret acted as agents for the company at both ports and sold capacity not needed for the company's products. Instead the paper group formed an alliance with SOL Continent Line, a division of Swedish Orient Line, which led to two of the three Wagenborg freighters continuing to operate between Zeebrugge and Gothenburg and also a weekly direct service from Finland to Zeebrugge, Tilbury and Antwerp.

Victorine *(J.J.Jager)*

Rodin *(George Holland)*

Spirit of Britain (*George Holland*)

Seven Sisters (*Nick Widdows*)

Having built up considerable traffic, CLdN/Cobelfret decided to launch their own three ship, six days per week service to Gothenburg. The return of the *Wilhelmine* from P&O, the *Celestine* from RMR Shipping and the *Longstone*, renamed the *Dorset*, from an Australian charter, enabled the service to be operated from the company's own resources. The *Dorset* was soon after sold to Finnlines and became their *Finnmerchant* but in January CLdN purchased the *Spaarneborg*, one of the three Wagenborg ships previously used on the route, and renamed her the *Somerset*.

In the summer, Transfennica introduced a Portsmouth call on the northbound run of their Zeebrugge - Bilbao freight service. Whilst this was moderately successful, the route overall failed to make a profit and was withdrawn at the end of the year.

Mann Lines' replacement for the *Estraden*, chartered to P&O Ferries from the beginning of January 2014, was the larger *Stena Foreteller*. At the same time, Mann Lines entered into an agreement with Stena Line to act as their sales agent and give them an access to the Northern Baltic market.

There were few changes on the Thames during 2014 apart from the ending of the Tilbury - Gothenburg service. Cobelfret ships made occasional calls at the mothballed Dartford terminal and the terminal itself remains well used for storage of Mercedes cars and vans which have been offloaded at Purfleet.

In October, Finnlines returned to Tilbury after a gap of eight years with a new weekly service to Finnish ports. This was later increased to twice weekly. The service calls also at Hull and Immingham.

Thames Clippers ordered a new catamaran passenger ferry from Australian builders Aluminium Boats, Brisbane, Australia. She was expected to be delivered in June 2015. During 2014, sponsorship of the company changed from the accountants KPGM to the credit card subsidiary of Bank of America, MBNA.

EASTERN CHANNEL

Ramsgate ferry port remained without a service following the ending of TransEuopa Ferries service in April 2013. Some of the land has been taken over by companies servicing the burgeoning wind farm industry off the Thanet coast and the chances of a service resuming remain remote.

Dover was again dominated by the seemingly never ending saga of MyFerryLink. In January 2015 the Competition Appeal Tribunal ruled that Eurotunnel must sell MyFerryLink in order for the service to continue. Whilst Eurotunnel decided to accept the verdict and sought a new buyer, the 'SCOP' (Société coopérative et participative - workers' co-operative) which provides the crews decided to appeal to the UK Court of Appeal to have the ruling overturned. On 15th May, the Court agreed with the SCOP and the ruling was overturned. The Competition & Mergers Authority were refused permission to appeal to the Supreme Court and the July deadline for MyFerryLink to cease operations was lifted. However, on 28th May, Eurotunnel announced it was ceasing its involvement with the SCOP from the beginning of July. On 7th June DFDS announced that it had submitted a binding offer to Eurotunnel for the charter or purchase of the ferries *Rodin* and *Berlioz* with an effective date of 2 July 2015. Eurotunnel announced that it intended to retain the *Nord Pas-de-Calais* to convey traffic which could not be conveyed through the Channel Tunnel, but it would not be operated by the SCOP, which was later placed in judicial administration.

P&O Ferries adopted a slightly revised livery with the letters 'P&O' in a new, sans serif typeface. Interestingly, the web address, www.poferries.com, is no longer shown, perhaps reflecting the fact that these days people tend to use search engines to access websites rather than typing in the full URL. In October, P&O secured a charter for their laid up freighter, the *European Seaway*, serving the RWEI Nordsee Ost wind farm project in the North Sea some 23 nautical miles off Helgoland. This ended in April 2015.

DFDS Seaways were reduced to a single ship operation between December 2014 and June 2015, following the ending of the chart of the *Dieppe Seaways*. The vessel had been purchased by a Stena subsidiary in May and although the charter continued, she was required to operate on the Holyhead - Dublin route from March 2015, replacing the *Stena Nordica* and the HSS *Stena Explorer*. The second vessel for DFDS at Dover was in fact the *Stena Nordica*. Renamed the *Malo Seaways*, she entered service in April 2015, enabling the *Calais Seaways* to go to Gdansk for a refit and the replacement of one of her engines. A two ship service resumed in June.

The future of the Newhaven - Dieppe looked uncertain in February 2014 when DFDS withdrew from the bidding to continue operating the service from January 2015, leaving the sponsor of the route, the Conseil General of the Seine-Maritime department with no bidder. However, in the autumn agreement was reached with the Danish company that in 2015 they would operate up to three sailings each way per day between May and September and deploy both Transmanche Ferries branded vessels, the *Côte d'Albtare* and *Seven Sisters*, on the route. The *Seven Sisters* spent most of 2014 on the Portsmouth - Le Havre service.

WESTERN CHANNEL AND SOLENT

In January 2014, Brittany Ferries announced the building of a new LNG powered vessel at STX France, St Nazaire, France to be delivered in 2016 - the 'Pegasus Project' However, due to funding problems no firm order was placed and the project was put on hold, as were plans to convert other vessels to LNG propulsion. Instead, the company opted to fit scrubbers to all vessels over winter 2014/2015 and 2015/2016.

Brittany Ferries launched a new Portsmouth - Le Havre service in March 2014 with their charter of the former LD Lines and DFDS vessel *Norman Voyager*. Renamed the *Etretat* the new service was launched under the 'économie' brand, being more of a 'no frills' service than their usual offering, with just a single all-purpose cafeteria rather than the mix of waiter service, cafeteria and tea bar found on some of their other vessels. Her roster included a weekend trip to Santander.

The vessel became available because DFDS decided to operate their Portsmouth - Le Havre service with the *Seven Sisters*, which had spent most of 2013 in reserve. However, with the competition from Brittany Ferries and the decision to deploy the *Seven Sisters* on Newhaven - Dieppe in 2015, DFDS concluded that their Le Havre service was uneconomic and decided to terminate the service at the end of 2014.

In January 2015 Brittany Ferries announced that a second vessel would operate on the Portsmouth - Le Havre service and also make a weekend return trip to Spain - Bilbao this time. The vessel would be the former DFDS Seaways' vessel *Sirena Seaways* which would be renamed the *Baie de Seine*. She was handed over to the French company in early April and entered service in May.

LD Lines had re-entered the UK market in their own right in November 2013 with the launch of a new Poole - Santander service. A second Visentini vessel, the former *Scintu*, was chartered and replaced the *Norman Asturias* on the St Nazaire - Gijon service. In January 2014 she was renamed the *Norman Atlantic* and Rosslare in Ireland was added to her roster. However, the start of March, after severe winter weather affected reliability, it was decided to make the Rosslare service summer only and the route resumed in June. The *Norman Asturias* took over the new Poole service and from January 2014 one of her two weekly trips to Spain was changed to operate Poole - Gijon. She then operated a round trip to St Nazaire, enabling the *Norman Atlantic* to operate a round trip to Rosslare. However, in September LD Lines decided to abandon both services and the charter of the two ships ended, effectively ending LD Lines participation in the UK ferry, market which started when they replaced P&O Ferries on the Portsmouth - Le Havre route in October 2005 and had also involved Dover - Boulogne, Dover - Dieppe and Newhaven - Dieppe services by both conventional and fast ferries. The parent company of LD Lines, Louis Dreyfus Armateurs (LDA), subsequently disposed of the 18% share in the DFDS Seaways Dover - Calais/Dunkirk, Newhaven - Dieppe and Marseille - Tunis routes. The *Norman Atlantic* subsequently caught fire on 28th December 2014 in the Adriatic Sea whilst on charter to ANEK Lines of Greece.

In August 2014, Condor Ferries purchased *Austal Hull 270* from builders Austal Ships of Australia. Built speculatively in 2010, she had not until then attracted a buyer. She was moved to the builder's yard in Cebu, Philippines for further work before arriving at Poole at the end of December. Renamed the *Condor Liberation*, she entered service between Poole and The Channel Island in late March. Replacing both the *Condor Express* and *Condor Vitesse*, her arrival meant the ending of services from Weymouth whose berth, repaired at some expense in 2013, was unsuitable for the new vessel. The *Condor Rapide* has been retained to operate service from the Channel Islands to St Malo.

Baie de Seine (*John Bryant*)

Normandie (*Brian D. Smith*)

In November 2014 Wightlink announced that their Lymington - Yarmouth service was to become hourly throughout the year, with one of the three ships used on the route transferred to Portsmouth - Fishbourne. When the new ships were introduced in 2008/09 it was not found possible to continue with the half hourly service previously operated and a 40 minute frequency was introduced. This rather spoiled connections with the half-hourly rail service from Brokenhurst. In recent years the service has been hourly with extras at peak times operated by a third ship - but this ship only operated three round trips per day during the summer period.

One of the Lymington ships - the *Wight Sun* - was moved to Portsmouth to replace the *St. Helen* which was withdrawn from service in April 2015 and sold to Delcomar of Italy. The *St. Helen* was the last British Rail Sealink ship still sailing in UK waters.

Red Funnel Ferries' refurbished *Red Falcon* entered service in Spring 2014. As well as new décor, seating and catering arrangements, additional covered passenger accommodation was built on the upper deck. During winter 2014/15 the *Red Osprey* received similar treatment and re-entered service at the end of March.

Gosport Ferry's new *Harbour Spirit* built by Tehnomont of Pula in Croatia was delivered by cargo ship in March 2015. She is similar to the 2001 built *Spirit of Gosport*. She entered service In May.

IRISH SEA

As previously mentioned, in January 2014 LD Lines inaugurated a new service from Rosslare to St Nazaire, using the *Norman Atlantic*. Initially intended to be a year round service it was soon decided that it would operate during the summer only, as it was found that good time-keeping in winter weather conditions was impossible. Along with all LD Lines' Atlantic and English Channel services, the route closed in September.

Celtic Link's Rosslare - Cherbourg service was taken over by Stena Line in March 2014 and the vessel used, the *Celtic Horizon*, was renamed the *Stena Horizon*.

Stena Line's HSS *Stena Explorer* operated as normal during the summer between Holyhead and Dun Laoghaire but did not operate during the Christmas/New Year period as in previous years and it was later announced that she would not return in 2015. Instead the Holyhead - Dublin service was to be enhanced by the introduction of the bigger and faster *Stena Superfast X*, the former *Dieppe Seaways* of DFDS Seaways and *SeaFrance Moliere* of SeaFrance. Following a major refit she entered service in March 2015.

Irish Ferries second ship for the Dublin - Holyhead route, the *Cartour Epsilon*, operated on the Rosslare - Pembroke Dock service during December 2013 but moved to her proper route in January 2014, being renamed the *Epsilon*. She also undertakes a weekly trip from Dublin to Cherbourg.

Seatruck Ferries returned the *Anglia Seaways* to her owners DFDS in May 2014 and her place on the Heysham - Warrenpoint service was taken by the *Seatruck Pace*, which had returned for a charter carrying windfarm equipment. All services were from that point covered by the company's own vessels.

In April 2014, the Isle of Man Steam Packet Company took the Seatruck ro-ro *Arrow*, a vessel they had often used in the past, on long term charter. Although not required at all times, the charter ensured that she was available at times she was needed - for example, during the TT Season and when one of the other ships was out of service. At other times she has been sub-chartered to other operators, in particular *Condor Ferries*.

IRELAND

In February 2015, The Department for Regional Development, Northern Ireland ordered a new ferry from Cammell Laird, Birkenhead for the service across the mouth of Strangford Loch. Similar to the 2001 built *Portaferry II*, she will replace the 1969 built Strangford Ferry in 2016. A similar vessel is to be ordered to replace the *Canna* on the service from Ballycastle to Rathlin Island.

The Lough Foyle Ferry Company's summer only Lough Swilly Service between Buncrana and Rathmullan in County Donegal, operated by the *Foyle Rambler,* did not resume in summer 2014 due to the withdrawal of subsidy. The vessel was sold to the Waterford Castle Hotel in the Republic of Ireland and renamed the *Mary Fitzgerald*. Built as a self steering vessel she was modified to allow for cable guidance. She replaced the 1959 built former Rhine ferry the *Loreley*.

SCOTLAND

Clydelink kept the *Cailin Oir* as Gourock - Kilcreggan back-up vessel through the first part of 2014. She returned to Ireland in April 2014 and did not return. Meanwhile, the vessel which previous operator, Clyde Marine, had specially built for the route, the *Seabus*, was renamed the *Chieftain* and now operates as part of the company's excursion and charter fleet.

Caledonian MacBrayne's second hybrid vessel, the *Lochinvar* was delivered almost a year after launch in May 2014. She operates on the summer only Tarbert - Portavadie service and on other routes during the winter. In August, the vessel's builders, Ferguson Shipbuilders, went into administration. Fortunately new owners purchased the yard and, as Ferguson Marine Engineering, in September secured the order for a third hybrid ferry to be operated by Caledonian MacBrayne from 2016.

The new Ullapool - Stornoway vessel, the *Loch Seaforth* was expected in July 2015 but due to various delays at the builders, FSG in Flensburg, was not delivered until November. Towards the end of the build process, the yard, which had been in financial difficulties for some time, was in danger of going into administration. As the ship would have become a disposable asset of the company, she was purchased by the customer, Caledonian Maritime Assets, in an uncompleted state and the yard continued to work on her. In the event the yard was purchased by a Norwegian company and was able to continue.

However, even when she was delivered it was not possible for her to operate as planned as berth modifications at Ullapool had not been undertaken. She eventually entered service in March 2015 using the old linkspan. The new linkspan was installed in April and May 2015 and vehicle services were diverted to Uig, operated by the *Isle of Lewis*. Meanwhile the chartered freight ship, the *Clipper Ranger*, continued in service.

The *Coruisk* was again stationed at Gourock during winter 2014/15 to operate on the service to Dunoon when weather conditions stopped the two passenger ferries operating and also had her own peak hour workings.

Caledonian MacBraynes last 'Clyde streaker', the *Saturn*, which had been laid up since 2011, finally found a buyer in February 2015 in the form of Pentland Ferries of Orkney who have renamed her the *Orcadia*.

Bruce Watt, who operated the 1969 built *Western Isles* between Mallaig and Inverie on the Knoydart peninsular retired in September 2013. A new operator called Western Isles Cruises took over the vessel in spring 2014.

Nick Widdows

Norbank *(Gordon Hislip)*

Clansman *(Stuart Mackillop)*

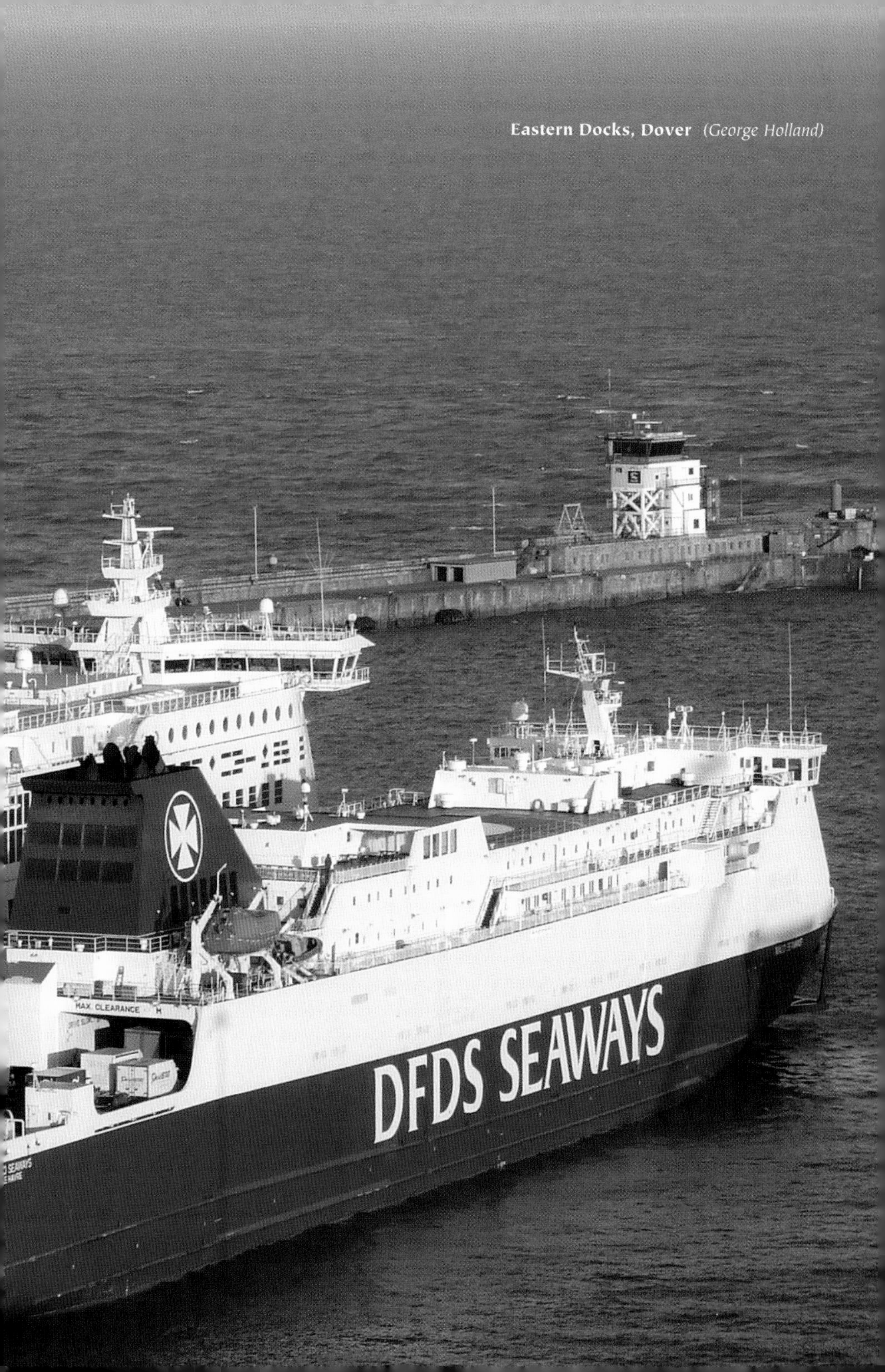

Eastern Docks, Dover *(George Holland)*

SECTION 1 - GB AND IRELAND - MAJOR PASSENGER OPERATORS

BRITTANY FERRIES

THE COMPANY Brittany Ferries is the trading name of BAI SA, a French private sector company and the operating arm of the Brittany Ferries Group. The UK operations are run by BAI (UK) Ltd, a UK private sector company, wholly owned by the Brittany Ferries Group.

MANAGEMENT Group Managing Director Martine Jourdren, Commercial Director, Passengers Mike Bevens, Commercial Director, Freight Simon Wagstaff.

ADDRESS Millbay Docks, Plymouth, Devon PL1 3EW.

TELEPHONE Passenger - Administration Plymouth +44 (0)871 244 0500, Portsmouth +44 (0)871 244 0600, Reservations All Services +44 (0)871 244 1400, Freight - Administration & Enquiries +44 (0)871 244 0411, Reservations +44 (0)871 244 0912.

FAX Freight - Administration & Reservations +44 (0)871 244 0912.

INTERNET Passenger - Website www.brittanyferries.com (English, French, Spanish, German), Freight Website www.brittanyferriesfreight.co.uk (English)

ROUTES OPERATED Conventional Ferries All year Plymouth - Roscoff (6 hrs (day), 7 hrs - 9 hrs (night); ARMORIQUE, PONT-AVEN; up to 2 per day (Summer), 1 per day (Winter)), Poole - Cherbourg (4 hrs 15 mins; BARFLEUR; 1 per day), Portsmouth - St Malo (8 hrs 45 mins (day), 10 hrs 45 mins (night); BRETAGNE; (1 per day), Portsmouth - Caen (Ouistreham) (6 hrs (day), 6 hrs - 8 hrs (night); NORMANDIE, MONT ST MICHEL; 3 per day), Portsmouth - Le Havre (5 hrs 30 mins; BAIE DE SEINE, ETRETAT, 9 per week), Portsmouth - Santander (Spain) (24 hrs; CAP FINISTERE, ETRETAT, PONT-AVEN; up to 3 per week, Portsmouth - Bilbao (Spain) (24/32 hrs; BAIE DE SEINE, CAP FINISTERE; up to 3 per week, Summer only Plymouth - Santander (Spain) (19 hrs 30 mins; PONT-AVEN; 1 per week (April - October)), Cork - Roscoff (14 hrs; PONT-AVEN; 1 per week (March - November)). Fast Ferries Summer only Plymouth - Cherbourg (3 hrs; NORMANDIE EXPRESS; 1 per day (April-September)), Portsmouth - Le Havre (3 hrs 45 mins; NORMANDIE EXPRESS; Sat & Sun (May - September); 1 per day). Note: The Portsmouth - Le Havre service and sailings to Spain operated by the BAIE DE SEINE and ETRETAT are branded 'économie'.

1	ARMORIQUE	29468 t	09	23.0k	167.0m	1500P	470C	65L	BA2	FR	9364980
2	BAIE DE SEINE	22382t	03	22.0k	199.4m	596P	316C	154T	A	FR	9212163
3	BARFLEUR	20133t	92	19.0k	158.0m	1212P	590C	112T	BA2	FR	9007130
4	BRETAGNE	24534t	89	19.5k	151.0m	1926P	580C	84T	BA	FR	8707329
5	CAP FINISTERE	32728t	01	28.0k	203.9m	1608P	1000C	140T	BA	FR	9198927
6	ETRETAT	26500t	08	23.5k	186.5m	800P	185C	120L	A	FR	9420423
7	MONT ST MICHEL	35592t	02	21.2k	173.0m	2200P	880C	166T	BA2	FR	9238337
8	NORMANDIE	27541t	92	20.5k	161.0m	2120P	600C	126T	BA2	FR	9006253
9»	NORMANDIE EXPRESS	6581t	00	40.0k	97.2m	900P	260C	-	A	FR	8814134
10	PONT-AVEN	41748t	04	26.0k	184.3m	2400P	650C	85L	BA	FR	9268708

ARMORIQUE Built by STX Europe, Helsinki, Finland for Brittany Ferries to operate between Plymouth and Roscoff.

BAIE DE SEINE Built as the GOLFO DEI DELFINI by Stocznia Szczecinska, Szczecin, Poland for Lloyd Sardegna of Italy for service between Italy and Sardinia. However, due to late delivery the order was cancelled. In 2002 purchased by DFDS Seaways, and, during Winter 2002/03, passenger accommodation was enlarged and refitted, increasing passenger capacity from 308 to 596. In June 2003, renamed the DANA SIRENA, she replaced unmodified sister vessel, the DANA GLORIA on the Esbjerg – Harwich service. In February 2013 she was renamed the SIRENA SEAWAYS. At the end of September 2014 the route ceased and she moved to the Paldiski (Estonia) - Kapellskär route, replacing the PATRIA SEAWAYS. In December she was replaced by the LIVERPOOL SEAWAYS and laid up. During the early part of 2015 she performed relief work in the Baltic. In April 2015 she was

Is there **_any_** better way to discover France or Spain?

chartered to *Brittany Ferries* for five years and renamed the BAIE DE SEINE. She entered service in May.

BARFLEUR Built as the BARFLEUR by Kvaerner Masa-Yards, Helsinki for the *Truckline* (freight division of *Brittany Ferries*) Poole - Cherbourg service to replace two passenger vessels and to inaugurate a year-round passenger service. In 1999 the *Truckline* branding was dropped for passenger services and she was repainted into full *Brittany Ferries* livery. In 2005 operated partly Cherbourg - Poole and partly Cherbourg - Portsmouth but in 2006 returned to operating mainly to Poole. In February 2010, she was laid up. The conventional car ferry service ended the following month. In March 2010, she resumed service on the Poole - Cherbourg route. In September 2011 she was withdrawn again. In April 2012 chartered to *DFDS Seaways* to operate between Dover and Calais and renamed the DEAL SEAWAYS. In November 2012 returned to *Brittany Ferries* and renamed the BARFLEUR. Resumed the Poole - Cherbourg service in March 2013, replacing the COTENTIN but offering a service for both freight and passengers.

BRETAGNE Built by Chantiers de l'Atlantique, St Nazaire for the Plymouth - Santander and Cork - Roscoff services (with two sailings per week between Plymouth and Roscoff). In 1993 she was transferred to the Portsmouth - St Malo service. In 2004 also operated between Portsmouth and Cherbourg. In 2005 operated between Plymouth and Roscoff. In 2006 returned to the Portsmouth - St Malo route.

CAP FINISTERE Built as the SUPERFAST V by Howaldtswerke Deutsche Werft AG, Kiel, Germany for *Attica Enterprises* (now *Attica Group*) for use by *Superfast Ferries* of Greece. Initially operated between Patras and Ancona and in January 2007 switched to the Patras - Igoumenitsa - Bari route. In 2008 the route became Patras - Igoumenitsa - Ancona. In 2010 sold to *Brittany Ferries*, renamed the CAP FINISTERE and in March placed on the Portsmouth - Santander service, also operating some sailings between Portsmouth and Cherbourg. In 2011 began operating also between Portsmouth and Bilbao and only operated between Portsmouth and Cherbourg during the winter period. Now operates on Portsmouth – Santander and Portsmouth – Bilbao routes only.

ETRETAT Built as the NORMAN VOYAGER by CN Visentini, Porto Viro, Italy for *Epic Shipping* of the UK and chartered to *LD Lines*. Operated between Le Havre and Portsmouth and Le Havre and Rosslare. In September 2009 sub-chartered to *Celtic Link Ferries*. Initially operated between Cherbourg and Portsmouth and Cherbourg and Rosslare but the Portsmouth service was abandoned in November 2009. In October 2011 returned to *LD Lines* and placed on the St Nazaire - Gijon route. In November moved to the Portsmouth - Le Havre service and, following the establishment of the joint *LD Lines/DFDS* venture, the charter was transferred to *DFDS Seaways*. In April 2012 sold to *Stena RoRo*; she continued to be chartered to *DFDS*. In March 2014 chartered to *Brittany Ferries* and placed on the new 'économie' services between Portsmouth and Le Havre and Portsmouth and Santander. Renamed the ETRETAT.

MONT ST MICHEL Built by Van der Giessen-de Noord, Krimpen aan den IJssel, Rotterdam for *Brittany Ferries*. Used on the Portsmouth - Caen route.

NORMANDIE Built by Kvaerner Masa-Yards, Turku, Finland for *Brittany Ferries*. Used on the Portsmouth - Caen route.

NORMANDIE EXPRESS Incat Evolution 10 catamaran built as the INCAT TASMANIA. In November 2000 chartered to *TranzRail* of New Zealand and renamed THE LYNX. Placed on the Wellington – Picton service. In July 2003 replaced by 1997-built Incat 86m craft INCAT 046, given the marketing name 'The Lynx' and laid up. In Spring 2005 chartered to *Brittany Ferries* to operate on their Cherbourg – Portsmouth and Caen – Portsmouth services and renamed the NORMANDIE EXPRESS. In 2007 purchased by *Brittany Ferries*. In 2015 operates to Cherbourg and Le Havre.

PONT-AVEN Built by Jos L Meyer Werft, Papenburg, Germany for *Brittany Ferries* to operate on the Plymouth - Roscoff, Plymouth - Santander and Cork - Roscoff routes.

Armorique *(John Bryant)*

Barfleur *(Kevin Mitchell)*

CONDOR FERRIES

THE COMPANY *Condor Ferries Ltd* is a Channel Islands private sector company owned by the *Condor Group*, Guernsey which is owned by *Macquarie European Infrastructure*.

MANAGEMENT Managing Director Simon Edsall, **Sales and Marketing Director** Alicia Andrews, **Marketing Manager** Justin Amey, **Sales Manager** Jonathan Godson.

ADDRESS **Head Office** New Jetty Offices, White Rock, St Peter Port, Guernsey GYI 2LL, **Sales and Marketing** Condor House, New Harbour Road South, Hamworthy, Poole BH15 4AJ.

TELEPHONE **Administration** *Guernsey* +44 (0)1481 728620, *Poole* +44 (0)1202 207207, **Passenger Reservations** +44 (0)845 609 1024, **Freight Reservations** +44 (0)1481 728521.

FAX **Administration** *Guernsey* +44 (0)1481 712555; *Poole* +44 (0)1202 685184.

INTERNET **Email** *Passenger* reservations@condorferries.co.uk

Freight len.lepage@condorferries.co.uk **Website** www.condorferries.com *(English, French, German)*

ROUTES OPERATED *Conventional Passenger Ferry* Portsmouth to Guernsey (from 7 hrs) and Jersey (from 9 hrs) (*COMMODORE CLIPPER*; daily except Sun). *Fast Ferries* Poole - Guernsey (from 2 hrs 40 mins) and Jersey (from 4 hrs) (*CONDOR LIBERATION*; up to 2 per day), Guernsey (2 hrs) and Jersey (1 hr 20 mins) to St Malo (*CONDOR RAPIDE*; 1 per day). *Freight Ferry* Portsmouth - Guernsey - Jersey (10 hrs 30 min; *COMMODORE GOODWILL*; 1 per day), Guernsey - Jersey - St Malo (13 hrs; *COMMODORE GOODWILL*; 1 per week).

1	COMMODORE CLIPPER	14000t	99	18.0k	129.1m	500P	100C	92T	A	BS	9201750
2F	COMMODORE GOODWILL	11166t	96	17.3k	126.4m	12P	-	92T	A	BS	9117985
3»	CONDOR LIBERATION	6307t	10	39.0k	102.0m	873P	245C	12L	A	BS	9551363
4»	CONDOR RAPIDE	5007t	97	40.5k	86.6m	870P	200C	-	A	BS	9161560

COMMODORE CLIPPER Ro-pax vessel built by Van der Giessen-de Noord, Krimpen aan den IJssel, Rotterdam for *Commodore Ferries* to operate between Portsmouth and the Channel Islands. She replaced the ISLAND COMMODORE, a freight-only vessel. Her passenger capacity is normally restricted to 300 but is increased to 500 when the fast ferries are unable to operate.

COMMODORE GOODWILL Built by Koninklijke Scheldegroep BV, Vlissingen, The Netherlands for *Commodore Ferries*.

CONDOR LIBERATION Austal 102-metre Trimaran built speculatively by Austal Ships Pty, Fremantle, Australia as AUSTAL HULL 270. Laid up. In August 2014 sold to *Condor Ferries*. During autumn and early winter 2014/15 she was modified by Austal Ships in their shipyard at Balamban, Cebu, Philippines and in March 2015 renamed the CONDOR LIBERATION and placed on the Poole - Channel Islands service.

CONDOR RAPIDE Incat 86m catamaran built at Hobart, Tasmania, Australia as the INCAT 045. Chartered to *Transport Tasmania* of Australia and operated between Melbourne (Victoria) and Devonport (Tasmania). In 1999 she was chartered to the *Royal Australian Navy*, renamed the HMAS JERVIS BAY and took part in moving Australian troops from Darwin to Dili (East Timor) as part of the United Nations operation. She operated over 75 trips between the two points carrying personnel and equipment for the United Nations Transitional Administration in East Timor (UNTAET). The charter ended in May 2001 and she was renamed the INCAT 045 and laid up. In Spring 2003 she was chartered to *Traghetti Isole Sarde (TRIS)* of Italy, renamed the WINNER and operated between Genoa and Palau (Sardinia). In Autumn 2003 the charter ended, she resumed the name INCAT 045 and was laid up at Portland, Dorset. In 2004 chartered to *SpeedFerries* and renamed the SPEED ONE. In May 2008 purchased by *SpeedFerries*. In November 2008 the services ceased and the company went into administration. She was laid up at Tilbury. In May she was sold at auction to *Epic Shipping* of the UK and renamed the SEA LEOPARD. In April 2010 sold to *Condor Ferries* and renamed the CONDOR RAPIDE. Entered service in May 2010.

Condor Liberation *(Kevin Mitchell)*

Commodore Clipper *(Matt Davies)*

Finlaggan (*Stuart Mackillop*)

Lord of the Isles (*Stuart Mackillop*)

DAVID MACBRAYNE GROUP

THE COMPANY David MacBrayne Limited is a Scottish registered company, wholly owned by the Scottish Ministers. Its ferry operations are conducted through two subsidiary companies - Argyll Ferries Ltd and CalMac Ferries Ltd (trading as Caledonian MacBrayne). The majority of CalMac Ferries vessels are owned by Caledonian Maritime Assets Limited, a separate company which is also owned by the Scottish Ministers.

ARGYLL FERRIES

MANAGEMENT Managing Director Martin Dorchester, Public Affairs Manager David Cannon.

ADDRESS Ferry Terminal, Gourock PA19 1QP.

TELEPHONE Administration +44 (0)1475 650100, Customer services 0800 066 5000.

FAX Administration +44 (0)1475 650336,

INTERNET Email info@argyllferries.co.uk Website www.argyllferries.co.uk (English)

ROUTE OPERATED All-year passenger-only ferry Gourock - Dunoon (20 mins; ALI CAT, ARGYLL FLYER, CORUISK of Caledonian MacBrayne (winter only) 1 or 2 per hour.

| 1p | ALI CAT | 74t | 99 | - | 19.8m | 250P | 0C | 0L | - | UK | |
| 2p | ARGYLL FLYER | 300t | 01 | 19.5k | 29.9m | 227P | 0C | 0L | - | UK | 9231016 |

ALI CAT Catamaran built for Solent & Wight Line Cruises of Ryde, Isle of Wight. She operated a passenger service from Cowes to Hamble and Warsash and cruises from Cowes. At times chartered to Wightlink to cover for the fast catamarans. In 2002 chartered to Red Funnel Ferries who had contracted with Caledonian MacBrayne to operate passenger-only services between Gourock and Dunoon in the morning and evening peaks. In June 2011 purchased by and operated by Argyll Ferries.

ARGYLL FLYER Built as the QUEEN OF ARAN II by OCEA, Les Sables d'Olonne, France for Inis Mór Ferries. In 2007 sold to Aran Island Ferries and renamed the BANRION CHONAMARA. In June 2011 sold to Argyll Ferries, renamed the ARGYLL FLYER and replaced the car ferry SATURN on the Gourock - Dunoon service.

CALEDONIAN MACBRAYNE

MANAGEMENT Managing Director Martin Dorchester, Marketing and e.Commerce Manager Cathy Craig, Public Affairs Manager David Cannon.

ADDRESS Ferry Terminal, Gourock PA19 1QP.

TELEPHONE Administration +44 (0)1475 650100, Vehicle Reservations +44 (0)800 066 5000.

FAX Administration +44 (0)1475 650336, Vehicle Reservations +44 (0)1475 635235.

INTERNET Email enquiries@calmac.co.uk Website www.calmac.co.uk (English)

ROUTES OPERATED All-year vehicle ferries (frequencies are for Summer – services are listed alphabetically, by mainland port or larger island port where service is between two islands), Ardmhor (Barra) - Eriskay (40 mins; LOCH ALAINN; up to 5 per day), Ardrossan - Brodick (Arran) (55 mins; CALEDONIAN ISLES, ISLE OF ARRAN; up to 6 per day), Colintraive - Rhubodach (Bute) (5 mins; LOCH DUNVEGAN; frequent service), Kennacraig - Port Askaig (Islay) (2 hrs 5 mins; FINLAGGAN, HEBRIDEAN ISLES; up to 4 per day), Kennacraig - Port Ellen (Islay) (2 hrs 20 mins; FINLAGGAN, HEBRIDEAN ISLES; service currently suspended due to harbour works), Largs - Cumbrae Slip (Cumbrae) (10 mins; LOCH RIDDON, LOCH SHIRA,; every 30 or 15 mins), Leverburgh (Harris) - Berneray (1 hr 10 mins; LOCH PORTAIN; 3-4 per day), Lochaline - Fishnish (Mull) (15 mins; LOCH FYNE; up to 14 per day), Mallaig - Armadale (Skye) (23 mins; CORUISK (Summer), LOCHNEVIS (Winter); up to 9 per day (2 in Winter)), Oban - Castlebay (Barra) (5 hrs (direct); CLANSMAN, LORD OF THE ISLES; 1 per day), Oban - Lochboisdale (South Uist) (5 hrs (if direct), 7 hrs (via Barra); CLANSMAN, LORD OF THE ISLES; 4 per week), Oban - Coll - Tiree (2 hrs 45 min to Coll, 3 hrs 50 min to Tiree via Coll; *CLANSMAN, LORD OF THE ISLES*; 1 per day), Oban - Colonsay (2 hrs 15 mins; *CLANSMAN, LORD OF THE ISLES*; 5 per week), Oban - Craignure (Mull) (45 mins; *ISLE OF MULL*; up to 7 per day), Oban - Lismore (50 mins; *EIGG, LOCH STRIVEN*; up to 4 per day), Sconser (Skye) - Raasay (15 mins; *HALLAIG*; up to 11 per day), Tarbert (Loch Fyne) - Portavadie (25 mins; *LOCHINVAR*; up to 12 per day), Tayinloan - Gigha (20 mins; *LOCH RANZA*; up to 10 per day), Tobermory (Mull) - Kilchoan (35 mins; *LOCH LINNHE*; up to 7 per day), Uig (Skye) - Lochmaddy (North Uist) (1 hr 45 mins; *HEBRIDES*; 1 or 2 per day), Uig (Skye) - Tarbert (Harris) (1 hr 40 mins; *HEBRIDES*; 1 or 2 per day), Ullapool - Stornoway (Lewis) (2 hrs 45 mins; *LOCH SEAFORTH, ISLE OF LEWIS*; up to 4 per day (one freight only)), Wemyss Bay - Rothesay (Bute) (35 mins; *ARGYLE, BUTE*; hourly), **All-year passenger and restricted vehicle ferries** (frequencies are for Summer) Fionnphort (Mull) - Iona (5 mins; *LOCH BUIE*; frequent), Mallaig - Eigg - Muck - Rum - Canna - Mallaig (round trip 7 hrs (all islands); *LOCHNEVIS*; at least 1 sailing per day - most islands visited daily). **Note** Although these services are operated by vehicle ferries, special permission is required to take a vehicle and tourist cars are not normally conveyed, **Summer-only vehicle ferries** Ardrossan - Campbeltown (2 hrs 30 mins; *ISLE OF ARRAN*; 3 per week), Claonaig - Lochranza (Arran) (30 mins; *LOCH TARBERT*; up to 9 per day), Kennacraig - Port Askaig - Colonsay - Oban (3 hrs 35 mins; *HEBRIDEAN ISLES*; 1 per week), **Winter-only vehicle ferry** Tarbert (Loch Fyne) - Lochranza (Arran) (1 hr; *varies*; 1 per day).

1	ARGYLE	2643t	07	14.0k	69.0m	450P	60C	-	BAS	UK	9365178
2	BUTE	2612t	05	14.0k	69.0m	450P	60C	-	AS	UK	9319741
3	CALEDONIAN ISLES	5221t	93	15.0k	94.3m	1000P	120C	10L	BA	UK	9051284
4	CLANSMAN	5499t	98	16.5k	99.0m	638P	90C	6L	BA	UK	9158953
5	CORUISK	1599t	03	14.0k	65.0m	250P	40C	-	BA	UK	9274836
6	EIGG	69t	75	8.0k	24.3m	75P	6C	-	B	UK	
7	FINLAGGAN	5626t	11	16.5k	89.9m	550P	88C	-	BA	UK	9482902
8	HALLAIG	499t	13	9.0k	43.5m	150P	23C	2L	BA	UK	9652832
9	HEBRIDEAN ISLES	3040t	85	15.0k	85.1m	494P	68C	10L	BAS	UK	8404812
10	HEBRIDES	5506t	00	16.5k	99.0m	612P	110C	6L	BA	UK	9211975
11	ISLE OF ARRAN	3296t	84	15.0k	85.0m	446P	68C	8L	BA	UK	8219554
12	ISLE OF CUMBRAE	201t	77	8.5k	37.7m	139P	18C	-	BA	UK	7521625
13	ISLE OF LEWIS	6753t	95	18.0k	101.2m	680P	123C	10L	BA	UK	9085974
14	ISLE OF MULL	4719t	88	15.0k	90.1m	962P	80C	20L	BA	UK	8608339
15	LOCH ALAINN	396t	98	10.0k	43.0m	150P	24C	-	BA	UK	9147722
16	LOCH BHRUSDA	246t	96	8.0k	35.4m	150P	18C	-	BA	UK	9129483
17	LOCH BUIE	295t	92	9.0k	35.5m	250P	9C	-	BA	UK	9031375
18	LOCH DUNVEGAN	549t	91	9.0k	54.2m	200P	36C	-	BA	UK	9006409
19	LOCH FYNE	549t	91	9.0k	54.2m	200P	36C	-	BA	UK	9006411
20	LOCH LINNHE	206t	86	9.0k	35.5m	199P	12C	-	BA	UK	8512308
21	LOCH PORTAIN	950t	03	10.5k	50.0m	200P	32C	-	BA	UK	9274824
22	LOCH RANZA	206t	87	9.0k	35.7m	199P	12C	-	BA	UK	8519887
23	LOCH RIDDON	206t	86	9.0k	35.5m	199P	12C	-	BA	UK	8519875
24	LOCH SEAFORTH	8478t	14	19.2k	116.0m	700P	143C	20L	BA	UK	9665437
25	LOCH SHIRA	1024t	07	13.0k	43.0m	250P	24C	-	BA	UK	9376919
26	LOCH STRIVEN	206t	86	9.0k	35.7m	199P	12C	-	BA	UK	8512293
27	LOCH TARBERT	211t	92	9.0k	34.5m	149P	18C	-	BA	UK	9039389
28	LOCHINVAR	523t	14	9.0k	43.5m	150P	23C	2L	BA	UK	9652844
29	LOCHNEVIS	941t	00	13.0k	49.1m	190P	14C	-	A	UK	9209063
30	LORD OF THE ISLES	3504t	89	16.0k	84.6m	506P	56C	16L	BAS	UK	8710869
31	RAASAY	69t	76	8.0k	24.3m	75P	6C	-	B	UK	

Note In the following list, Gaelic names are shown in parenthesis.

ARGYLE (*EARRA-GHÀIDHEAL*), BUTE (*EILEAN BHÒID*) Built by Stocznia Remontowa, Gdansk, Poland to operate on the Wemyss Bay - Rothesay route.

Coruisk *(John Hendy)*

CALEDONIAN ISLES *(EILEANAN CHALEDONIA)* Built by Richards Shipyard, Lowestoft, UK for the Ardrossan - Brodick (Arran) service.

CLANSMAN *(FEAR-CINNIDH)* Built by Appledore Shipbuilders Ltd, Appledore, UK to replace the LORD OF THE ISLES on the Oban - Coll and Tiree and Oban - Castlebay and Lochboisdale services in the summer. She also serves as winter relief vessel on the Stornoway, Tarbert, Lochmaddy, Mull/Colonsay and Brodick routes.

CORUISK *(COIR' UISG')* Built by Appledore Shipbuilders Ltd, Appledore, UK to operate on the Mallaig - Armadale route during the summer. She operates on the Upper Clyde as a relief vessel during the winter. Between December 2013 and March 2014 operated for *Argyle Ferries* in lieu of the ALI CAT during peak periods and when that vessel could not sail due to adverse weather.

EIGG *(EILEAN EIGE)* Built by James Lamont & Co, Port Glasgow, UK. Since 1976 she has been employed mainly on the Oban - Lismore service. In 1996 she was transferred to the Tobermory (Mull) - Kilchoan route, very occasionally making sailings to the Small Isles (Canna, Eigg, Muck and Rum) for special cargoes. In 1999 her wheelhouse was raised to make it easier to see over taller lorries and she returned to the Oban - Lismore route. At present she continues to operate some sailings because of difficulties in operating the larger 'Loch class' vessels at the slipways at some states of the tide.

FINLAGGAN *(FIONN LAGAN)* Built by Stocznia Remontowa, Gdansk, Poland for the Kennacraig - Islay service.

HALLAIG *(HALLAIG)* Built by Ferguson Shipbuilders, Port Glasgow, UK to replace the LOCH STRIVEN on the Sconser - Raasay service. The vessel has both diesel and battery electric propulsion and can be 'plugged in' to a land supply on Raasay overnight.

HEBRIDEAN ISLES *(EILEANAN INNSE GALL)* Built by Cochrane Shipbuilders, Selby UK for the Uig - Tarbert/Lochmaddy service. She was used initially on the Ullapool - Stornoway and Oban - Craignure/Colonsay services pending installation of link-span facilities at Uig, Tarbert and Lochmaddy. She took up her regular role in May 1986. From May 1996 she no longer operated direct services in summer between Tarbert and Lochmaddy, this role being taken on by the new Harris - North Uist services of the LOCH BHRUSDA. In 2001 she was replaced by the HEBRIDES and transferred to the Islay service. In Autumn 2002 she operated between Scrabster and Stromness for *NorthLink Orkney and Shetland Ferries* before port modifications at Scrabster enabled the HAMNAVOE to enter service in Spring 2003. She then returned to the Islay service. She also relieved on the *NorthLink* Pentland Firth service between 2004 and 2007.

HEBRIDES *(INNSE GALL)* Built by Ferguson Shipbuilders Ltd, Port Glasgow, UK for the Uig - Tarbert and Uig - Lochmaddy services.

ISLE OF ARRAN *(EILEAN ARAINN)* Built by Ferguson Ailsa, Port Glasgow, UK for the Ardrossan - Brodick service. In 1993 transferred to the Kennacraig - Port Ellen/Port Askaig service, also undertaking the weekly Port Askaig - Colonsay - Oban summer service. From then until 1997/98 she also relieved on the Brodick, Coll/Tiree, Castlebay/Lochboisdale, Craignure and Tarbert/Lochmaddy routes in winter. In 2001 she was replaced by the HEBRIDEAN ISLES and became a reserve for the larger vessels. She has operated on the two-ship Islay service in summer since 2003; this service is now all-year-round. Following the delivery of the FINLAGGAN in May 2011 she became a spare vessel, and operates extra services between Ardrossan and Brodick and Ardrossan and Campbeltown during the peak summer period.

ISLE OF CUMBRAE *(EILEAN CHUMRAIGH)* Built by Ailsa Shipbuilding Ltd, Troon, UK for the Largs - Cumbrae Slip (Cumbrae) service. In 1986 she was replaced by the LOCH LINNHE and the LOCH STRIVEN and transferred to the Lochaline - Fishnish (Mull) service. She used to spend most of the winter as secondary vessel on the Kyle of Lochalsh - Kyleakin service; however, this ceased following the opening of the Skye Bridge in 1995. In 1997 she was transferred to the Colintraive - Rhubodach service. In Summer 1999 she was transferred to the Tarbert - Portavadie service. In May 2014 replaced by the new LOCHINVAR and laid up.

ISLE OF LEWIS *(EILEAN LEÒDHAIS)* Built by Ferguson Shipbuilders Ltd, Port Glasgow, UK for the Ullapool - Stornoway service. In February 2015 replaced by the new LOCH SEAFORTH. During peak summer period 2015 she will operate an additional sailing between Ullapool and Stornoway.

Isle of Lewis (*Matt Davies*)

Loch Seaforth (*Peter Therkildsen*)

ISLE OF MULL *(AN T-EILEAN MUILEACH)* Built by Appledore Ferguson, Port Glasgow, UK for the Oban - Craignure (Mull) service. She also operates some Oban - Colonsay sailings and until 1997/98 was the usual winter relief vessel on the Ullapool - Stornoway service. She has also deputised on the Oban - Castlebay/Lochboisdale and Oban - Coll/Tiree routes.

LOCH ALAINN *(LOCH ÀLAINN)* Built by Buckie Shipbuilders Ltd, Buckie, UK for the Lochaline - Fishnish service. Launched as the LOCH ALINE but renamed the LOCH ALAINN before entering service. After a brief period on the service for which she was built, she was transferred to the Colintraive - Rhubodach route. In 1998 she was transferred to the Largs - Cumbrae Slip service. In 2007 moved to the Ardmhor (Barra) - Eriskay service. She relieves the larger 'Loch' class vessels in the winter, with her own service covered by the LOCH BHRUSDA.

LOCH BHRUSDA *(LOCH BHRÙSTA)* Built by McTay Marine, Bromborough, Wirral, UK to inaugurate a new Otternish (North Uist) - Leverburgh (Harris) service. In 2001 the service became Berneray - Leverburgh. In 2003 she moved to the Eriskay - Barra service, previously operated by *Comhairle Nan Eilean Siar* vessels. In 2007 she became a spare vessel on the Clyde. Note 'Bhrusda' is pronounced "Vroosta".

LOCH BUIE *(LOCH BUIDHE)* Built by J W Miller & Sons Ltd, St Monans, Fife, UK for the Fionnphort (Mull) - Iona service to replace the MORVERN (see *Arranmore Island Ferry Services*) and obviate the need for a relief vessel in the summer. Due to height restrictions, loading arrangements for vehicles taller than private cars are stern-only. Only islanders' cars and service vehicles (eg mail vans, police) are carried; no tourist vehicles are conveyed.

LOCH DUNVEGAN *(LOCH DÙNBHEAGAN)* Built by Ferguson Shipbuilders Ltd, Port Glasgow, UK for the Kyle of Lochalsh - Kyleakin service. On the opening of the Skye Bridge in October 1995 she was withdrawn from service and offered for sale. In Autumn 1997, she returned to service on the Lochaline - Fishnish route. In 1998 she was due to be transferred to the Colintraive - Rhubodach route but this was delayed because of problems in providing terminal facilities. She operated on the Clyde and between Mallaig and Armadale during the early summer and spent the rest of that summer laid up. In 1999 she was transferred to the Colintraive - Rhubodach route.

LOCH FYNE *(LOCH FINE)* Built by Ferguson Shipbuilders Ltd, Port Glasgow, UK for the Kyle of Lochalsh - Kyleakin service (see the LOCH DUNVEGAN). In Autumn 1997, she also served on the Lochaline - Fishnish route and was transferred to this route as regular vessel in 1998.

LOCH LINNHE *(AN LINNE DHUBH)* Built by Richard Dunston (Hessle) Ltd, Hessle, UK. Until 1997 she was used mainly on the Largs - Cumbrae Slip (Cumbrae) service and until Winter 1994/95 she was usually used on the Lochaline - Fishnish service during the winter. Since then she has relieved on various routes in winter. In Summer 1998 she operated mainly on the Tarbert - Portavadie route. In 1999 she was transferred to the Tobermory - Kilchoan service in summer.

LOCH PORTAIN *(LOCH PORTAIN)* Built by McTay Marine, Bromborough, Wirral, UK (hull constructed in Poland) to replace the LOCH BHRUSDA on the Berneray - Leverburgh service.

LOCH RANZA *(LOCH RAONASA)* Built by Richard Dunston (Hessle) Ltd, Hessle, UK for the Claonaig - Lochranza (Arran) seasonal service and used a relief vessel in the winter. In 1992 she was replaced by the LOCH TARBERT and transferred to the Tayinloan - Gigha service.

LOCH RIDDON *(LOCH RAODAIN)* Built by Richard Dunston (Hessle) Ltd, Hessle, UK. Until 1997 she was used almost exclusively on the Colintraive - Rhubodach service. In 1997, she was transferred to the Largs - Cumbrae Slip service. In January 2014 she became regular vessel on the Oban - Lismore service. However, after problems with using the slipways, she became the second vessel on the Largs - Cumbrae Slip service.

LOCH SEAFORTH *(LOCH SHIPHOIRT)* Built by Flensburger Schiffbau-Gesellschaft, Flensburg, Germany for the Stornoway - Ullapool service, replacing the ISLE OF LEWIS and freight vessel MUIRNEAG.

LOCH SHIRA *(LOCH SIORA)* Built by Ferguson Shipbuilders, Port Glasgow, UK for the Largs - Cumbrae Slip route.

LOCH STRIVEN (LOCH SROIGHEANN) Built by Richard Dunston (Hessle) Ltd, Hessle, UK. Used mainly on the Largs - Cumbrae Slip service until 1997. In Winter 1995/96 and 1996/97 she was used on the Tarbert - Portavadie and Claonaig - Lochranza routes. In 1997 she took over the Sconser - Raasay service. In winter 2014 replaced by the HALLAIG. In summer 2014 operating between Oban and Lismore.

LOCH TARBERT (LOCH AN TAIRBEIRT) Built by J W Miller & Sons Ltd, St Monans, Fife, UK for the Claonaig - Lochranza service. She was the winter relief vessel on the Largs - Cumbrae Slip route between 1994/95 and 2007/08.

LOCHINVAR (LOCH AN BARR) As the HALLAIG. Operates on the Tarbert - Portavadie route.

LOCHNEVIS (LOCH NIBHEIS) Built by Ailsa Shipbuilding, Troon, UK to replace the LOCHMOR on the Mallaig - Small Isles service and the winter Mallaig - Armadale service. Although a vehicle ferry, cars are not normally carried to the Small Isles; the ro-ro facility is used for the carriage of agricultural machinery and livestock and it is possible to convey a vehicle on the ferry from which goods can be unloaded directly onto local transport rather than transhipping at Mallaig.

LORD OF THE ISLES (RIGH NAN EILEAN) Built by Appledore Ferguson, Port Glasgow, UK to replace the CLAYMORE on the Oban - Castlebay and Lochboisdale services and also the COLUMBA (1420t, 1964) on the Oban - Coll and Tiree service. She took over the Mallaig - Armadale and Mallaig - Outer Isles services in July 1998 but returned to her previous routes during the winter period. In Spring 2003 the Mallaig – Armadale service was taken over by the PIONEER standing in for the new CORUISK and she operated services from Oban to South Uist and Barra. She now serves Colonsay, Coll, Tiree, Barra, Craignure and Lochboisdale from Oban.

RAASAY (EILEAN RATHARSAIR) Built by James Lamont & Co Ltd, Port Glasgow, UK for and used primarily on the Sconser (Skye) - Raasay service. In 1997 she was replaced by the LOCH STRIVEN, became a spare/relief vessel and inaugurated in October 2003 the winter service between Tobermory (Mull) and Kilchoan (Ardnamurchan).

Under Construction

| 33 | NEWBUILDING 1 | | 499t | 16 | 9.0k | 43.5m | 150P | 23C | 2L | BA | UK | |

NEWBUILDING 1 Under construction by Ferguson Marine Engineering, Port Glasgow. Sister vessel of the HALLAIG and LOCHINVAR. Route to be decided.

To be ordered

| 34 | NEWBUILDING 2 | - | 17 | 16.5k | 100.0m | 1000P | 127C | 16L | BA | UK | - |
| 35 | NEWBUILDING 3 | - | 17 | 16.5k | 100.0m | 1000P | 127C | 16L | BA | UK | - |

NEWBUILDING 2, NEWBUILDING 3 Tenders being sought by Caledonian Maritime Assets for two new vessels to operate on the Ardrossan - Brodick and Uig - Tarbert - Lochmaddy services. They are likely to supplement rather than replace the existing vessels.

DFDS SEAWAYS

THE COMPANY DFDS Seaways is a business unit within DFDS A/S, a Danish private sector company. Services from Dover, Newhaven and Marseilles are operated by DFDS Seaways France which was inaugurated in March 2013 following the establishment of a DFDS Seaways/LD Lines joint venture in November 2012. It is 82% owned by DFDS and 18% by Louis Dreyfus Armateurs. The Newhaven - Dieppe route is branded as Transmanche Ferries, operating under a franchise awarded by Syndicat Mixte de L'Activité Transmanche in Dieppe.

MANAGEMENT President and CEO DFDS A/S Niels Smedegaard, Head of Shipping Division Peder Gellert Pedersen, Managing Director, DFDS Seaways PLC Sean Potter, Head of North Sea Business Area Kell Robdrup, Head of English Channel Business Area Carsten Jensen, Head of Passenger Business Area Brian Thorsted Hansen.

ADDRESS International Ferry Terminal, North Shields NE29 6EA.

TELEPHONE Administration +44 (0)191 296 5546, **Passenger Reservations** 0871 882 0881, Freight Reservations see website.

FAX **Freight Reservations** see website.

INTERNET Websites *Passenger* www.dfdsseaways.co.uk *(Chinese, Danish, Dutch, English, German, Italian, Japanese, Norwegian, Polish, Swedish) Freight* freight.dfdsseaways.com *(English) Corporate* www.dfds.com *(English)*

ROUTES OPERATED *Passenger ferries* Newcastle (North Shields) - IJmuiden (near Amsterdam, The Netherlands) (15 hrs; *KING SEAWAYS, PRINCESS SEAWAYS;* daily). ROUTES OPERATED Dover - Dunkerque (2 hrs; *DELFT SEAWAYS, DOVER SEAWAYS, DUNKERQUE SEAWAYS,* 12 per day), Dover - Calais (1 hr 30 mins; *CALAIS SEAWAYS, MALO SEAWAYS;* 10 per day), Newhaven - Dieppe (4 hrs; *COTE D'ALBATRE, SEVEN SISTERS;* up to 3 per day (ships continue to be branded *Transmanche Ferries). Freight only ferries* Zeebrugge (Belgium) - Rosyth (Scotland) (20 hrs; *FINLANDIA SEAWAYS;* 3 per week), Esbjerg - Immingham (18 hrs; *ARK DANIA, ARK GERMANIA;* 6 per week), Cuxhaven - Immingham (19 hrs; *CLIPPER POINT, HAFNIA SEAWAYS;* 4/5 per week), Gothenburg - Immingham (26 hrs (direct), *45 hrs (via Brevik (Fri)); *BEGONIA SEAWAYS, FIONIA SEAWAYS, FREESIA SEAWAYS;* 7 per week), Brevik - Immingham (25 hrs (direct), 42 hrs (via Gothenburg); *BEGONIA SEAWAYS, FIONIA SEAWAYS, FREESIA SEAWAYS;* 2 per week), Gothenburg - Brevik (Norway) - Ghent (Belgium) (Gothenburg 32 hrs, Brevik 32 hrs; *MAGNOLIA SEAWAYS, PETUNIA SEAWAYS, PRIMULA SEAWAYS;* 5 per week), Vlaardingen - Immingham (14 hrs; *FICARIA SEAWAYS, JUTLANDIA SEAWAYS;* 6 per week), Vlaardingen - Felixstowe (7 hrs; *BRITANNIA SEAWAYS, SELANDIA SEAWAYS, SUECIA SEAWAYS;* 3 per day). Marseilles – Tunis (currently freight only) (3 per week; *ARK FUTURA),* Note the Marseilles - Tunis route is outside the scope of this book but is included for completeness.

Note Freight vessels are sometimes moved between routes.

1F	ANGLIA SEAWAYS	13073t	00	18.5k	142.5m	12P	-	114T	A	DK	9186649
2F	ARK DANIA	25000t	14	20.0k	195.2m	12P	-	206T	A	DK	9609964
3F	ARK FUTURA	18725t	96	19.7k	183.3m	12P	-	164T	AS	DK	9129598
4F	ARK GERMANIA	25000t	14	20.0k	195.2m	12P	-	206T	A	DK	9609952
5F	BEGONIA SEAWAYS	37722t	04	22.5k	230.0m	12P	-	340T	AS	DK	9262089
6F	BRITANNIA SEAWAYS	24196t	00	21.1k	197.5m	12P	-	200T	AS	DK	9153032
7	CALAIS SEAWAYS	28833t	91	21.0k	163.6m	1850P	600C	100L	BA2	FR	8908466
8F	CLIPPER POINT	14759t	08	22.0k	142.0m	12P	-	120T	A	CY	9350666
9	COTE D'ALBATRE	18425t	06	22.0k	112.0m	600P	300C	62L	BA	FR	9320128
10	DELFT SEAWAYS	35923t	06	25.5k	187.0m	780P	200C	120L	BA2	UK	9293088
11	DOVER SEAWAYS	35923t	06	25.8k	187.0m	780P	200C	120L	BA2	UK	9318345
12	DUNKERQUE SEAWAYS	35923t	05	25.8k	187.0m	780P	200C	120L	BA2	UK	9293076
13F	FICARIA SEAWAYS	37939t	04	22.5k	230.0m	12P	-	340T	AS	DK	9320568
14F	FIONIA SEAWAYS	25609t	09	20.0k	184.8m	12P	-	250T	AS	UK	9395343
15F	FREESIA SEAWAYS	37722t	04	22.5k	230.0m	12P	-	340T	AS	DK	9274848
16F	HAFNIA SEAWAYS	25609t	08	20.0k	184.8m	12P	-	250T	AS	UK	9357602
17F	JUTLANDIA SEAWAYS	25609t	10	20.0k	184.8m	12P	-	250T	AS	UK	9395355
18	KING SEAWAYS	31788t	87	20.0k	161.6m	1400P	600C	104T	BA	DK	8502406
19F	MAGNOLIA SEAWAYS	32289t	03	22.5k	199.8m	12P	-	280T	AS	DK	9259496
20	MALO SEAWAYS	24206t	01	25.7k	169.8m	405P	375C	90L	BA2	FR	9215505
21F	PETUNIA SEAWAYS	32289t	04	22.5k	199.8m	12P	-	280T	AS	DK	9259501
22F	PRIMULA SEAWAYS	32289t	04	22.5k	199.8m	12P	-	280T	AS	DK	9259513
23	PRINCESS SEAWAYS	31356t	86	18.5k	161.0m	1600P	600C	100T	BA	DK	8502391
24F	SELANDIA SEAWAYS	24196t	98	21.0k	197.5m	12P	-	206T	A	DK	9157284
25	SEVEN SISTERS	18425t	06	22.0k	112.0m	600P	300C	62L	BA	FR	9320130
26F	SUECIA SEAWAYS	24196t	99	21.0k	197.5m	12P	-	206T	AS	DK	9153020

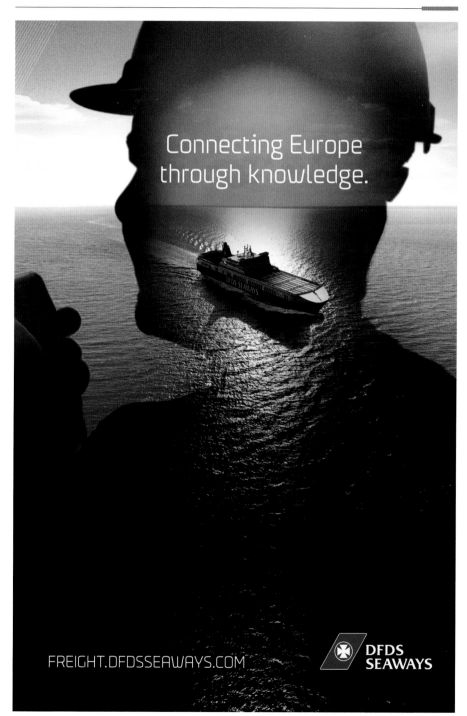

ANGLIA SEAWAYS Built as the MAERSK ANGLIA by Guangzhou Shipyard International, Guangzhou, China for *Norfolkline*. Entered service as the GUANGZHOU 7130011 (unofficially the 'China II') but renamed shortly afterwards. Operated on the Scheveningen (from 2007 Vlaardingen) - Felixstowe service. In June 2009 moved to the Heysham - Dublin route. In August 2010 renamed the ANGLIA SEAWAYS. In January 2011 service withdrawn. In February 2011 chartered to *Seatruck Ferries* to inaugurate their new Heysham - Dublin service. In January 2012 returned to *DFDS Seaways* and placed on the Vlaardingen - Immingham route as an extra vessel. In April 2012 moved to the Zeebrugge - Rosyth service but proved too slow. In May chartered to *Seatruck Ferries* to operate between Heysham and Belfast. In August, this service ceased and she was switched to the Heysham - Dublin route and in September to the Heysham - Warrenpoint route. In April 2014 returned to *DFDS Seaways* and placed on Kiel - St Petersburg service. In July 2014 transferred to the Travemünde - Klaipéda route and in September to the Vlaardingen - Immingham service, providing additional capacity. In March 2015 placed on the charter market.

ARK DANIA, ARK GERMANIA Built by P + S Werften GmbH, Stralsund, Germany. They are used for the German/Danish joint ARK Project providing NATO transport but are also available for *DFDS* use and charter when not required. They have a crane for loading containers on the weather deck. In December 2012 the order for these vessels was cancelled due to late delivery. Following negotiations with the shipyard it was agreed that they would be completed under a new contract which was signed in February 2013. Both vessels were delivered to *DFDS* in April 2014, the ARK GERMANIA almost complete, the ARK DANIA still incomplete. The latter vessel was towed to the Fayard shipyard, Odense, to be completed. The ARK GERMANIA entered service a few days after delivery, the ARK DANIA in November 2014.

ARK FUTURA Built as the DANA FUTURA by C N Visentini di Visentini Francesco & C, Donada, Italy for *DFDS*. In 2001 she was renamed the TOR FUTURA. Initially operated mainly between Esbjerg and Harwich, but latterly operated mainly between Esbjerg and Immingham. In 2004 chartered to *Toll Shipping* of Australia. Later time-chartered to the *Danish MoD* for 5.5 years. However, when not required for military service she has been chartered to other operators such as *P&O Ferries*, *Cobelfret Ferries* and *Van Uden Ro-Ro* and used on *DFDS Tor Line* services. In 2006 sold to *DFDS Lys Line Rederi A/S* of Norway, a *DFDS* subsidiary and chartered back. In April 2011 renamed the ARK FUTURA. In August 2014 placed on the Marseilles - Tunis service.

BEGONIA SEAWAYS Built as the TOR BEGONIA by Flensburger Schiffbau-Gesellschaft, Flensburg, Germany for *DFDS Tor Line*. Operates on the Gothenburg - Immingham/Brevik route. In Summer 2009 lengthened by 30m by MWB Motorenwerke Bremerhaven AG, Germany. In July 2012 renamed the BEGONIA SEAWAYS.

BRITANNIA SEAWAYS Built as the TOR BRITANNIA by Fincantieri-Cantieri Navali Italiani SpA, Ancona, Italy for *DFDS Tor Line*. Operated on the Gothenburg - Immingham route until 2004 when she was transferred to the Esbjerg - Immingham route. In January 2010 chartered to *Norfolkline* to operate between Vlaardingen and Felixstowe. In May 2011 renamed the BRITANNIA SEAWAYS.

CALAIS SEAWAYS Built as the PRINS FILIP by NV Boelwerf SA, Temse, Belgium for *Regie voor Maritiem Transport (RMT)* of Belgium for the Ostend - Dover service. Although completed in 1991, she did not enter service until May 1992. In 1994 the British port became Ramsgate. Withdrawn in 1997 and laid up for sale. In 1998 she was sold to *Stena RoRo* and renamed the STENA ROYAL. In November 1998 she was chartered to *P&O Ferries* to operate as a freight-only vessel on the Dover - Zeebrugge route. In Spring 1999 it was decided to charter the vessel on a long-term basis and she was repainted into *P&O Stena Line* (later *P&O Ferries*) colours and renamed the P&OSL AQUITAINE. In Autumn 1999 she was modified to make her suitable to operate between Dover and Calais and was transferred to that route, becoming a passenger vessel again. In 2002 renamed the PO AQUITAINE and in 2003 the PRIDE OF AQUITAINE. In September 2005 sold to *LD Lines* and renamed the NORMAN SPIRIT. In October, inaugurated a Le Havre - Portsmouth service, replacing that previously operated by *P&O Ferries*. In November 2009 moved to the Dover - Boulogne route. In March 2010 chartered to *TransEuropa Ferries*, placed on the Ostend - Ramsgate service (as part of a joint venture) and renamed the OSTEND SPIRIT. In May 2011 returned to the Portsmouth - Le Havre route and renamed the NORMAN SPIRIT. In November 2011 chartered to *DFDS Seaways* to add extra capacity to their Dover - Dunkerque route. In February 2012 transferred to the new Dover - Calais route, joint with *DFDS*

Princess Seaways (*Matt Davies*)

Malo Seaways (*George Holland*)

Calais Seaways (*John Hendy*)

Anglia Seaways (*Cees de Bijl*)

Seaways. Ownership transferred to *DFDS Seaways* in late 2012. In March 2013 refurbished, repainted into *DFDS Seaways* colours and renamed the CALAIS SEAWAYS.

COTE D'ALBATRE Built by Astilleros Barreras SA, Vigo, Spain for *Transmanche Ferries* to operate between Newhaven and Dieppe. In February 2009 she was moved to the Boulogne - Dover and Dieppe - Dover routes. In September 2009 moved to the Le Havre - Portsmouth route. In April 2011 replaced by the NORMAN SPIRIT. The vessel has had periods laid up when not required on the Newhaven – Dieppe route.

DELFT SEAWAYS, DOVER SEAWAYS, DUNKERQUE SEAWAYS Built as the MAERSK DELFT, DOVER SEAWAYS and MAERSK DUNKERQUE by Samsung Heavy Industries, Koje (Geoje) Island, South Korea for *Norfolkline* to operate between Dover and Dunkerque. In July and August 2010 renamed the DELFT SEAWAYS, DOVER SEAWAYS and DUNKERQUE SEAWAYS. In November 2012 the DOVER SEAWAYS was moved to the Dover - Calais route.

FICARIA SEAWAYS Built as the TOR FICARIA by Flensburger Schiffbau-Gesellschaft, Flensburg, Germany for *DFDS Tor Line*. Operated on the Gothenburg - Immingham/Brevik service. In Summer 2009 lengthened by 30m by MWB Motorenwerke Bremerhaven AG, Germany. In July 2011 renamed the FICARIA SEAWAYS. In March 2015 placed on the Vlaardingen - Immingham service.

FIONIA SEAWAYS Built as the TOR FIONIA by Jinling Shipyard, Nanjing, China for *Macoma Shipping Ltd* of the UK. Launched as the JINGLING 3. She was time-chartered to *DFDS Tor Line* for ten years (with an option on a further three). Delivered in May 2009 and initially replaced the TOR BEGONIA, TOR FICARIA and TOR FREESIA while they were being lengthened. In October 2011 renamed the FIONIA SEAWAYS. In March 2015 placed on the Gothenburg - Immingham service.

FREESIA SEAWAYS Built as the TOR FREESIA by Flensburger Schiffbau-Gesellschaft, Flensburg, Germany for *DFDS Tor Line*. Operates on the Gothenburg - Immingham/Brevik service. In Summer 2009 lengthened by 30m by MWB Motorenwerke Bremerhaven AG, Germany. In August 2012 renamed the FREESIA SEAWAYS.

HAFNIA SEAWAYS Built as the TOR HAFNIA by Jinling Shipyard, Nanjing, China for *Macoma Shipping Ltd* of the UK and time-chartered to *DFDS Tor Line* for ten years. Until 2013, mainly operated on the Immingham - Esbjerg route. In March 2011 renamed the HAFNIA SEAWAYS. In February 2013 transferred to the Vlaardingen - Immingham route. In January 2015 chartered to *Cobelfret Ferries* for four weeks. Currently operates on the Cuxhaven - Immingham service.

JUTLANDIA SEAWAYS Built as the TOR JUTLANDIA by Jinling Shipyard, Nanjing, China for *Macoma Shipping Ltd* of the UK and time-chartered to *DFDS Tor Line* for ten years. In July 2011 renamed the JUTLANDIA SEAWAYS. Currently operates on the Immingham - Esbjerg route. In late summer 2014 to be replaced by the ARK DANIA and moved to another route.

KING SEAWAYS Built as the NILS HOLGERSSON by Schichau Seebeckwerft AG, Bremerhaven, Germany for *Rederi AB Swedcarrier* of Sweden for their service between Trelleborg and Travemünde, joint with *TT-Line* of Germany (trading as *TT-Line*). In 1992 purchased by *Brittany Ferries* for entry into service in Spring 1993. After a major rebuild, she was renamed the VAL DE LOIRE and introduced onto the Plymouth - Roscoff, Plymouth - Santander and Cork - Roscoff routes. In 2004 transferred to the Portsmouth - St Malo and Portsmouth – Cherbourg services. In 2005 operated mainly Portsmouth - St Malo. In 2006 sold to *DFDS*, renamed the KING OF SCANDINAVIA and placed on the Newcastle – IJmuiden route. In January 2011 renamed the KING SEAWAYS.

MAGNOLIA SEAWAYS Built as the TOR MAGNOLIA by Flensburger Schiffbau-Gesellschaft, Flensburg, Germany for *DFDS Tor Line*. In July 2011 renamed the MAGNOLIA SEAWAYS. Currently operates on the Gothenburg – Ghent route.

MALO SEAWAYS Built as the EUROPEAN AMBASSADOR by Mitsubishi Heavy Industries, Shimonoseki, Japan for *P&O Irish Sea* for their Liverpool - Dublin service. Service transferred to from Liverpool to Mostyn in November 2001. Also operated between Dublin and Cherbourg once a week. In 2004 the Mostyn route closed and she was sold to *Stena RoRo*. Chartered to *Stena Line* to operate between Karlskrona and Gdynia and renamed the STENA NORDICA. In 2008 transferred to the Holyhead - Dublin service. In 2009 transferred to UK registry. In February 2015 replaced by the

STENA SUPERFAST X and chartered to *DFDS Seaways France*. Renamed the MALO SEAWAYS and placed on the Dover - Calais route in April 2015.

PETUNIA SEAWAYS Built as the TOR PETUNIA by Flensburger Schiffbau-Gesellschaft, Flensburg, Germany for *DFDS Tor Line*. In July 2011 renamed the PETUNIA SEAWAYS. Currently operates on the Gothenburg – Ghent route.

PRIMULA SEAWAYS Built as the TOR PRIMULA by Flensburger Schiffbau-Gesellschaft, Flensburg, Germany for *DFDS Tor Line*.. In July 2010 renamed the PRIMULA SEAWAYS. Currently operates on the Gothenburg – Ghent route.

PRINCESS SEAWAYS Built by Schichau Seebeckwerft AG, Bremerhaven, Germany as the PETER PAN for *TT-Line* for the service between Travemünde and Trelleborg. In 1992 sold to *TT Line* of Australia (no connection) for use on their service between Port Melbourne (Victoria) and Devonport (Tasmania) and renamed the SPIRIT OF TASMANIA. In 2002 sold to *Nordsjøferger K/S* of Norway and renamed the SPIR. After modification work she was, in 2003, renamed the FJORD NORWAY and chartered to *Fjord Line*. Placed on the Bergen - Egersund - Hanstholm route. In 2005 placed on the Bergen - Stavanger - Newcastle route, but operated once a week to Hanstholm. In October 2006 sold to *DFDS* and renamed the PRINCESS OF NORWAY, remaining on the Newcastle - Norway service but no longer serving Hanstholm. In May 2007 moved to the Newcastle - IJmuiden route. In February 2011 renamed the PRINCESS SEAWAYS.

SELANDIA SEAWAYS Built as the TOR SELANDIA by Fincantieri-Cantieri Navali Italiani SpA, Ancona, Italy for *DFDS Tor Line*. Operated on the Gothenburg - Immingham route until 2004 when she was moved to the Gothenburg – Ghent route. In 2005 she moved to the Gothenburg – Harwich route. In July the UK terminal moved to Tilbury. In August 2010 renamed the SELANDIA SEAWAYS. Currently operates on the Rotterdam - Felixstowe route.

SEVEN SISTERS Built by Astilleros Barreras SA, Vigo, Spain for *Transmanche Ferries* to operate between Newhaven and Dieppe. In recent years generally held as a reserve vessel. In March 2014 transferred to the Portsmouth - Le Havre service. She continues to carry *Transmanche Ferries* branding. In 2015 returned to the Newhaven - Dieppe service as second vessel. The vessel has had periods laid up when not required on the Newhaven – Dieppe route.

SUECIA SEAWAYS Built as the TOR SUECIA by Fincantieri-Cantieri Navali Italiani SpA, Ancona, Italy for *DFDS Tor Line*. Operated on the Gothenburg - Immingham route until 2004 when she was transferred to the Esbjerg - Immingham route. Later transferred to the Danish flag. In March 2010 chartered to *Norfolkline* to operate between Vlaardingen and Felixstowe and continued on the route when it was taken over by *DFDS*. In June 2011 renamed the SUECIA SEAWAYS.

IRISH FERRIES

THE COMPANY *Irish Ferries* is an Irish Republic private sector company, part of the *Irish Continental Group*. It was originally mainly owned by the state-owned *Irish Shipping* and partly by *Lion Ferry AB* of Sweden. *Lion Ferry* participation ceased in 1977 and the company was sold into the private sector in 1987. Formerly state-owned *B&I Line* was taken over in 1991 and from 1995 all operations were marketed as *Irish Ferries*.

MANAGEMENT Irish Continental Group Chief Executive Office Eamonn Rothwell, **Irish Ferries Limited Managing Director** Andrew Sheen.

ADDRESS PO Box 19, Ferryport, Alexandra Road, Dublin 1, Irish Republic.

TELEPHONE Administration +353 (0)1 607 5700, **Reservations** *Ireland* +353 (0)818300 400, *Rosslare Harbour* +353 (0)53 913 3158, *Holyhead* +44 (0)8717 300200, *Pembroke Dock* +44 (0)8717 300500, *National* 44 (0)8717 300400, **24 hour information** +353 (0)818300 400 (Ireland) or 44 (0)8717 300400 (UK).

FAX Administration & Reservations *Dublin* +353 (0)1 607 5660, *Rosslare* +353 (0)53 913 3544.

INTERNET Email info@irishferries.com **Website** www.irishferries.com *(English, French, German, Italian)*

Hafina Seaways (*Rob de Visser*)

Epsilon (*Matt Davies*)

ROUTES OPERATED Conventional Ferries Dublin - Holyhead (3 hrs 15 mins; *EPSILON*; *ULYSSES*; 2-4 per day), Rosslare - Pembroke Dock (4 hrs; *ISLE OF INISHMORE*; 4 per day), Dublin - Cherbourg (17-19 hrs; *EPSILON*; 1 per week), Rosslare - Cherbourg (France) (17 hrs 30 mins; *OSCAR WILDE*; average of 3 per week), Rosslare - Roscoff (France) (16 hrs; *OSCAR WILDE*; 1 or 2 per week (seasonal)). Fast Ferry Dublin - Holyhead (1 hr 49 min; *JONATHAN SWIFT*; 2 per day) marketed as 'DUBLIN*swift*'.

1	EPSILON	26375t	11	24.0k	177.5m	500P	500C	190T	A	IT	9539054
2	ISLE OF INISHMORE	34031t	97	21.3k	182.5m	2200P	802C	152T	BA2	CY	9142605
3»	JONATHAN SWIFT	5989t	99	37.0k	86.6m	800P	200C	-	BA	CY	9188881
4	KAITAKI	22365t	95	19.0k	181.6m	1650P	600C	130T	BA2	UK	9107942
5	OSCAR WILDE	31914t	87	22.0k	166.3m	1458P	580C	90T	BA	BS	8506311
6	ULYSSES	50938t	01	22.0k	209.0m	1875P	1342C	300T	BA2	CY	9214991

EPSILON Built as the CARTOUR EPSILON by CN Visentini, Porto Viro, Italy. Chartered to *Caronte & Tourist SPA* of Italy. In November 2013 chartered to *Irish Ferries*. In February 2014 renamed the EPSILON.

ISLE OF INISHMORE Built by Van der Giessen-de Noord, Krimpen aan den IJssel, Rotterdam for *Irish Ferries* to operate on the Holyhead - Dublin service. In 2001 replaced by the ULYSSES and moved to the Rosslare - Pembroke Dock route. She also relieves on the Dublin - Holyhead route when the ULYSSES receives her annual overhaul.

JONATHAN SWIFT Austal Auto-Express 86 catamaran built by Austal Ships Pty, Fremantle, Australia for *Irish Ferries* for the Dublin - Holyhead route.

KAITAKI Built as the ISLE OF INNISFREE by Van der Giessen-de Noord, Krimpen aan den IJssel, Rotterdam for *Irish Ferries* to operate on the Holyhead - Dublin route. In 1997 transferred to the Rosslare - Pembroke Dock service; for a short period, before modifications at Pembroke Dock were completed, she operated between Rosslare and Fishguard. In Spring 2001 she was replaced by the ISLE OF INISHMORE and laid up. In July 2002 she was chartered to *P&O Portsmouth* for 5 years and renamed the PRIDE OF CHERBOURG. Entered service in October 2002. Withdrawn in October 2004. In January 2005, sub-chartered by *P&O* to *Stena RoRo*, renamed the STENA CHALLENGER and operated on the Karlskrona - Gdynia route. In June 2006 sub-chartered by *Stena RoRo* to *Toll Shipping* of New Zealand and renamed the CHALLENGER. In August 2006 she arrived in New Zealand and was placed on the Wellington - Picton route. In 2007 renamed the KAITAKI. . In 2009 charter extended until 2013 and in 2013 a new direct charter was agreed extending until June 2017.

OSCAR WILDE Built as the KRONPRINS HARALD by Oy Wärtsilä AB, Turku, Finland for *Jahre Line* of Norway for the Oslo - Kiel service. In 1991 ownership was transferred to *Color Line*. In early 2007 sold to *Irish Ferries* for delivery in September 2007. Chartered back to *Color Line* until that date. When delivered, renamed the OSCAR WILDE and in November placed on the Rosslare - Roscoff/Cherbourg routes.

ULYSSES Built by Aker Finnyards, Rauma, Finland for *Irish Ferries* for the Dublin - Holyhead service.

ISLE OF MAN STEAM PACKET COMPANY

THE COMPANY *The Isle of Man Steam Packet Company Limited* is an Isle of Man-registered company.

MANAGEMENT Chief Executive Officer Mark Woodward.

ADDRESS Imperial Buildings, Douglas, Isle of Man IM1 2BY.

TELEPHONE Administration + 44 (0)1624 645645, Reservations + 44 (0)1624 661661

FAX Administration + 44 (0)1624 645627.

INTERNET Email iom.reservations@steam-packet.com Website www.steam-packet.com *(English)*

ROUTES OPERATED Conventional Ferries *All year* Douglas (Isle of Man) - Heysham (3 hrs 30 mins; *BEN-MY-CHREE*; up to 2 per day), *November-March* Douglas - Liverpool (Birkenhead) (4 hrs 15 mins; *BEN-MY-CHREE*; 2 per week). Fast Ferries *March-October* Douglas - Liverpool (2 hrs 40 mins;

MANANNAN; up to 2 per day), Douglas - Belfast (2 hrs 55 mins; *MANANNAN*; up to 2 per week), Douglas - Dublin (2 hrs 55 mins; *MANANNAN*; up to 2 per week), Douglas - Heysham (2 hrs; *MANANNAN*; occasional), **Freight Ferry** Douglas - Heysham (3 hrs 30 mins; *ARROW*; as required)

1F	ARROW	7606t	98	17.0k	122.3m	12P	-	84T	A	IM	9119414
2	BEN-MY-CHREE	12747t	98	18.0k	124.9m	630P	275C	90T	A	IM	9170705
3»	MANANNAN	5743t	98	43.0k	96.0m	820P	200C	-	A	IM	9176072

ARROW Built as the VARBOLA by Astilleros de Huelva SA, Huelva, Spain for the *Estonian Shipping Company*. On completion, chartered to *Dart Line* and placed on the Dartford - Vlissingen route. In 1999 she was renamed the DART 6. At the end of August 1999, the charter was terminated and she was renamed the VARBOLA. She undertook a number of short-term charters, including *Merchant Ferries*. In 2000 long-term chartered to *Merchant Ferries* to operate between Heysham and Dublin. In 2003 the charter ended and she was chartered to *Dart Line* to replace the DART 9; she was placed initially on the Dartford - Vlissingen route but later transferred to the Dartford - Dunkerque route. Later sub-chartered to *NorseMerchant Ferries* and placed on the Heysham – Dublin route. In 2004 the charter transferred to *NorseMerchant Ferries*. In 2005 sold to *Elmira Shipping* of Greece and renamed the RR ARROW. In October 2007 sold to *Seatruck Ferries* but the charter to *Norfolkline* continued. Renamed the ARROW. In June 2009 returned to *Seatruck Ferries*. In April 2014 long term chartered to *IOMSP*. When not required she is sub-chartered to other operators.

BEN-MY-CHREE Built by Van der Giessen-de Noord, Krimpen aan den IJssel, Rotterdam for the *IOMSP Co* and operates between Douglas and Heysham. Additional passenger accommodation was added at her spring 2004 refit. In 2005 her passenger certificate was increased from 500 to 630. She operates some sailings between Douglas and Liverpool (Birkenhead) in the winter.

MANANNAN Incat 96m catamaran built at Hobart, Tasmania. Initially chartered to *Transport Tasmania* of Australia and operated between Port Melbourne (Victoria) and Georgetown (Tasmania). In 1999 chartered to *Fast Cat Ferries* of New Zealand and operated between Wellington (North Island) and Picton (South Island) under the marketing name 'Top Cat'. In 2000 she was laid up. In 2001 she was chartered to the *US Navy* and renamed the USS JOINT VENTURE (HSV-X1). In 2008 the charter was terminated and she was renamed the INCAT 050. Later purchased by *IOMSP*. Following conversion back to civilian use she was renamed the MANANNAN and entered service in May 2009.

MYFERRYLINK

THE COMPANY *MyFerryLink* is a French private sector company owned by *Groupe Eurotunnel SA*. Operations started in August 2012.

MANAGEMENT Managing Director (UK) Robin Wilkins.

ADDRESS *France* Tour LillEurope, 11 Parvis de Rotterdam, Euralille, 59777 Lille, France, **UK** Whitfield Court, Honeywood Close, Whitfield, Dover, Kent CT16 3PX.

TELEPHONE *Passenger reservations and information* 0844 2482 100 (from UK); 0811 654 765 (from Continental Europe), **Freight** + 33(0)3 21 46 80 40.

FAX UK - **Passenger** +44 (0)1304 828379, **Freight** + 33(0)3 21 46 80 39.

INTERNET Email clientservices@myferrylink.com (**Freight** freightsales@myferrylink.com) **Website** www.myferrylink.com (*English, French*)

ROUTE OPERATED Service suspended after 2nd July 2015. See Late News.

1	BERLIOZ	33940t	05	25.0k	186.0m	1900P	700C	120L	BA2	FR	9305843
2F+	NORD PAS-DE-CALAIS	7264t	87	21.5k	160.1m	100P	-	85L	BA2	FR	8512152
3	RODIN	33796t	01	25.0k	186.0m	1900P	700C	120L	BA2	FR	9232527

BERLIOZ Built as the SEAFRANCE BERLIOZ by Chantiers de l'Atlantique, St Nazaire for *SeaFrance*. Launched in March 2005. In November 2011 laid up. In June 2012 sold to *Eurotransmanche*, a *Groupe Eurotunnel* company. In July 2012 renamed the BERLIOZ. In August 2012 chartered to *MyFerryLink* and resumed operation between Calais and Dover.

Arrow (*Matt Davies*)

Nord Pas-de-Calais (*George Holland*)

NORD PAS-DE-CALAIS Built by Chantiers du Nord et de la Mediterranée, Dunkerque, France as the NORD PAS-DE-CALAIS at Dunkerque, France for *SNCF* for the Dunkerque (Ouest) - Dover train ferry service. Before being used on this service (which required the construction of a new berth at Dover (Western Docks)) in May 1988, she operated road freight services from Calais to Dover Eastern Docks. The train ferry service continued to operate following the opening of the Channel Tunnel in 1994, to convey road vehicles and dangerous loads which were banned from the Tunnel. However, it ceased in December 1995 and, after a refit, in February 1996 she was renamed the SEAFRANCE NORD PAS-DE-CALAIS and switched to the Calais - Dover service, primarily for road freight vehicles and drivers but also advertised as carrying up to 50 car passengers. Since the entry into service of a third multi-purpose ferry, she operated on a freight-only basis. In November 2011 laid up. In June 2012 sold to *Eurotransmanche*. In July renamed the NORD PAS-DE-CALAIS. In November 2012 chartered to *MyFerryLink* and resumed operation between Calais and Dover.

RODIN Built as the SEAFRANCE RODIN by Aker Finnyards, Rauma, Finland for *SeaFrance*. Launched in November 2001. In November 2011 laid up. In June 2012 sold to *Eurotransmanche*. In July 2012 renamed the RODIN. In August 2012 chartered to *MyFerryLink* and resumed operation between Calais and Dover.

NORTHLINK FERRIES

THE COMPANY *NorthLink Ferries* is a UK based company, wholly owned *Serco Group plc*. The service is operated on behalf of Scottish Ministers.

MANAGEMENT Managing Director Stuart Garrett, **Customer Service Director** Cheryl Fox.

ADDRESS Ferry Terminal, Ferry Road, Stromness, Orkney KW16 3BH.

TELEPHONE Customer Services 0845 6000 449, (International +44 (0)1856 885500), **Freight Reservations** 0845 6060 449.

FAX Administration +44 (0)1856 851795.

INTERNET Email info@northlinkferries.co.uk **Website** www.northlinkferries.co.uk *(English)*

ROUTES OPERATED *Passenger Ferries* Scrabster - Stromness (Orkney) (1 hr 30 min; *HAMNAVOE*; up to 3 per day), Aberdeen - Lerwick (Shetland) (direct) (12 hrs; *HJALTLAND, HROSSEY*; 3 northbound/4 southbound per week), Aberdeen - Kirkwall, Hatston New Pier (Orkney) (5 hrs 45 mins) - Lerwick (14 hrs; *HJALTLAND, HROSSEY*; 4 northbound/3 southbound per week). *Freight Ferries* Aberdeen - Kirkwall (Orkney) (12 hrs; *HELLIAR, HILDASAY*; 4 per week), Aberdeen - Lerwick (Shetland) (*HELLIAR, HILDASAY*; 4 per week).

1	HAMNAVOE	8780t	02	19.3k	112.0m	600P	95C	20L	BA	UK	9246061
2F	HELLIAR	7800t	98	17.0k	122.3m	12P	-	86T	A	IM	9119397
3F	HILDASAY	7606t	99	17.0k	122.3m	12P	-	84T	A	IM	9119426
4	HJALTLAND	11720t	02	24.0k	125.0m	600P	150C	30L	BA	UK	9244958
5	HROSSEY	11720t	02	24.0k	125.0m	600P	150C	30L	BA	UK	9244960

HAMNAVOE Built by Aker Finnyards, Rauma, Finland for *NorthLink Orkney and Shetland Ferries Ltd* to operate on the Scrabster - Stromness route. Did not enter service until Spring 2003 due to late completion of work at Scrabster to accommodate the ship. *Caledonian MacBrayne's* HEBRIDEAN ISLES covered between October 2002 and Spring 2003.

HELLIAR Built as the LEHOLA by Astilleros de Huelva SA, Huelva, Spain for the *Estonian Shipping Company*. Initially used on *ESCO* Baltic services. In 1998 chartered to *Czar Peter Line* to operate between Moerdijk (The Netherlands) and Kronstadt (Russia). In 1999 chartered to *Delom* of France to operate between Marseilles and Sete and Tunis. In 2000 she returned to *ESCO*, operating between Kiel and Tallinn. In 2003 chartered to *Scandlines AG* and transferred to subsidiary *Scandlines Estonia AS*. Operated Rostock - Helsinki – Muuga initially and later Rostock – Helsinki. Service finished at the end of 2004 and in 2005 she was chartered to *P&O Ferries* to operate between Hull and Rotterdam and Hull and Zeebrugge. In 2005 sold to *Elmira Shipping* of Greece. Later renamed the RR TRIUMPH. In 2006 transferred to *P&O Irish Sea* to operate between Liverpool and Dublin. In 2007 chartered to

Hjaltland (*NorthLink*)

Thorsvoe (*Miles Cowsill*)

Balearia of Spain and operated from Barcelona. In December 2007 purchased by *Seatruck Ferries* and renamed the TRIUMPH. In Spring 2008 she was sub-chartered to *Condor Ferries* to cover for the refit period of the COMMODORE GOODWILL. In June 2008 placed on the Liverpool - Dublin route and in July renamed the CLIPPER RACER. In February 2009 replaced by the new CLIPPER PACE. In April 2009 again chartered to *Balearia*. In January 2011 chartered to *NorthLink Ferries* and renamed the HELLIAR.

HILDASAY Built as the LEILI by Astilleros de Huelva SA, Huelva, Spain for the *Estonian Shipping Company*. Used on Baltic services. In 2002 chartered to *Crowley Maritime* of the USA and renamed the PORT EVERGLADES EXPRESS. In 2004 resumed the name LEILI and chartered to *NorseMerchant Ferries* to operate between Birkenhead and Dublin. In July 2005 moved to the Heysham - Belfast route and at the same time sold to *Elmira Shipping* of Greece and renamed the RR SHIELD. In 2007 sold to *Attica Group* of Greece and renamed the SHIELD. In January 2008 sold to *Seatruck Ferries* but continued to be chartered to *Norfolkline*. In June 2009 returned to *Seatruck Ferries*. In January 2009 chartered to *NorthLink Orkney and Shetland Ferries* and renamed the HILDASAY.

HJALTLAND, HROSSEY Built by Aker Finnyards, Rauma, Finland for *NorthLink Orkney and Shetland Ferries* to operate on the Aberdeen - Kirkwall - Lerwick route when services started in 2002.

ORKNEY FERRIES

THE COMPANY *Orkney Ferries Ltd* (previously the *Orkney Islands Shipping Company*) is a British company, owned by *Orkney Islands Council*.

MANAGEMENT Operations Director Capt N H Mills, **Ferry Services Manager** D I Sawkins.

ADDRESS Shore Street, Kirkwall, Orkney KW15 1LG.

TELEPHONE Administration + 44 (0)1856 872044, **Reservations** + 44 (0)1856 872044.

FAX Administration & Reservations + 44 (0)1856 872921.

INTERNET Email info@orkneyferries.co.uk **Website** www.orkneyferries.co.uk *(English)*

ROUTES OPERATED Kirkwall (Mainland) to Eday (1 hr 15 mins), Rapness (Westray) (1 hr 25 mins), Sanday (1 hr 25 mins), Stronsay (1 hr 35 mins), Papa Westray (1 hr 50 mins), North Ronaldsay (2 hrs 30 mins) ('North Isles service') (timings are direct from Kirkwall - sailings via other islands take longer; *EARL SIGURD, EARL THORFINN, VARAGEN*; 1/2 per day except Papa Westray which is twice weekly and North Ronaldsay which is weekly), Pierowall (Westray) - Papa Westray (25 mins; *GOLDEN MARIANA*; up to six per day (Summer service - passenger-only)), Kirkwall - Shapinsay (25 mins; *SHAPINSAY*; 6 per day), Houton (Mainland) to Lyness (Hoy) (35 mins; *HOY HEAD*; 5 per day), and Flotta (35 mins; *HOY HEAD*; 4 per day) ('South Isles service') (timings are direct from Houton - sailings via other islands take longer), Tingwall (Mainland) to Rousay (20 mins; *EYNHALLOW*; 6 per day), Egilsay (30 mins; *EYNHALLOW*; 5 per day) and Wyre (20 mins; *EYNHALLOW*; 5 per day) (timings are direct from Tingwall - sailings via other islands take longer), Stromness (Mainland) to Moaness (Hoy) (25 mins; *GRAEMSAY*; 2/3 per day) and Graemsay (25 mins; *GRAEMSAY*; 2/3 per day) (passenger/cargo service - cars not normally conveyed).

1	EARL SIGURD	771t	90	12.5k	45.0m	190P	26C	-	BA	UK	8902711
2	EARL THORFINN	771t	90	12.5k	45.0m	190P	26C	-	BA	UK	8902723
3	EYNHALLOW	104t	87	10.5k	28.8m	95P	11C	-	BA	UK	8960880
4p	GOLDEN MARIANA	33t	73	9.5k	15.2m	40P	0C	-	-	UK	
5	GRAEMSAY	90t	96	10.0k	20.6m	73P	2C	-	C	UK	
6	HOY HEAD	358t	94	11.0k	53.5m	125P	24C	3L	BA	UK	9081722
7	SHAPINSAY	199t	89	10.0k	32.6m	91P	16C	-	BA	UK	8814184
8	THORSVOE	385t	91	10.6k	35.0m	122P	16C	-	BA	UK	9014743
9	VARAGEN	928t	88	14.5k	49.9m	144P	33C	5L	BA	UK	8818154

EARL SIGURD, EARL THORFINN Built by McTay Marine, Bromborough, Wirral, UK to inaugurate ro-ro working on the 'North Isles service'.

EYNHALLOW Built by David Abels Boat Builders, Bristol, UK to inaugurate ro-ro services from Tingwall (Mainland) to Rousay, Egilsay and Wyre. In 1991 she was lengthened by 5 metres, to increase car capacity.

GOLDEN MARIANA Built by Bideford Shipyard Ltd, Bideford, UK for *A J G England* of Padstow as a dual-purpose passenger and fishing vessel. In 1975 sold to *M MacKenzie* of Ullapool, then to *Pentland Ferries, Wide Firth Ferry* in 1982, and *Orkney Islands Council* in 1986. Passenger-only vessel. Generally operates summer-only feeder service between Pierowall (Westray) and Papa Westray.

GRAEMSAY Built by Ailsa Shipbuilding, Troon UK to operate between Stromness (Mainland), Moaness (Hoy) and Graemsay. Designed to offer an all-year-round service to these islands, primarily for passengers and cargo. Between October 2009 and January 2010 lengthened by 4.4 metres.

HOY HEAD Built by Appledore Shipbuilders Ltd, Appledore, UK to replace the THORSVOE on the 'South Isles service'. During winter 2012/13 extended by 14 metres at Cammell Laird Shiprepairers & Shipbuilders, Birkenhead, England.

SHAPINSAY Built by Yorkshire Drydock Ltd, Hull, UK for the service from Kirkwall (Mainland) to Shapinsay. In April 2011 lengthened by 6 metres at the Macduff Shipyards, Macduff, Scotland to increase car capacity from 12 to 16 and re-engined.

THORSVOE Built by Campbeltown Shipyard, Campbeltown, UK for the 'South Isles service'. In 1994 replaced by the new HOY HEAD and became the main reserve vessel for the fleet.

VARAGEN Built by Cochrane Shipbuilders, Selby, UK for *Orkney Ferries*, a private company established to start a new route between Gills Bay (Caithness, Scotland) and Burwick (South Ronaldsay, Orkney). However, due to problems with the terminals it was not possible to maintain regular services. In 1991, the company was taken over by *Orkney Islands Shipping Company* and the VARAGEN became part of their fleet, sharing the 'North Isles service' with the EARL SIGURD and the EARL THORFINN and replacing the freight vessel ISLANDER (494t, 1969).

P&O FERRIES

THE COMPANY *P&O Ferries Holdings Ltd* is a private sector company, a subsidiary of *Dubai World*, owned by the Government of Dubai. In Autumn 2002 *P&O North Sea Ferries*, P&O Irish Sea, *P&O Portsmouth* and *P&O Stena Line* (*Stena Line* involvement having ceased) were merged into a single operation.

MANAGEMENT **Chief Executive Officer** Helen Deeble, **Fleet Director** John Garner, **Finance Director** Karl Howarth, **Human Resources Director** Lesley Cotton, **Ports Director** Sue Mackenzie, **Commercial Director** Janette Bell, **Company Secretary** Susan Kitchin.

ADDRESSES *Head Office and Dover Services* Channel House, Channel View Road, Dover, Kent CT17 9TJ, *Hull* King George Dock, Hedon Road, Hull HU9 5QA, *Larne* P&O Irish Sea, Larne Harbour, Larne, Co Antrim BT40 1AW *Rotterdam* Beneluxhaven, Rotterdam (Europoort), Postbus 1123, 3180 Rozenburg, Netherlands, *Zeebrugge* Leopold II Dam 13, Havendam, 8380 Zeebrugge, Belgium.

TELEPHONE **Administration** *UK* +44 (0)1304 863000, **Passenger Reservations** *UK* 08716 64 64 64, *France* +33 (0)825 12 01 56, *Belgium* +32 (0)70 70 77 71, *The Netherlands* +31 (0)20 20 08333, *Spain* +34 (0)902 02 04 61, *Luxembourg* +34 (0)20 80 82 94. **Freight Reservations** *UK* 0870 6000 868, *Irish Republic* +353 (0)1 855 0522.

FAX **Passenger Reservations** *UK East and South Coast* +44 (0)1304 863464, *West Coast* 44 (0)02828 872195, *The Netherlands* +31 (0)118 1225 5215, *Belgium* +32 (0)50 54 71 12, **Freight Reservations** *Cairnryan* +44 (0)1581 200282, *Larne* +44 (0)28 2827 2477..

INTERNET **Email** customer.services@poferries.com **Website** www.poferries.com *(English, French, Dutch, German)* www.poirishsea.com *(English)* www.poferriesfreight.com *(English, French, German)*

ROUTES OPERATED **Passenger - conventional ferries** Dover - Calais (1 hr 15 mins - 1 hr 30 mins; *PRIDE OF BURGUNDY, PRIDE OF CANTERBURY, PRIDE OF KENT, SPIRIT OF BRITAIN, SPIRIT OF FRANCE*; up to 25 per day), Hull - Zeebrugge (Belgium) (from 12 hrs 30 mins; *PRIDE OF BRUGES, PRIDE OF YORK*; 1 per day), Hull - Rotterdam (Beneluxhaven, Europoort) (The Netherlands) (from

10 Hrs; *PRIDE OF HULL, PRIDE OF ROTTERDAM*; 1 per day), Cairnryan - Larne (1 hr 45 min; *EUROPEAN CAUSEWAY, EUROPEAN HIGHLANDER*; 7 per day), Liverpool - Dublin (8 hrs; *EUROPEAN ENDEAVOUR, NORBANK, NORBAY*; up to 3 per day (some sailings are freight only). **Fast Ferry** (March-October) Cairnryan - Larne (1 hr; *EXPRESS*; 1 per day), Troon – Larne (1 hr 49 min; *EXPRESS* 2 per day). **Freight-only** Tilbury - Zeebrugge (8 hrs; *NORSKY, NORSTREAM* ; 10 per week), Middlesbrough (Teesport) - Rotterdam (Beneluxhaven, Europoort) (16 hrs; *ESTRADEN* ; 3 per week), Middlesbrough (Teesport) - Zeebrugge (15 hrs 30 mins; *BORE SONG, MISTRAL*; 6 per week).

1	BORE SONG	25235t	11	18.5k	195.0m	12P	-	210T	A2	FI	9443566
2F	ESTRADEN	18205t	99	19.0k	162.7m	12P	130C	170T	A	FI	9181077
3	EUROPEAN CAUSEWAY	20646t	00	22.7k	159.5m	410P	315C	84T	BA2	BS	9208394
5	EUROPEAN ENDEAVOUR	22152t	00	22.5k	180.0m	366P	-	120L	BA2	BS	9181106
5	EUROPEAN HIGHLANDER	21128t	02	22.6k	162.7m	410P	315C	84T	BA2	BS	9244116
6F+	EUROPEAN SEAWAY	22986t	91	21.0k	179.7m	200P	-	120L	BA2	UK	9007283
7»	EXPRESS	5902t	98	43.0k	91.3m	868P	195C	-	A	BS	9176046
8F	MISTRAL	10471t	98	22.0k	153.5m	12P	-	112T	A	FI	9183788
9	NORBANK	17464t	93	22.5k	166.7m	114P	-	125T	A	NL	9056583
10	NORBAY	17464t	92	21.5k	166.7m	114P	-	125T	A	BM	9056595
11F	NORSKY	19992t	99	20.0k	180.0m	12P	-	194T	A	FI	9186182
12F	NORSTREAM	19992t	99	20.0k	180.0m	12P	-	194T	A	FI	9186194
13	PRIDE OF BRUGES	31598t	87	18.5k	179.0m	1050P	310C	185T	A	NL	8503797
14	PRIDE OF BURGUNDY	28138t	92	21.0k	179.7m	1420P	465C	120L	BA2	UK	9015254
15	PRIDE OF CANTERBURY	30635t	91	21.0k	179.7m	2000P	537C	120L	BA2	UK	9007295
16	PRIDE OF HULL	59925t	01	22.0k	215.4m	1360P	205C	263T	AS	BS	9208629
17	PRIDE OF KENT	30635t	92	21.0k	179.7m	2000P	537C	120L	BA2	UK	9015266
18	PRIDE OF ROTTERDAM	59925t	00	22.0k	215.4m	1360P	205C	263T	AS	NL	9208617
19	PRIDE OF YORK	31785t	87	18.5k	179.0m	1050P	310C	185T	A	BS	8501957
20	SPIRIT OF BRITAIN	47592t	11	22.0k-	212.0m	2000P	194C	180L	BA2	UK	9524231
21	SPIRIT OF FRANCE	47592t	12	22.0k-	212.0m	2000P	194C	180L	BA2	UK	9533816

BORE SONG Built by Flensburger Schiffbau-Gesellschaft, Flensburg, Germany for *Bore Shipowners (Rettig Group Bore)* of Finland. In July 2011 chartered to *Mann Lines* to cover for the ESTRADEN'S refit. In September 2011 chartered to *P&O Ferries* and placed on the Middlesbrough - Zeebrugge route.

ESTRADEN Built as the ESTRADEN by Aker Finnyards, Rauma, Finland for *Rederi Ab Engship* (later *Bore Shipowners*) of Finland and chartered to *ArgoMann*. Later in 1999 renamed the AMAZON. In 2001 the charter was taken over by *Mann Lines* and in August she resumed the name ESTRADEN. In 2006 *Rederi AB Engship* was taken over by *Rettig Group Bore* and she remained on charter to *Mann Lines*. In January 2015 chartered to *P&O Ferries* to replace the WILHELMINE of *Cobelfret Ferries* on the Rotterdam - Middlesbrough (Teesport) service.

EUROPEAN CAUSEWAY Built by Mitsubishi Heavy Industries, Shimonoseki, Japan for *P&O Irish Sea* for the Cairnryan - Larne service.

EUROPEAN ENDEAVOUR Built as the MIDNIGHT MERCHANT by Astilleros Españoles SA, Seville, Spain for *Cenargo* (then owners of *NorseMerchant Ferries*). On delivery, chartered to *Norfolkline* to operate as second vessel on the Dover - Dunkerque (Ouest) service. In 2002 modified to allow two-deck loading. In 2006 chartered to *Acciona Trasmediterranea* of Spain and renamed the EL GRECO. Used on Mediterranean and Canary Island services. In 2007 sold to *P&O Ferries* and renamed the EUROPEAN ENDEAVOUR. Operated on the Dover - Calais route and as a re-fit relief vessel on Irish Sea routes. In May 2010 laid up. In February 2011 moved to the Liverpool - Dublin route.

EUROPEAN HIGHLANDER Built by Mitsubishi Heavy Industries, Shimonoseki, Japan for *P&O Irish Sea* for the Cairnryan - Larne service.

EUROPEAN SEAWAY Built by Schichau Seebeckwerft AG, Bremerhaven, Germany for *P&O European Ferries* for the Dover - Zeebrugge freight service. In 2000 a regular twice-daily freight-only Dover-Calais service was established, using this vessel which continued to operate to Zeebrugge at night.

In 2001 car passengers (not foot or coach passengers) began to be conveyed on the Dover - Zeebrugge service. In 2003 the Zeebrugge service ended and she operated only between Dover and Calais in a freight-only mode. In 2004 withdrawn and laid up. In January 2005 returned to the Dover - Calais route. In July 2012 chartered to GLID, a joint venture between Centrica Renewable Energy Limited and EIG, for use by technicians working on the North Sea Lynn and Inner Dowsing wind farm array four miles off Skegness. In October 2012 returned to the Dover - Calais service. In April 2013 laid up at Tilbury. In August 2014 chartered as a wind farm accommodation and support vessel near the North German coast. In April 2015 returned to layup at Tilbury.

EXPRESS Incat 91m catamaran built at Hobart, Tasmania, Australia for *Buquebus* of Argentina as the CATALONIA 1 and used by *Buquebus España* on their service between Barcelona (Spain) and Mallorca. In April 2000 chartered to *P&O Portsmouth* and renamed the PORTSMOUTH EXPRESS. During Winter 2000/01 she operated for *Buquebus* between Buenos Aires (Argentina) and Piriapolis (Uruguay) and was renamed the CATALONIA. Returned to *P&O Portsmouth* in Spring 2001 and was renamed the PORTSMOUTH EXPRESS. Returned to *Buquebus* in Autumn 2001 and then returned to *P&O Portsmouth* in Spring 2002. Laid up in Europe during Winter 2002/03 and renamed the CATALONIA. She returned to *P&O Ferries* in Spring 2003 trading under the marketing name 'Express'. In November she was renamed the EXPRESS. In 2004 she operated as the 'Cherbourg Express'. In 2005 transferred to *P&O Irish Sea* and operated on the Larne - Cairnryan/Troon service. Currently chartered until autumn 2015.

MISTRAL Built by J J Sietas KG, Hamburg, Germany for *Godby Shipping AB* of Finland. Chartered to *Transfennica*. In 2003 chartered to UPM-Kymmene Oy of Finland and operated between Rauma and Santander. In 2005 chartered to *Finnlines*. Until the end of 2007 used on a Helsinki - Hamina - Zeebrugge service only available northbound for general traffic. From January 2008 operated on *UPM-Kymmene Seaways'* service from Hamina to Lübeck, Amsterdam and Tilbury. In June 2013 charter ended. During the ensuing period she undertook several short charters. In October 2014 chartered to *P&O Ferries* as second ship on the Zeebrugge - Middlesbrough (Teesport) service; she has also operated between Tilbury and Zeebrugge.

NORBANK Built by Van der Giessen-de Noord, Krimpen aan den IJssel, Rotterdam, The Netherlands for *North Sea Ferries* for the Hull - Rotterdam service. She was originally built for and chartered to *Nedlloyd* but the charter was taken over by *P&O* in 1996 and she was bought by *P&O* in 2003. She retains Dutch crew and registry. In May 2001 moved to the Felixstowe - Europoort route. In January 2002 transferred to *P&O Irish Sea* and operated on the Liverpool - Dublin route.

NORBAY Built by Van der Giessen-de Noord, Krimpen aan den IJssel, Rotterdam, The Netherlands for *North Sea Ferries* for the Hull - Rotterdam service. Owned by *P&O*. In January 2002 transferred to *P&O Irish Sea* and operated on the Liverpool - Dublin route.

NORSKY, NORSTREAM Built by Aker Finnyards, Rauma, Finland for *Bore Line* of Finland and chartered to *P&O North Sea Ferries*. They generally operated on the Teesport - Zeebrugge service. In September 2011, the NORSTREAM was moved to the Tilbury - Zeebrugge route. In January 2013, the NORSKY was also moved to the Tilbury - Zeebrugge route.

PRIDE OF BRUGES Built as the NORSUN by NKK, Tsurumi, Japan for the Hull - Rotterdam service of *North Sea Ferries*. She was owned by *Nedlloyd* and was sold to *P&O* in 1996 but retains Dutch crew and registry. In May 2001 replaced by the PRIDE OF ROTTERDAM and in July 2001, after a major refurbishment, she was transferred to the Hull - Zeebrugge service, replacing the NORSTAR (26919t, 1974). In 2003 renamed the PRIDE OF BRUGES.

PRIDE OF BURGUNDY Built by Schichau Seebeckwerft AG, Bremerhaven, Germany for *P&O European Ferries* for the Dover - Calais service. When construction started she was due to be a sister vessel to the EUROPEAN SEAWAY (see Section 3) called the EUROPEAN CAUSEWAY and operate on the Zeebrugge freight route. However, it was decided that she should be completed as a passenger/freight vessel (the design allowed for conversion) and she was launched as the PRIDE OF BURGUNDY. In 1998, transferred to *P&O Stena Line* and renamed the P&OSL BURGUNDY. In 2002 renamed the PO BURGUNDY and in 2003 renamed the PRIDE OF BURGUNDY. In 2004 she operated mainly in freight-only mode. In 2005 returned to full passenger service.

Pride of Canterbury *(John Hendy)*

Pride of Burgundy *(George Holland)*

Norsky *(J.J.Jager)*

Pride of York *(J.J.Jager)*

Mistral *(P&O Ferries)*

European Highlander *(Miles Cowsill)*

PRIDE OF CANTERBURY Built as the EUROPEAN PATHWAY by Schichau Seebeckwerft AG, Bremerhaven, Germany for *P&O European Ferries* for the Dover - Zeebrugge freight service. In 1998 transferred to *P&O Stena Line*. In 2001 car/foot passengers were again conveyed on the route. In 2002/03 rebuilt as a full passenger vessel and renamed the PRIDE OF CANTERBURY; now operates between Dover and Calais.

PRIDE OF HULL Built by Fincantieri-Cantieri Navali Italiani SpA, Venice, Italy for *P&O North Sea Ferries* to replace (with the PRIDE OF ROTTERDAM) the NORSEA and NORSUN plus the freight vessels NORBAY and NORBANK on the Hull - Rotterdam service.

PRIDE OF KENT Built as the EUROPEAN HIGHWAY by Schichau Seebeckwerft AG, Bremerhaven, Germany for *P&O European Ferries* for the Dover - Zeebrugge freight service. In 1998 transferred to *P&O Stena Line*. In Summer 1999 she operated full-time between Dover and Calais. She returned to the Dover - Zeebrugge route in the autumn when the P&OSL AQUITAINE was transferred to the Dover - Calais service. In 2001 car/foot passengers were again conveyed on the route. In 2002/03 rebuilt as a full passenger vessel and renamed the PRIDE OF KENT; now operates between Dover and Calais.

PRIDE OF ROTTERDAM Built by Fincantieri-Cantieri Navali Italiani SpA, Venice, Italy. Keel laid as the PRIDE OF HULL but launched as the PRIDE OF ROTTERDAM. Owned by Dutch interests until 2006 when she was sold to *P&O Ferries*. Further details as the PRIDE OF HULL.

PRIDE OF YORK Built as the NORSEA by Govan Shipbuilders Ltd, Glasgow, UK for the Hull - Rotterdam service of *North Sea Ferries* (jointly owned by *P&O* and *The Royal Nedlloyd Group* of The Netherlands until 1996). In December 2001 she was replaced by the new PRIDE OF HULL and, after a two-month refurbishment, in 2002 transferred to the Hull - Zeebrugge service, replacing the NORLAND (26290t, 1974). In 2003 renamed the PRIDE OF YORK.

SPIRIT OF BRITAIN, SPIRIT OF FRANCE Built by STX Europe, Rauma, Finland for the Dover - Calais service. Car capacity relates to dedicated car deck only; additional cars can be accommodated on the freight decks as necessary.

PENTLAND FERRIES

THE COMPANY *Pentland Ferries* is a UK private sector company.

MANAGEMENT **Managing Director** Andrew Banks, **Designated Person Ashore** Kathryn Banks.

ADDRESS Pier Road, St Margaret's Hope, South Ronaldsay, Orkney KW17 2SW.

TELEPHONE **Administration & Reservations** + 44 (0)1856 831226.

FAX **Administration & Reservations** + 44 (0)1856 831697.

INTERNET **Email** sales@pentlandferries.co.uk **Website** www.pentlandferries.co.uk *(English)*

ROUTE OPERATED Gills Bay (Caithness) - St Margaret's Hope (South Ronaldsay, Orkney) (1 hour; *PENTALINA*; up to 4 per day).

1	ORCADIA	899t	78	13.0k	69.5m	-	40C	-	AS	UK	7615490
2	PENTALINA	2382t	08	17.1k	59.0m	345P	70C	9L	A	UK	9437969

ORCADIA Built as the SATURN by Ailsa Shipbuilding, Troon for *Caledonian MacBrayne* and initially used on the Wemyss Bay - Rothesay services. Between 1986 and 2005 she usually rotated on this service and services from Gourock; until 2000 this, in summer, included Clyde cruising but this was not repeated in 2001. In the summers 2005 - 2010, she operated additional peak summer sailings between Ardrossan and Brodick with a maximum capacity of 250 passengers. In October 2010 she took over the Gourock - Dunoon service. In June 2011 replaced by *Argyll Ferries* passenger ferries. During Summer 2011 she operated additional sailings between Ardrossan and Brodick. In September returned to the Gourock - Dunoon route to provide additional capacity for the Cowal Games. She was then laid up. In February 2015 sold to *Pentland Ferries* and renamed the ORCADIA.

PENTALINA Catamaran built by FBMA Marine, Cebu, Philippines for *Pentland Ferries*.

RED FUNNEL FERRIES

THE COMPANY Red Funnel Ferries is the trading name of the *Southampton, Isle of Wight and South of England Royal Mail Steam Packet Company Limited*, a British private sector company. The company was acquired by *JP Morgan International Capital Corporation* in 2000; it was purchased by the management in 2004 and in 2007 it was sold to *Infracapital Partners LP* – the infrastructure fund of the *Prudential Group*.

MANAGEMENT Managing Director Tom Docherty, Commercial Director Colin Hetherington.

ADDRESS 12 Bugle Street, Southampton SO14 2JY.

TELEPHONE Administration +44 (0)23 8024 8500, Reservations UK 0844 844 9988, *Elsewhere* +44 (0)23 8001 9192.

FAX Administration & Reservations UK +44 (0)23 8024 8501.

INTERNET Email post@redfunnel.co.uk Website www.redfunnel.co.uk *(English)*

ROUTES OPERATED Conventional Ferries Southampton - East Cowes (55 mins; *RED EAGLE, RED FALCON, RED OSPREY*; hourly). Fast Passenger Ferries Southampton - West Cowes (22 mins; *RED JET 3, RED JET 4, RED JET 5*; every hour or half hour).

1	RED EAGLE	3953t	96	13.0k	93.2m	895P	200C	18L	BA	UK	9117337
2	RED FALCON	3953t	94	13.0k	93.2m	895P	200C	18L	BA	UK	9064047
3»p	RED JET 3	213t	98	33.0k	32.9m	190P	0C	0L	-	UK	9182758
4»p	RED JET 4	342t	03	35.0k	39.8m	277P	0C	0L	-	UK	9295854
5»p	RED JET 5	209t	99	35.0k	35.0m	177P	0L	0L	-	UK	8954415
6	RED OSPREY	3953t	94	13.0k	93.2m	895P	200C	18L	BA	UK	9064059

RED EAGLE Built by Ferguson Shipbuilders, Port Glasgow, UK for the Southampton - East Cowes service. During Winter 2004/05 stretched by 10 metres and height raised by 3 metres at Gdansk, Poland.

RED FALCON Built by Ferguson Shipbuilders, Port Glasgow, UK for the Southampton - East Cowes service. In 2004 stretched by 10 metres and height raised by 3 metres at Gdansk, Poland. In spring 2014 she received a £2m upgrade.

RED JET 3 FBM Marine catamaran built at Cowes, UK for the Southampton - West Cowes service.

RED JET 4 North West Bay Ships Pty Ltd catamaran built in Hobart, Tasmania, Australia for the Southampton - West Cowes service.

RED JET 5 Built by Pequot River Shipworks, New London, Connecticut, USA to FBM Marine design as the BO HENGY for *Bahamas Fast Ferries* of The Bahamas. In May 2009 sold to *Red Funnel Ferries* and renamed the RED JET 5.

RED OSPREY Built by Ferguson Shipbuilders, Port Glasgow, UK for the Southampton - East Cowes service. In 2003 stretched by 10 metres and height raised by 3 metres at Gdansk, Poland. In spring 2015 she received a £2.2m upgrade.

Red Eagle *(Andrew Cooke)*

Red Jet 3 and Red Jet 4 *(Andrew Cooke)*

SHETLAND ISLANDS COUNCIL

THE COMPANY Shetland Islands Council is a British local government authority.

MANAGEMENT Ferry Services Manager Jim Mouatt, Marine Superintendent Kevin Main.

ADDRESS Port Administration Building, Sella Ness, Mossbank, Shetland ZE2 9QR.

TELEPHONE Administration +44 (0)1806 244234, 244266, Reservations Yell Sound & Bluemull +44 (0)1595 745804, Fair Isle +44 (0)1595 760363, Whalsay +44(0)1595 745804, Skerries +44 (0)1595 745804, Papa Stour +44 (0)1595 745804.

TELEPHONE Administration +44 (0)1806 244234, 244266, Reservations Yell Sound & Bluemull +44 (0)1595 745804, Fair Isle +44 (0)1595 760363, Whalsay +44(0)1595 745804, Skerries +44 (0)1595 745804, Papa Stour +44 (0)1595 745804.

FAX +44 (0)1806 244232.

INTERNET Email ferries@sic.shetland.gov.uk Website: www.shetland.gov.uk/ferries (English)

ROUTES OPERATED Yell Sound Service Toft (Mainland) - Ulsta (Yell) (20 mins; DAGALIEN, DAGGRI; up to 26 per day), Bluemull Sound Service (Gutcher (Yell) - Belmont (Unst) (10 mins; BIGGA, FIVLA, GEIRA; up to 28 per day), Gutcher – Hamars Ness (Fetlar) (25 mins; BIGGA, FIVLA, GEIRA; up to 8 per day), Bressay Lerwick (Mainland) - Maryfield (Bressay) (5 mins; LEIRNA; up to 23 per day), Whalsay Laxo/Vidlin (Mainland) - Symbister (Whalsay) (30-45 mins; HENDRA, LINGA; up to 18 per day), Skerries Vidlin (Mainland) – Out Skerries (1 hr 30 mins; FILLA; up to 10 per week), Out Skerries – Lerwick (3 hours; FILLA; 2 per week), Fair Isle (Grutness (Mainland) - Fair Isle (3 hrs; GOOD SHEPHERD IV; 2 per week), Papa Stour West Burrafirth (Mainland) – Papa Stour (40 mins; SNOLDA; up to 7 per week).

1	BIGGA	274t	91	11.0k	33.5m	96P	21C	4L	BA	UK	9000821
2	DAGALIEN	1861t	04	12.0k	61m	145P	30C	4L	BA	UK	9291626
3	DAGGRI	1861t	04	12.0k	61m	145P	30C	4L	BA	UK	9291614
4	FILLA	356t	03	12.0k	35.5m	30P	10C	2L	BA	UK	9269192
5	FIVLA	230t	85	11.0k	29.9m	95P	15C	4L	BA	UK	8410237
6	GEIRA	226t	88	10.8k	29.9m	95P	15C	4L	BA	UK	8712489
7	GOOD SHEPHERD IV	76t	86	10.0k	18.3m	12P	1C	0L	C	UK	
8	HENDRA	248	82	11.0k	33.8m	100P	18C	4L	BA	UK	8200254
9	LEIRNA	420t	92	9.0k	35.1m	100P	20C	4L	BA	UK	9050199
10	LINGA	658t	01	11.0k	35.8m	100P	16C	2L	BA	UK	9242170
11	SNOLDA	130t	83	9.0k	24.4m	12P	6C	1L	A	UK	8302090
12•	THORA	147t	75	8.5k	25.3m	93P	10C	2L	BA	UK	7347354

BIGGA Built by JW Miller & Sons Ltd, St Monans, Fife, UK. Used on the Toft - Ulsta service. In 2005 moved to the Bluemull Sound service.

DAGALIEN, DAGGRI Built by Stocznia Polnócna, Gdansk, Poland to replace the BIGGA and HENDRA on Toft - Ulsta service.

FILLA Built by Stocznia Polnócna, Gdansk, Poland for the Lerwick /Vidlin - Out Skerries service. She looks like an oil rig supply vessel and is capable of transporting fresh water for replenishing the tanks on the Skerries in case of drought.

FIVLA Built by Ailsa Shipbuilding, Troon, UK. Now a spare vessel, though often used on the Bluemull service.

GEIRA Built by Richard Dunston (Hessle), Hessle, UK. Formerly used on the Laxo - Symbister route. Replaced by the HENDRA in 2005 and moved to the Bluemull Sound service.

GOOD SHEPHERD IV Built by JW Miller & Sons Ltd, St Monans, Fife, UK. Used on the service between Grutness (Mainland) and Fair Isle. Vehicles conveyed by special arrangement and generally consist

Daggri (*Miles Cowsill*)

Stena Europe (*Andrew Cooke*)

of agricultural vehicles. She is pulled up on the marine slip on Fair Isle at the conclusion of each voyage.

HENDRA Built by McTay Marine, Bromborough, Wirral, UK for the Laxo - Symbister service. In 2002 transferred to the Toft - Ulsta service. In 2004 replaced by new vessels DAGGRI and DAGALIEN and moved to the Bluemull Sound service. In May 2005 returned to the Laxo - Symbister service as second vessel.

LEIRNA Built by Ferguson Shipbuilders, Port Glasgow, UK. Used on the Lerwick - Maryfield (Bressay) service.

LINGA Built by Stocznia Polnócna, Gdansk, Poland. Used on the Laxo - Symbister service.

SNOLDA Built as the FILLA by Sigbjorn Iversen, Flekkefjord, Norway. Used on the Lerwick (Mainland) - Out Skerries and Vidlin (Mainland) - Out Skerries services. At other times she operated freight and charter services around the Shetland Archipelago. She resembles a miniature oil rig supply vessel. Passenger capacity was originally 20 from 1st April to 31st October inclusive but is now 12 all year. In 2003 renamed the SNOLDA; replaced by the new FILLA and, in 2004, transferred to the West Burrafirth - Papa Stour route.

THORA Built by Tórshavnor Skipasmidja, Tórshavn, Faroe Islands. After a period as a spare vessel, in 1998 she took over the Laxo - Symbister service from the withdrawn KJELLA (158t, 1957). Withdrawn again in 2001 and became a spare vessel. Now laid up for sale.

STENA LINE

THE COMPANY *Stena Line Limited* is incorporated in Great Britain and registered in England and Wales. *Stena Line BV* is a Dutch company. The ultimate parent undertaking is *Stena AB* of Sweden.

MANAGEMENT Area Director, North Sea Pim de Lange, Area Director, Irish Sea Michael McGrath.

ADDRESS *UK* Stena House, Station Approach, Holyhead, Anglesey LL65 1DQ, *The Netherlands* PO Box 2, 3150 AA, Hook of Holland, The Netherlands.

TELEPHONE Administration *UK* +44 (0)1407) 606631, *The Netherlands* +31 (0)174 389333, Reservations *UK* 0844 7707070 (from UK only), *The Netherlands* +31 (0)174 315811.

FAX Administration & Reservations *UK* +44 (0)1407 606811, *The Netherlands* +31 (0)174 387045, Telex 31272.

INTERNET Email info@stenaline.com Website www.stenaline.co.uk *(English)*

ROUTES OPERATED Conventional Ferries Cairnryan - Belfast (2 hrs 15 mins; *STENA SUPERFAST VII, STENA SUPERFAST VII*; up to 6 per day, Port of Liverpool (Twelve Quays River Terminal, Birkenhead) - Belfast (8 hrs; *STENA HIBERNIA (freight only), STENA LAGAN, STENA MERSEY*; 1 per day (Mon), 2/3 per day (Sun, Tue-Sat)), Holyhead - Dublin (3 hrs 15 mins; *STENA ADVENTURER, STENA SUPERFAST X*; 4 per day), Fishguard - Rosslare (3 hrs 30 mins; *STENA EUROPE*; 2 per day), Rosslare - Cherbourg (20 hrs; *STENA HORIZON*; 3 per week), Harwich - Hook of Holland (The Netherlands) (7 hrs 30 mins; *STENA BRITANNICA, STENA HOLLANDICA*; 2 per day), Freight Ferries Heysham - Belfast (7 hrs; *STENA PERFORMER, STENA PRECISION*; 2 per day), Harwich - Rotterdam (8 hrs; *CAPUCINE, SEVERINE*; 11 per week), Killingholme - Hook of Holland (11 hrs; *STENA TRANSIT, STENA TRANSPORTER*; 1 per day), Killingholme - Rotterdam (13 hrs; *STENA SCOTIA*; 3 per week).

1F	CAPUCINE	16342t	11	16.0k	150.0m	12P	-	140T	A	UK	9539066
2F	SEVERINE	16342t	12	16.0k	150.0m	12P	-	140T	A	NL	9539078
3	STENA ADVENTURER	43532t	03	22.0k	210.8m	1500P	-	210L	BA2	UK	9235529
4	STENA BRITANNICA	63600t	10	22.0k	240.0m	1200P	-	300T	BA2	UK	9419175
5	STENA EUROPE	24828t	81	20.5k	149.0m	2076P	456C	60T	BA	UK	7901760
6»•	STENA EXPLORER	19638t	96	40.0k	126.6m	1500P	375C	50L	A	UK	9080194
7F	STENA HIBERNIA	13017t	96	18.6k	142.5m	12P	-	114T	A	NL	9121637
8	STENA HOLLANDICA	63600t	10	22.5k	240.0m	1200P	-	300T	BA2	NL	9419163

9	STENA HORIZON	26500t	06	23.5k	186.5m	1000P	200C	120L	A	IT	9332559
10	STENA LAGAN	27510t	05	23.5k	186.5m	980P	160C	135T	A	UK	9329849
11	STENA MERSEY	27510t	05	23.5k	186.5m	980P	160C	135T	A	UK	9329851
12F	STENA PERFORMER	19722t	12	21.0k	142.0m	12P	-	151T	A	IM	9506227
13F	STENA PRECISION	19722t	12	21.0k	142.0m	12P	-	151T	A	IM	9506239
14F	STENA SCOTIA	13017t	96	18.6k	142.5m	12P	-	114T	A	NL	9121625
15	STENA SUPERFAST VII	30285t	01	26.6k	203.3m	717P	695C	110L	BA2	UK	9198941
16	STENA SUPERFAST VIII	30285t	01	26.6k	203.3m	717P	695C	110L	BA2	UK	9198953
17	STENA SUPERFAST X	30285t	02	22.0k	203.3m	1200P	480C	110L	BA2	UK	9211511
18F+	STENA TRANSIT	34700t	11	22.2k	212.0m	300P	-	290T	A2	NL	9469388
19F+	STENA TRANSPORTER	34700t	11	22.2k	212.0m	300P	-	290T	A2	NL	9469376

CAPUCINE, SEVERINE Built by the Kyokuyo Shipyard, Shimonoseki, Japan for CLdN. Initially operated on their Ipswich - Rotterdam service. This service was suspended in August 2012. In September, they were chartered to *Stena Line* and placed on the Harwich - Rotterdam service.

STENA ADVENTURER Ro-pax vessel built by Hyundai Heavy Industries, Ulsan, South Korea, for *Stena RoRo* and chartered to *Stena Line* to operate between Holyhead and Dublin.

STENA BRITANNICA Built by Waden Yards in Wismar and Warnemünde, Germany, for *Stena Rederi* (bow sections constructed at Warnemünde and stern and final assembly at Wismar). Replaced the 2003 built STENA BRITANNICA on the Harwich - Hook of Holland service.

STENA EUROPE Built as the KRONPRINSESSAN VICTORIA by Götaverken Arendal AB, Gothenburg, Sweden for *Göteborg-Frederikshavn Linjen* of Sweden (trading as *Sessan Linjen*) for their Gothenburg - Frederikshavn service. Shortly after delivery, the company was taken over by *Stena Line* and services were marketed as *Stena-Sessan Line* for a period. In 1982 she was converted to an overnight ferry by changing one vehicle deck into two additional decks of cabins and she was switched to the Gothenburg - Kiel route (with, during the summer, daytime runs from Gothenburg to Frederikshavn and Kiel to Korsør (Denmark)). In 1989 she was transferred to the Oslo - Frederikshavn route and renamed the STENA SAGA. In 1994, transferred to *Stena Line BV*, renamed the STENA EUROPE and operated between Hook of Holland and Harwich. She was withdrawn in June 1997, transferred to the *Lion Ferry* (a *Stena Line* subsidiary) Karlskrona - Gdynia service and renamed the LION EUROPE. In 1998 she was transferred back to *Stena Line* (remaining on the same route) and renamed the STENA EUROPE. In early 2002 the cabins installed in 1982 were removed and other modifications made and she was transferred to the Fishguard - Rosslare route.

STENA EXPLORER Finnyards HSS1500 built at Rauma, Finland for *Stena RoRo* and chartered to *Stena Line*. Operated on the Holyhead - Dún Laoghaire route until September 2014. Will not operate during 2015; laid up for sale or scrapping.

STENA HIBERNIA Built as the ` by Miho Shipyard, Shimizu, Japan for *Norfolkline*. Used on the Scheveningen (from 2007 Vlaardingen) - Felixstowe service. In October 2009 moved to the Heysham-Belfast service. In July 2010 renamed the HIBERNIA SEAWAYS. In July 2011 renamed the STENA HIBERNIA. In September 2012 transferred to *Stena RoRo*. In November chartered to *Stena Line* and placed on the Birkenhead - Belfast service.

STENA HOLLANDICA Built by Nordic Yards in Wismar and Warnemünde, Germany, for *Stena Rederi* (bow sections constructed at Warnemünde and stern and final assembly at Wismar) to replace the previous STENA HOLLANDICA on the Harwich - Hook of Holland service. Entered service May 2010.

STENA HORIZON Built as the CARTOUR BETA by CN Visentini, Porto Viro, Italy for Levantina Trasporti of Italy. Chartered to *Caronte & Tourist* of Italy and operated between Messina and Salerno (Sicily). In October 2011 chartered to *Celtic Link Ferries*, renamed the CELTIC HORIZON and placed on the Rosslare - Cherbourg route. In March 2014 service and charter taken over by *Stena Line*. Renamed the STENA HORIZON.

STENA LAGAN, STENA MERSEY Built as the LAGAN VIKING and MERSEY VIKING by CN Visentini, Donada, Italy for *Levantina Trasporti* of Italy. Chartered to *NorseMerchant Ferries* and placed on the Birkenhead - Belfast route. In 2008 sold to *Norfolkline*, then resold to *Epic Shipping* and chartered back.

Stena Superfast X *(Gordon Hislip)*

Stena Mersey *(Matt Davies)*

In August 2010, following *Norfolkline's* purchase by *DFDS Seaways*, they were renamed the LAGAN SEAWAYS and MERSEY SEAWAYS respectively. Between January and July 2011 they were operated by *Stena Line Irish Sea Ferries*, a 'stand-alone' company pending consideration of the take-over by the UK and Irish competition authorities. In July 2011 the take-over was confirmed and in August 2011 they were renamed the STENA LAGAN and STENA MERSEY. In April 2012 they were sold to *Stena RoRo*; they continue to be operated by *Stena Line*.

STENA PERFORMER Built as the SEATRUCK PERFORMANCE by Flensburger Schiffbau-Gesellschaft, Flensburg, Germany for *Seatruck Ferries*. In September 2012 chartered to *Stena Line* to operate between Heysham and Belfast and renamed the STENA PERFORMER.

STENA PRECISION Built as the SEATRUCK PRECISION by Flensburger Schiffbau-Gesellschaft, Flensburg, Germany for *Seatruck Ferries*. In September 2012 chartered to *Stena Line* to operate between Heysham and Belfast and renamed the STENA PRECISION.

STENA SCOTIA Built as the MAERSK EXPORTER by Miho Shipyard, Shimizu, Japan for *Norfolkline*. Used on the Scheveningen (from 2007 Vlaardingen) - Felixstowe service until March 2009 when she was moved to the Heysham - Belfast route. In July 2010 renamed the SCOTIA SEAWAYS. In July 2011 renamed the STENA SCOTIA. In September 2013 transferred to *Stena RoRo* and placed on the charter market. In September 2014 chartered to *Stena Line* and inaugurated a new service between Rotterdam and Killingholme

STENA SUPERFAST VII, STENA SUPERFAST VIII Built as the SUPERFAST VII and SUPERFAST VIII by Howaldtswerke Deutsche Werft AG, Kiel, Germany for *Attica Enterprises* (now *Attica Group*) for use by *Superfast Ferries* between Rostock and Hanko. In 2006 sold to *Tallink*. The Finnish terminal was transferred to Helsinki and daily return trips between Helsinki and Tallinn were introduced. These ceased in September 2008. The operation was ceased for the winter season in December 2009 and 2010. Service resumed at the end of April 2010 and 2011. In August 2011 chartered to *Stena Line* for three years (with an option to extend by one year) and renamed the STENA SUPERFAST VII, STENA SUPERFAST VIII. In November 2011, after a major refit, they were placed on a service between Cairnryan and Belfast (replacing the Stranraer - Belfast service).

STENA SUPERFAST X Built as the SUPERFAST X by Howaldtswerke Deutsche Werft AG, Kiel, Germany for *Attica Enterprises* (now *Attica Group*) for use by *Superfast Ferries*. In May 2002 she and the SUPERFAST IX (see ATLANTIC VISION, *Tallink*, Section 6) began operating between Rosyth (Scotland) and Zeebrugge. In 2004 fitted with additional cabins and conference/seating areas. In 2007 sold to *Veolia Transportation* and renamed the JEAN NICOLI. Chartered to *CoTuNav* of Tunisia and operated between France/Italy and Tunisia. Later chartered to *ANEK Lines* of Greece and operated on the Patras - Corfu - Igoumenitsa - Venice route. In July 2008 chartered to *SeaFrance* and renamed the SEAFRANCE MOLIERE. After modifications she was placed on the Dover - Calais route. In November 2011 laid up. In January 2012 offered for sale or charter. In July 2012 sold to *Scapino Shipping Ltd* of Monaco and renamed the MOLIERE. In October 2012 chartered to the *DFDS/LD Lines* joint venture and, in November, renamed the DIEPPE SEAWAYS and introduced onto the Dover - Calais service. In May 2014 sold to *Stena Line North Sea Ltd*. In December 2014 charter ended. Refurbished and, in March 2015, chartered to *Stena Line*, renamed the STENA SUPERFAST X and placed on the Holyhead - Dublin route.

STENA TRANSIT, STENA TRANSPORTER Built by Samsung Heavy Industries, Koje, South Korea. Used on the Hook of Holland - Killingholme service.

WESTERN FERRIES

THE COMPANY *Western Ferries (Clyde) Ltd* is a British private sector company.

MANAGEMENT **Managing Director** Gordon Ross.

ADDRESS Hunter's Quay, Dunoon, Argyll PA23 8HJ.

TELEPHONE **Administration** + 44 (0)1369 704452, **Reservations** Not applicable.

INTERNET **Email** enquiries@western-ferries.co.uk **Website** www.western-ferries.co.uk *(English)*

Stena Hollandica *(Rob de Visser)*

Sound of Soay *(Matthew Punter)*

White Light (*Andrew Cooke*)

ROUTE OPERATED McInroy's Point (Gourock) - Hunter's Quay (Dunoon) (20 mins; *SOUND OF SCARBA, SOUND OF SEIL, SOUND OF SHUNA, SOUND OF SOAY*; every 20 mins (15 mins in peaks)).

1	SOUND OF SCARBA	489t	01	11.0k	49.95m	220P	40C	4/5L	BA	UK	9237424
2	SOUND OF SEIL	497t	13	11.0k	49.95m	220P	54C	4/5L	BA	UK	9665217
3	SOUND OF SHUNA	489t	03	11.0k	49.95m	220P	40C	4/5L	BA	UK	9289441
4	SOUND OF SOAY	497t	13	11.0k	49.95m	220P	54C	4/5L	BA	UK	9665229

SOUND OF SCARBA, SOUND OF SHUNA Built by Ferguson Shipbuilders, Port Glasgow, UK for *Western Ferries*.

SOUND OF SEIL, SOUND OF SOAY Built by Cammell Laird Shiprepairers & Shipbuilders, Birkenhead, UK for *Western Ferries*.

SOUND OF SEIL, SOUND OF SOAY Under construction by Cammell Laird Shiprepairers & Shipbuilders, Birkenhead, UK to replace the SOUND OF SANDA and SOUND OF SCALPAY.

WIGHTLINK

THE COMPANY *Wightlink* is a British private sector company, owned by the *Balfour Beatty Infrastructure Partners LLP*. The routes and vessels were previously part of *Sealink (British Rail)* but were excluded from the purchase of most of the *Sealink* operations by *Stena Line* in 1990. They remained in *Sea Containers'* ownership until purchased by *CINVen* Ltd, a venture capital company in 1995. The company was the subject of a management buy-out financed by the *Royal Bank of Scotland* in 2001 and was sold to the *Macquarie Group* of Australia in 2005. It was purchased by *Balfour Beatty Infrastructure Partners LLP* in February 2015.

MANAGEMENT **Chief Executive** Russell Kew, **Marketing Manager** Kerry Jackson, **Commercial Director** Clive Tilley.

ADDRESS Gunwharf Road, Portsmouth PO1 2LA.

TELEPHONE **Administration and Reservations** 0871 376 1000 (from UK only), +44 (0)23 9285 5230 (from overseas).

INTERNET **Email** bookings@wightlink.co.uk **Website** www.wightlink.co.uk (*English, Dutch, French, German*)

ROUTES OPERATED **Conventional Ferries** Lymington - Yarmouth (Isle of Wight) (approx 35 mins; *WIGHT LIGHT, WIGHT SKY*, hourly), Portsmouth - Fishbourne (Isle of Wight) (approx 35 mins; *ST. CECILIA, ST. CLARE, ST. FAITH, WIGHT SUN*; half-hourly or hourly depending on time of day). **Fast Passenger Ferries** Portsmouth - Ryde (Isle of Wight) (passenger-only) (under 20 mins; *WIGHT RYDER I, WIGHT RYDER II*; 2 per hour).

1	ST. CECILIA	2968t	86	12.0k	77.0m	771P	142C	12L	BA	UK	8518546
2	ST. CLARE	5359t	01	13.0k	86.0m	878P	186C	-	BA	UK	9236949
3	ST. FAITH	3009t	89	12.5k	77.0m	771P	142C	12L	BA	UK	8907228
5	WIGHT LIGHT	1500t	08	11.0k	62.4m	360P	65C	-	BA	UK	9446972
6»p	WIGHT RYDER I	520t	09	20.0k	40.9m	260P	0C	-	-	UK	9512537
7»p	WIGHT RYDER II	520t	09	20.0k	40.9m	260P	0C	-	-	UK	9512549
8	WIGHT SKY	1500t	08	11.0k	62.4m	360P	65C	-	BA	UK	9446984
9	WIGHT SUN	1500t	09	11.0k	62.4m	360P	65C	-	BA	UK	9490416

ST. CECILIA, ST FAITH Built by Cochrane Shipbuilders, Selby, UK for *Sealink British Ferries* for the Portsmouth - Fishbourne service.

ST. CLARE Built by Stocznia Remontowa, Gdansk, Poland for the Portsmouth - Fishbourne service. She is a double-ended ferry with a central bridge. She will be modified for double deck loading during winter 2016/17.

Wight Ryder 1 (*Miles Cowsill*)

Wight Sun (*Nick Widdows*)

WIGHT LIGHT, WIGHT SKY, WIGHT SUN Built by Brodogradilište Kraljevica, Croatia for the Lymington - Yarmouth route. In March 2015 the WIGHT SUN was transferred to the Portsmouth - Fishbourne service.

WIGHT RYDER I, WIGHT RYDER II Catamarans built by FBMA Marine, Balamban, Cebu, Philippines. Operate on the Portsmouth - Ryde service.

Note: When one of the 'Wight Riders' is unavailable a replacement vessel is often chartered. This is generally the SOLENT CAT of *Solent & Wightline Cruises* - 74t, 2000, 13k, 20.1m, 250 passengers, catamaran.

To be ordered

| 10 | NEWBUILDING | - | 17 | - | - | 1000P | 178C | - | BA2 | UK | - |

NEWBUILDING To be ordered during 2015 for delivery in 2017. To be dual powered - LNG and diesel.

SECTION I – GB & IRELAND PASSENGER OPERATIONS

Glenachulish *(John Hendy)*

SECTION 2 - MINOR FERRY OPERATORS
ARGYLL AND BUTE COUNCIL

THE COMPANY Argyll and Bute Council is a British local government authority.

MANAGEMENT Executive Director of Development and Infrastructure Pippa Milne, Head of Economic Development and Strategic Transportation Fergus Murray, Operations Manager Clive Hayward.

ADDRESS Whitegates Offices, Whitegates Road, Lochgilphead, Argyll PA31 8SY.

TELEPHONE Administration +44 (0)1546 604673.

FAX Administration +44 (0)1546 604738.

INTERNET Email clive.hayward@argyll-bute.gov.uk Website www.argyll-bute.gov.uk/transport-and-streets/ferry-travel

ROUTES OPERATED Vehicle ferries Seil - Luing (5 mins; BELNAHUA; approx half-hourly), Port Askaig (Islay) - Feolin (Jura) (5 mins; EILEAN DHIURA; approx half-hourly). Passenger-only ferries Port Appin – Lismore (10 mins; THE LISMORE; approx hourly), Ellenabeich – Easdale (5 mins; EASDALE; approx quarter-hourly).

1	BELNAHUA	35t	72	8.0k	17.1m	40P	5C	1L	BA	UK
2p	EASDALE	-	93	6.5k	6.4m	11P	0C	0L	-	UK
3	EILEAN DHIURA	86t	98	9.0k	25.6m	50P	13C	1L	BA	UK
4p	THE LISMORE	12t	88	8.0k	9.7m	20P	0C	0L	-	UK

BELNAHUA Built by Campbeltown Shipyard, Campbeltown, UK for Argyll County Council for the Seil - Luing service. In 1975, following local government reorganisation, transferred to Strathclyde Regional Council. In 1996, transferred to Argyll and Bute Council.

EASDALE Built for Strathclyde Regional Council for the Ellenabeich - Easdale passenger-only service. In 1996, following local government reorganisation, transferred to Argyll and Bute Council.

EILEAN DHIURA Built by McTay Marine, Bromborough, Wirral, UK for Argyll and Bute Council to replace the Western Ferries (Argyll) SOUND OF GIGHA on the Islay - Jura route. ASP Ship Management manage and operate this vessel on behalf of Argyll and Bute Council.

THE LISMORE Built for Strathclyde Regional Council for the Port Appin – Lismore passenger-only service. In 1996, following local government reorganisation, transferred to Argyll and Bute Council.

ARRANMORE FAST FERRIES

THE COMPANY Arranmore Fast Ferries is an Irish Republic private sector company.

MANAGEMENT Managing Director Seamus Boyle.

ADDRESS Leabgarrow, Arranmore, County Donegal, Irish Republic.

TELEPHONE Administration & Reservations +353 (0)87 3171810.

INTERNET Email: info.fastferry@gmail.com Website www.arranmorefastferry.com (English). App can be downloaded from Twitter - @Arranmore Ferry

ROUTE OPERATED Burtonport (County Donegal) - Leabgarrow (Arranmore Island) (20 mins; MORVERN; up to 8 per day).

1	MORVERN	83t	73	8.0k	26.6m	96P	10C	-	B	IR
2P	OCEAN WARRIOR	18t	89	18.0k	14.3m	12P	0C	-	-	IR
3	RENFREW ROSE	65t	84	-	17.5m	12P	3C	-	B	IR

MORVERN Built by James Lamont & Co Ltd, Port Glasgow, UK for Caledonian MacBrayne. After service on a number of routes she was, after 1979, the main vessel on the Fionnphort (Mull) - Iona service.

In 1992 she was replaced by the LOCH BUIE and became a spare vessel. In 1995 sold to *Arranmore Island Ferry Services*. In 2001 sold to *Bere Island Ferries*. In February 2010 refurbished by Bere Island Boatyard and sold to *Arranmore Charters*. Extended in June 2012.

OCEAN WARRIOR An ex Tyne class lifeboat. Originally at *RNLI* Headquarters, Poole, Dorset. Bought by *Arranmore Fast Ferries* in 2014.

RENFREW ROSE Built by MacCrindle Shipbuilding Ltd, Ardrossan for *Strathclyde PTE* (later *Strathclyde Partnership for Transport*). Built as a small car ferry but operated passenger only between Renfrew and Yoker (apart from carrying ambulances in earlier days before they became too heavy). In March 2010 laid up. In June 2012 sold to *Arranmore Fast Ferries* for use as a passenger/car ferry.

ARRANMORE ISLAND FERRY SERVICES

THE COMPANY *Arranmore Island Ferry Services (Bád Farrantoireacht Arainn Mhór)* is an Irish Republic company, supported by *Roinn na Gaeltachta (The Gaeltacht Authority)*, a semi-state-owned body responsible for tourism and development in the Irish-speaking areas of The Irish Republic.

MANAGEMENT Managing Director Dominic Sweeney.

ADDRESS Cara na nOilean, Burtonport Pier, Letterkenny, Co. Donegal Irish Republic.

TELEPHONE Administration & Reservations + 353 (0)7495 20532, + 353 (0)7495 42233,

INTERNET Email arranmoreferry@gmail.com Website www.arranmoreferry.com *(English)*

ROUTE OPERATED Burtonport (County Donegal) - Leabgarrow (Arranmore Island) (15 mins; COLL, RHUM; up to 10 per day (Summer), 8 per day (Winter)).

1	COLL	69t	74	8.0k	25.3m	96P	6C	-	B	IR
2	RHUM	69t	73	8.0k	25.3m	96P	6C	-	B	IR

COLL Built by James Lamont & Co Ltd, Port Glasgow, UK for *Caledonian MacBrayne*. For several years she was employed mainly in a relief capacity. In 1986 she took over the Tobermory (Mull) - Kilchoan service from a passenger-only vessel; the conveyance of vehicles was not inaugurated until 1991. In 1996 she was transferred to the Oban - Lismore route. In 1998 she was sold to *Arranmore Island Ferry Services*.

RHUM Built by James Lamont & Co Ltd, Port Glasgow, UK for *Caledonian MacBrayne*. Until 1987, she was used primarily on the Claonaig - Lochranza (Arran) service. After that time she served on various routes. In 1994 she inaugurated a new service between Tarbert (Loch Fyne) and Portavadie. In 1997 she operated between Kyles Scalpay and Scalpay until the opening of the new bridge on 16th December 1997. In 1998 she was sold to *Arranmore Island Ferry Services*.

BERE ISLAND FERRIES

THE COMPANY *Bere Island Ferries Ltd* is an Irish Republic private sector company.

MANAGEMENT Operator Colum Harrington.

ADDRESS Ferry Lodge, West End, Bere Island, Beara, County Cork, Irish Republic.

TELEPHONE Administration + 353 (0)27 75009, Reservations Not applicable, Mobile + 353 (0)86 2423140.

FAX Administration + 353 (0)27 75000, Reservations Not applicable.

INTERNET Email biferry@eircom.net Website www.bereislandferries.com *(English)*

1F	KIRSTY M	109t	66	10.5k	23.7m	0P	-	1L	B	IR
2	OILEAN NA H-OIGE	69t	80	7.0k	18.6m	75P	4C	-	B	IR
3	SANCTA MARIA	67t	83	7.0k	18.6m	75P	4C	-	B	IR

KIRSTY M Landing craft (Klasse 521) built as the LCM 12 SPROTTE by Rheinwerft Walsum, Walsum, Germany for the German Navy. In 1993 withdrawn and sold to a German firm and converted to a civilian ferry. She was later sold to *Mainstream Salmon Farm (Aquascot Seafarms Ltd)*, Orkney, renamed the KIRSTY M and used as a work boat. In December 2009 sold to *Bere Island Ferries* and converted back to ferry operation. She is used in a freight-only mode and doesn't have a licence to carry passengers.

OILEAN NA H-OIGE Built as the EILEAN NA H-OIGE by Lewis Offshore Ltd, Stornoway, UK for *Western Isles Islands Council* (from 1st April 1996 the *Western Isles Council* and from 1st January 1998 *Comhairle Nan Eilean Siar*) for their Ludaig (South Uist) - Eriskay service. From 2000 operated from a temporary slipway at the Eriskay causeway. This route ceased in July 2001 following the full opening of the causeway and she was laid up. In 2002 she was moved to the Eriskay - Barra service. In 2003 replaced by the LOCH BHRUSDA of *Caledonian MacBrayne* and laid up. Later sold to *Bere Island Ferries* and renamed the OILEAN NA H-OIGE (same name - "The Island of Youth" - in Irish rather than Scots Gaelic).

SANCTA MARIA Built as the EILEAN BHEARNARAIGH by George Brown & Company, Greenock, UK for *Western Isles Islands Council* for their Otternish (North Uist) - Berneray service. From 1996 until 1999 she was operated by *Caledonian MacBrayne* in conjunction with the LOCH BHRUSDA on the service between Otternish and Berneray and during the winter she was laid up. Following the opening of a causeway between North Uist and Berneray in early 1999, the ferry service ceased and she became reserve vessel for the Eriskay route. This route ceased in July 2001 following the opening of a causeway and she was laid up. In 2002 operated between Eriskay and Barra as reserve vessel. In 2003 sold to *Transalpine Redemptorists Inc*, a community of monks who live on Papa Stronsay, Orkney. Used for conveying supplies to the island - not a public service. In 2008 sold to *Bere Island Ferries*. Entered service in May 2009.

BK MARINE

THE COMPANY *BK Marine* is a UK company.

MANAGEMENT **Managing Director** Gordon Williamson.

ADDRESS Herrislea House Hotel, Veensgarth, Tingwall, Shetland ZE2 9SB.

TELEPHONE **Administration & Reservations** +44 (0)1595 840208.

INTERNET **Website** www.bkmarine.co.uk *(English)*

ROUTE OPERATED *All year* Foula - Walls (Mainland) (2 hours; *NEW ADVANCE*; 2 per week (Winter), 3 per week (Summer)), *Summer only* Foula - Scalloway (3 hrs 30 mins; *NEW ADVANCE*; alternate Thursdays).

1	NEW ADVANCE	25t	96	8.7k	9.8m	12P	1C	0L	C	UK

NEW ADVANCE Built by Richardson's, Stromness, Orkney, UK for *Shetland Islands Council* for the Foula service. Although built at Penryn, Cornwall, she was completed at Stromness. She has a Cygnus Marine GM38 hull and is based on the island where she can be lifted out of the water. Vehicle capacity is to take residents' vehicles to the island - not for tourist vehicles. In 2004 it was announced that the vessel and service would be transferred to the *Foula Community*. However, it was then found that under EU rules the route needed to be offered for competitive tender. In July 2006 the contract was awarded to *Atlantic Ferries Ltd* who began operations in October 2006. In August 2011 replaced by *BK Marine*.

CLARE ISLAND FERRY COMPANY

THE COMPANY *Clare Island Ferry Company* is owned and operated by the O'Grady family, natives of Clare Island, Irish Republic, who have been operating the Clare Island Mail Boat Ferry service since 1880.

MANAGEMENT **Managing Director** Chris O'Grady.

ADDRESS Clare Island Ferry Co Ltd, Clare Island, Co Mayo, Republic Of Ireland.

TELEPHONE/FAX *May-September* +353 (0)98 23737 *Winter* +353 (0)98 25212, +353 (0)86 8515003.

INTERNET Email clareislandferry@anu.ie Website www.clareislandferry.com *(English)*

ROUTE OPERATED Roonagh (Co Mayo) - Clare Island (15 mins; *CLEW BAY QUEEN, PIRATE QUEEN*; *Winter* 1 to 2 trips per day, *Summer* up to 5 per day, Roonagh - Inishturk (50 mins; *CLEW BAY QUEEN, PIRATE QUEEN*; *Winter* 1 per day *Summer* up to 2 per day. Tourist vehicles are not normally carried.

| 1 | CLEW BAY QUEEN | 64t | 72 | 10.0k | 21.9m | 96P | 6C | - | B | IR | |
| 2p | PIRATE QUEEN | 73t | 96 | 10.5k | 19.8m | 96P | 0C | - | - | IR | |

CLEW BAY QUEEN Built as the KILBRANNAN by James Lamont & Co Ltd, Port Glasgow, UK for *Caledonian MacBrayne*. Used on a variety of routes until 1977, she was then transferred to the Scalpay (Harris) - Kyles Scalpay service. In 1990 she was replaced by the CANNA and, in turn, replaced the CANNA in her reserve/relief role. In 1992 sold to *Arranmore Island Ferry Services* and renamed the ÁRAINN MHÓR. She was subsequently sold to *Údarás na Gaeltachta* and leased back to *Arranmore Island Ferry Services*. In 2008 she was sold to *Clare Island Ferry Company* and renamed the CLEW BAY QUEEN. She operates a passenger and heavy freight service to both Clare Island and Inishturk all year round. In winter passenger capacity is reduced to 47 with 3 crew. Fitted with crane for loading and unloading cargo.

PIRATE QUEEN Built by Arklow Marine Services in 1996 for *Clare Island Ferry Company*. She operates a daily passenger and light cargo service to Clare Island and Inishturk all year round. In winter passenger capacity is reduced to 47 with 3 crew. Fitted with crane for loading and unloading cargo.

CROMARTY FERRY COMPANY

THE COMPANY The *Cromarty Ferry Company* operate under contract to *The Highland Council*.

MANAGEMENT Managing Director Tom Henderson.

ADDRESS Udale Farm, Poyntzfield By Dingwall, Ross-Shire IV7 8LY.

TELEPHONE +44 (0)1381 610269, Mobile +44 (0)7717 207875, Ferry Mobile:07879 401659 (working hours only).

FAX +44 (0)1381 610408.

INTERNET Email via website Website www.cromarty-ferry.co.uk *(English)*

ROUTE OPERATED *June-October* Cromarty - Nigg (Ross-shire) (10 mins; *CROMARTY QUEEN*; SERVICE CURRENTLY SUSPENDED)

| 1 | CROMARTY QUEEN | 68t | 10 | 9.0k | 17.3m | 50P | 4C | - | B | UK | |

CROMARTY QUEEN Built by Southampton Marine Services for *Cromarty Ferry Company*.

CROSS RIVER FERRIES

THE COMPANY *Cross River Ferries Ltd* is an Irish Republic company, part of the *Doyle Shipping Group*.

MANAGEMENT Operations Manager Eoin O'Sullivan.

ADDRESS Westlands House, Rushbrooke, Cobh, County Cork, Irish Republic.

TELEPHONE Administration +353 (0)21 42 02 900 Reservations Not applicable.

INTERNET Website www.scottcobh.ie/pages/ferry.html *(English)*

ROUTE OPERATED Carrigaloe (near Cobh, on Great Island) - Glenbrook (Co Cork) (4 mins; *CARRIGALOE, GLENBROOK*; frequent service 07.00 - 00.15 (one or two vessels used according to demand)).

| 1 | CARRIGALOE | 225t | 70 | 8.0k | 49.1m | 200P | 27C | - | BA | IR | 7028386 |

Corran (*Brian Maxted*)

Rhum (*Brian Maxted*)

2	GLENBROOK	225t	71	8.0k	49.1m	200P	27C	-	BA	IR	7101607

CARRIGALOE Built as the KYLEAKIN by Newport Shipbuilding and Engineering Company, Newport (Gwent), UK for the *Caledonian Steam Packet Company* (later *Caledonian MacBrayne*) for the Kyle of Lochalsh - Kyleakin service. In 1991 sold to *Marine Transport Services Ltd* and renamed the CARRIGALOE. She entered service in March 1993. In Summer 2002 chartered to the *Lough Foyle Ferry Company*, returning in Spring 2003.

GLENBROOK Built as the LOCHALSH by Newport Shipbuilding and Engineering Company, Newport (Gwent), UK for the *Caledonian Steam Packet Company* (later *Caledonian MacBrayne*) for the Kyle of Lochalsh - Kyleakin service. In 1991 sold to *Marine Transport Services Ltd* and renamed the GLENBROOK. She entered service in March 1993.

THE HIGHLAND COUNCIL

THE COMPANY *The Highland Council* (previously *Highland Regional Council*) is a Scottish Local Authority.

MANAGEMENT **Area Community Services Manager** Cameron Kemp, **Ferry Foremen** Allan McCowan and Donald Dixon.

ADDRESS *Area Office* Lochybridge Depot, Carr's Corner Industrial Estate, Fort William PH33 6TQ, *Ferry Office* Ferry Cottage, Ardgour, Fort William PH33 7AA.

TELEPHONE Administration *Area Office* +44 (0)1397 709000, *Corran* +44 (0)1855 841243, *Camusnagaul* – Now run by private operator *Highland Ferries* by vessel CAILIN AN AISEAG.

INTERNET   Email   communityservices@highland.gov.uk   Website www.highland.gov.uk/info/1526/public_and_community_transport/111/public_transport/3 (English)

ROUTES OPERATED **Vehicle Ferries** Corran - Ardgour (5 mins; *CORRAN, MAID OF GLENCOUL*; half-hourly), **Passenger-only Ferry** Fort William - Camusnagaul (10 mins; *CAILIN AN AISEAG*; frequent).

1p	CAILIN AN AISEAG	-	80	7.5k	9.8m	26P	0C	0L	-	UK	
2	CORRAN	351t	01	10.0k	42.0m	150P	30C	2L	BA	UK	9225990
3	MAID OF GLENCOUL	166t	75	8.0k	32.0m	116P	16C	1L	BA	UK	7521613

CAILIN AN AISEAG Built by Buckie Shipbuilders Ltd, Buckie, UK for *Highland Regional Council* and used on the Fort William - Camusnagaul passenger-only service. In 2006 the service transferred to *Geoff Ward* under contract with a different vessel. In 2013 resumed service under new operator *Highland Ferries*.

CORRAN Built by George Prior Engineering Ltd, Hull, UK for *The Highland Council* to replace the MAID OF GLENCOUL as main vessel.

MAID OF GLENCOUL Built by William McCrindle Ltd, Shipbuilders, Ardrossan, UK for *Highland Regional Council* for the service between Kylesku and Kylestrome. In 1984 the ferry service was replaced by a bridge and she was transferred to the Corran - Ardgour service. In April 1996, ownership transferred to *The Highland Council*. In 2001 she became the reserve vessel.

ISLES OF SCILLY STEAMSHIP COMPANY

THE COMPANY *Isles of Scilly Steamship Company* is a British private sector company.

MANAGEMENT **Chief Executive** Robert Goldsmith, **Marketing & Communications Manager** Sharon Sandercock.

ADDRESS *Scilly* PO Box 10, Hugh Town, St Mary's, Isles of Scilly TR21 0LJ, *Penzance* Steamship House, Quay Street, Penzance, Cornwall, TR18 4BZ.

TELEPHONE Administration & Reservations +44 (0) 1736 334220.

INTERNET Email sales@islesofscilly-travel.co.uk **Website** www.islesofscilly-travel.co.uk(*English)*

ROUTES OPERATED *Passenger services:* Penzance - St Mary's (Isles of Scilly) (2 hrs 40 mins; *SCILLONIAN III*; 1 per day), St Mary's - Tresco/St Martin's/St Agnes/Bryher; *LYONESSE LADY, SWIFT LADY (inter-island boats)*; irregular), *Freight service:* GRY MARITHA; Freight from Penzance Monday, Wednesday and Fridays (weather dependant, all year round).

1F	GRY MARITHA	590t	81	10.5k	40.3m	6P	5C	1L	C	UK	8008462
2	LYONESSE LADY	40t	91	9.0k	15.5m	4P	1C	0L	AC	UK	
3	SCILLONIAN III	1346t	77	15.5k	67.7m	485P	5C	-	C	UK	7527796
4F	SWIFT LADY	-	04	30.0k	8.4m	0P	0C	0L	-	UK	

GRY MARITHA Built by Moen Slip AS, Kolvereid, Norway for *Gjofor* of Norway. In design she is a coaster rather than a ferry. In 1990 she was sold to the *Isles of Scilly Steamship Company*. She operates a freight and passenger service all year (conveying most goods to and from the Islands). During the winter she provides the only sea service to the islands, the SCILLONIAN III being laid up.

LYONESSE LADY Built Lochaber Marine Ltd of Corpach, Fort William, Scotland, for inter-island ferry work.

SCILLONIAN III Built by Appledore Shipbuilders Ltd, Appledore, UK for the Penzance - St Mary's service. She operates from late March to November and is laid up in the winter. She is the last major conventional passenger/cargo ferry built for UK waters and probably Western Europe. Extensively refurbished during Winter 1998/99 and 2012/13. She can carry cars in her hold and on deck, as well as general cargo/perishables, boats, trailer tents and passenger luggage.

SWIFT LADY Stormforce 8.4 RIB (Rigid Inflatable Boat) built by Redbay Boats of Cushendall, Co Antrim, Northern Ireland for inter-island ferry work conveying mail and as back-up to the LYONESSE LADY.

KERRERA FERRY

THE COMPANY *Kerrera Ferry Ltd* is a UK company.

MANAGEMENT **Managing Director** Duncan MacEachen.

ADDRESS The Ferry, Isle of Kerrera, by Oban PA34 4SX.

TELEPHONE **Administration** +44 (0)1631 563665.

INTERNET Email kerreraferry@hotmail.com **Website** www.kerrera-ferry.co.uk *(English)*

ROUTE OPERATED Gallanach (Argyll) - Kerrera (5 mins; *GYLEN LADY*; on demand 10.30 - 12.30 and 14.00 - 18.00, Easter - October, other times by arrangement).

1	GYLEN LADY	9t	99	8.0k	10.0m	12P	1C	-	B	UK

GYLEN LADY Built by Corpach Boatyard, Corpach, UK to inaugurate a vehicle ferry service to the Isle of Kerrera, replacing an open passenger boat.

KNOYDART SEABRIDGE

THE COMPANY *Knoydart Seabridge* is a British company.

MANAGEMENT **Operator** Jon Sellars.

ADDRESS Knoydart Seabridge, Knoydart, Mallaig PH41 4PL.

TELEPHONE **Administration & Reservations** +44 (0)1687 462 916.

INTERNET Email jon@sandaig.com **Website** www.knoydartferry.com *(English)*

ROUTE OPERATED Mallaig - Inverie (Knoydart). The MERI 3 can take one car but only residents' vehicles are permitted.

1	MERI 3	11t	85	10.0k	12.0m	12P	1C	-	B	UK	
2p	THE ODYSSEY	6t	06	35.0k	10.5m	10P	-	-	-	UK	
3p	VANGUARD	12t	06	16.0k	13.0m	12P	-	-	-	UK	
4p	VENTURER	12t	06	16.0k	13.0m	12P	-	-	-	UK	

MERI 3 Built by Lohi Boats, Finland. She is a miniature beach landing draft.

THE ODYSSEY ProCharter 3 built by ProCharter, Wadebridge, Cornwall.

VANGUARD, VENTURER Interceptor 41 built by Safehaven Marine, Cobh, Republic of Ireland.

LOUGH FOYLE FERRY COMPANY

THE COMPANY *Lough Foyle Ferry Company Ltd* is an Irish Republic Company.

MANAGEMENT **Managing Director** Jim McClenaghan.

ADDRESS The Pier, Greencastle, Co Donegal, Irish Republic.

TELEPHONE **Administration** +353 (0)74 93 81901.

FAX **Administration** +353 (0)74 93 81903.

INTERNET **Email** info@loughfoyleferry.com **Website** www.loughfoyleferry.com *(English)*

ROUTES OPERATED *March-October* Greencastle (Inishowen, Co Donegal, Irish Republic) - Magilligan (Co Londonderry, Northern Ireland) (10 mins; *FOYLE VENTURE*; hourly).

1	FOYLE VENTURE	324t	78	10.0k	47.9m	300P	44C	-	BA	IR	7800033

FOYLE VENTURE Built as the SHANNON WILLOW by Scott & Sons (Bowling) Ltd, Bowling, Glasgow, UK for *Shannon Ferry Ltd*. In 2000 replaced by the SHANNON BREEZE and laid up for sale. In 2003 sold to the *Lough Foyle Ferry Company Ltd* and renamed the FOYLE VENTURE.

MURPHY'S FERRY SERVICE

THE COMPANY *Murphy's Ferry Service* is privately operated.

MANAGEMENT **Operator** Brendan Murphy.

ADDRESS Lawrence Cove, Bere Island, Co Cork, Irish Republic.

TELEPHONE **Administration** +353 (0)87 2386095.

FAX **Administration** +353 (0)27 75014.

INTERNET **Email** info@murphysferry.com **Website** www.murphysferry.com *(English)*

ROUTE OPERATED Castletownbere (Pontoon - 3 miles to east of town centre) - Bere Island (Lawrence Cove, near Rerrin) (20 mins; *IKOM K*; up to 8 per day).

1	IKOM K	55t	99	10.0k	16.0m	60P	4C	1L	B	IR	

IKOM K Built by Arklow Marine Services, Arklow, Irish Republic for *Murphy's Ferry Service*.

PASSAGE EAST FERRY

THE COMPANY *Passage East Ferry Company Ltd* is an Irish Republic private sector company.

MANAGEMENT **Manager** Gary O Hanlon, **Company Secretary** Derek Donnelly.

ADDRESS Barrack Street, Passage East, Co Waterford, Irish Republic.

TELEPHONE **Administration** +353 (0)51 382480, **Reservations** Not applicable.

FAX **Administration** +353 (0)51 382598, **Reservations** Not applicable.

INTERNET **Email** passageferry@yahoo.ie **Website** www.passageferry.ie *(English)*

SECTION 2 – Minor Ferry Operators

ROUTE OPERATED Passage East (County Waterford) - Ballyhack (County Wexford) (7 mins; *FBD TINTERN*; frequent service).

1	FBD TINTERN	236t	71	9.0k	54.8m	130P	30C	-	BA	IR

FBD TINTERN Built as the STADT LINZ by Schiffswerft Oberwinter, Oberwinter/Rhein, Germany for *Rheinfähre Linz - Remagen GmbH* of Germany and operated on the Rhine between Linz and Remagen. In 1990 renamed the ST JOHANNES. In 1997 sold to *Fähren Bremen-Stedingen GmbH*, renamed the VEGESACK and operated across the Weser between Lemwerder and Vegesack. In 2003 she became a reserve vessel and in 2004 was renamed the STEDINGEN (the name previously carried by the ferry sold to *Lough Foyle Ferry Company*). Later sold to *Schraven BV* of The Netherlands and refurbished. In Autumn 2005 sold to *Passage East Ferry* and renamed the FBD TINTERN.

RATHLIN ISLAND FERRY

THE COMPANY *Rathlin Island Ferry Ltd* is a UK private sector company owned by Ciarán and Mary O'Driscoll of County Cork, Irish Republic.

MANAGEMENT Managing Director Ciarán O'Driscoll.

ADDRESS Ballycastle Ferry Terminal, 18 Bayview Road, Ballycastle, County Antrim BT54 6BT.

TELEPHONE Administration & Reservations +44 (0)28 2076 9299.

INTERNET Email info@rathlinballycastleferry.com Website www.rathlinballycastleferry.com *(English)*

ROUTE OPERATED Vehicle Ferry Ballycastle - Rathlin Island (45 min; *CANNA*; up to 4 per day). Passenger-only Fast Ferry (20 min; *RATHLIN EXPRESS*; up to 5 per day). The service is operated on behalf of the *Northern Ireland Department of Regional Development*.

1	CANNA	69t	76	8.0k	24.3m	140P	6C	1L	B	UK
2»p	RATHLIN EXPRESS	31t	09	18.0k	17.7m	98P	0C	0L	-	UK
3»p	ST SORNEY	12t	99	17.0k	12.2m	38P	0C	0L	-	IR

CANNA Built by James Lamont & Co Ltd, Port Glasgow, UK for *Caledonian MacBrayne*. She was the regular vessel on the Lochaline - Fishnish (Mull) service. In 1986 she was replaced by the ISLE OF CUMBRAE and until 1990 she served in a relief capacity in the north, often assisting on the Iona service. In 1990 she was placed on the Kyles Scalpay (Harris) - Scalpay service (replaced by a bridge in Autumn 1997). In Spring 1997 *Caledonian MacBrayne* was contracted to operate the Ballycastle - Rathlin Island route and she was transferred to this service. In June 2008 she was chartered by *Caledonian Maritime Assets Limited* to *Rathlin Island Ferry Ltd* who took over the operation of the service.

RATHLIN EXPRESS Built by Arklow Marine Services, Arklow, Irish Republic for *Rathlin Island Ferry Ltd*.

ST SORNEY A Lochin 40 cruiser built by Ryan & Roberts, Limerick, Ireland. In 2008 placed on the Ballycastle - Rathlin Island service. Now reserve vessel.

SHANNON FERRY

THE COMPANY *Shannon Ferry Group Ltd* is an Irish Republic private company owned by eighteen shareholders on both sides of the Shannon Estuary.

MANAGEMENT Managing Director Eugene Maher.

ADDRESS Ferry Terminal, Killimer, County Clare, Irish Republic.

TELEPHONE Administration +353 (0)65 9053124, Reservations Phone bookings not available; Online booking available at www.shannonferries.com

FAX Administration +353 (0)65 9053125, Reservations Fax bookings not available; Online booking available at www.shannonferries.com

INTERNET Email enquiries@shannonferries.com Website www.shannonferries.com *(English)*

ROUTE OPERATED Killimer (County Clare) - Tarbert (County Kerry) (20 mins; *SHANNON BREEZE*, *SHANNON DOLPHIN*; hourly (half-hourly during May, June, July, August and September)).

| 1 | SHANNON BREEZE | 611t | 00 | 10.0k | 80.8m | 350P | 60C | - | BA | IR | 9224910 |
| 2 | SHANNON DOLPHIN | 501t | 95 | 10.0k | 71.9m | 350P | 52C | - | BA | IR | 9114933 |

SHANNON BREEZE, SHANNON DOLPHIN Built by Appledore Shipbuilders, Appledore, UK for *Shannon Ferry Group Ltd.*

SKYE FERRY

THE COMPANY The *Skye Ferry* is owned by the *Isle of Skye Ferry Community Interest Company*, a company limited by guarantee.

MANAGEMENT Ferry Development Officer Jo Crawford.

ADDRESS 6 Coulindune, Glenelg, Kyle, Ross-shire, IV40 8JU.

TELEPHONE Administration +44 (0)7881 634726.

INTERNET Email info@skyeferry.co.uk Website www.skyeferry.com *(English)*

ROUTE OPERATED *Easter - October only* Glenelg - Kylerhea (Skye) (10 mins; *GLENACHULISH*; frequent service).

| 1 | GLENACHULISH | 44t | 69 | 9.0k | 20.0m | 12P | 6C | - | BSt | UK | |

GLENACHULISH Built by Ailsa Shipbuilding Company, Troon, UK for the *Ballachulish Ferry Company* for the service between North Ballachulish and South Ballachulish, across the mouth of Loch Leven. In 1975 the ferry was replaced by a bridge and she was sold to *Highland Regional Council* and used on a relief basis on the North Kessock - South Kessock and Kylesku - Kylestrome routes. In 1983 she was sold to *Murdo MacKenzie*, who had operated the Glenelg – Skye route as ferryman since 1959. The vessel was eventually bought by *Roddy MacLeod* and the service resumed in September 1990. The *Isle of Skye Ferry Community Interest Company* reached agreement with *Mr MacLeod* that he would operate the ferry in 2006. In 2007 she was sold to the Company. During winter 2012 she was chartered to *The Highland Council* to operate between North and South Strome following a road closure due to a rock fall. She is the last turntable ferry in operation.

STRANGFORD LOUGH FERRY SERVICE

THE COMPANY The *Strangford Lough Ferry Service* is operated by the *DRD TransportNI*, a Northern Ireland Government Department (formerly operated by *Department of the Environment (Northern Ireland)*).

MANAGEMENT Ferry Manager Michael Murray.

ADDRESS Strangford Lough Ferry Service, The Slip, Strangford, Co Down BT30 7NE.

TELEPHONE Administration +44 0300 200 7898, Reservations Not applicable.

INTERNET Website www.nidirect.gov.uk/strangford-ferry-timetable *(English)*

ROUTE OPERATED Strangford - Portaferry (County Down) (10 mins; *PORTAFERRY II*, *STRANGFORD FERRY*; half-hourly).

| 1 | PORTAFERRY II | 312t | 01 | 12.0k | 38.2m | 260P | 28C | - | BA | UK | 9237436 |
| 2 | STRANGFORD FERRY | 186t | 69 | 10.0k | 32.9m | 263P | 20C | - | BA | UK | 6926311 |

PORTAFERRY II Built by McTay Marine, Bromborough, Wirral, UK for *DRD (Northern Ireland)*.

STRANGFORD FERRY Built by Verolme Dockyard Ltd, Cork, Irish Republic for *Down County Council*. Subsequently transferred to the *DOE (Northern Ireland)* and then the *DRD (Northern Ireland)*. Following delivery of the PORTAFERRY II, she became reserve ferry.

Under Construction

SECTION 2 – Minor Ferry Operators

| 3 | NEWBUILDING | 312t | 16 | 12.0k | 38.2m | 260P | 28C | - | BA | UK |

NEWBUILDING Under construction by Cammell Laird, Birkenhead for DRD *(Northern Ireland)*, UK to replace the STRANGFORD FERRY.

C TOMS & SON LTD

THE COMPANY *C Toms & Son Ltd* is a British private sector company.

MANAGEMENT **Managing Director** Allen Toms.

ADDRESS East Street, Polruan, Fowey, Cornwall PL23 1PB.

TELEPHONE **Administration** +44 (0)1726 870232.

INTERNET **Email** enquiries@ctomsandson.co.uk **Website** www.ctomsandson.co.uk *(English)*

ROUTE OPERATED *Car Ferry* Fowey - Bodinnick (Cornwall) (5 mins; *GELLAN, JENACK*; frequent), *Passenger Ferry* Fowey - Polruan (Cornwall) (5 mins; *KALEY, LADY DIANA, LADY JEAN, TAMSIN, THREE COUSINS*; frequent).

1	GELLAN	50t	03	4.5k	36.0m	50P	10C	-	BA	UK
2	JENACK	60t	00	4.5k	36.0m	50P	15C	-	BA	UK
3P	KALEY	7.6t	03	-	9.5m	48P	0C	-	-	UK
4P	LADY DI	-	81	-	8.2m	36P	0C	-	-	UK
5P	LADY JEAN	-	-	-	-	12P	0C	-	-	UK
6P	THREE COUSINS	-	14	-	-	12P	0C	-	-	UK

GELLAN, JENACK Built by C Toms & Sons Ltd, Fowey, UK.

KALEY, LADY DIANA, LADY JEAN, THREE COUSINS Built by C Toms & Sons Ltd, Fowey, UK.

VALENTIA ISLAND CAR FERRY

THE COMPANY *Valentia Island Car Ferry* is the trading name of *Valentia Island Ferries Ltd*, an Irish Republic private sector company.

MANAGEMENT **Manager** Richard Foran.

ADDRESS Valentia Island, County Kerry, Irish Republic.

TELEPHONE **Administration** +353 (0)66 76141, **Reservations** Not applicable.

FAX **Administration** +353 (0)66 76377, **Reservations** Not applicable.

INTERNET **Email** reforan@indigo.ie **Website** www.facebook.com (search for Valentia Island Car Ferry *(English)*

ROUTE OPERATED Reenard (Co Kerry) - Knightstown (Valentia Island) (5 minutes; *GOD MET ONS III*; frequent service, 1st April - 30th September).

| 1 | GOD MET ONS III | 95t | 63 | - | 43.0m | 95P | 18C | - | BA | IR |

GOD MET ONS III Built by BV Scheepswerven Vh HH Bodewes, Millingen, The Netherlands for *FMHE Res* of The Netherlands for a service across the River Maas between Cuijk and Middelaar. In 1987 a new bridge was opened and the service ceased. She was latterly used on contract work in the Elbe and then laid up. In 1996 acquired by *Valentia Island Ferries* and inaugurated a car ferry service to the island. **Note** This island never had a car ferry service before. A bridge was opened at the south end of the island in 1970; before that a passenger/cargo service operated between Reenard Point and Knightstown.

WOOLWICH FREE FERRY

THE COMPANY The *Woolwich Free Ferry* is operated by *Briggs Marine*, a British private sector company on behalf of *Transport for London*.

MANAGEMENT Ferry Manager Jeremy Mccarthy.

ADDRESS New Ferry Approach, Woolwich, London SE18 6DX.

TELEPHONE Administration +44 (0)20 8853 9400, Reservations Not applicable.

FAX Administration +44 (0)20 8316 6096, Reservations Not applicable.

INTERNET Website www.tfl.gov.uk/modes/river/woolwich-ferry *(English)*

ROUTE OPERATED Woolwich - North Woolwich (free ferry) (5 mins; *ERNEST BEVIN, JAMES NEWMAN, JOHN BURNS*; every 10 mins (weekdays - two ferries in operation), every 15 mins (weekends - one ferry in operation)). Note One ferry is always in reserve/under maintenance.

1	ERNEST BEVIN	1194t	63	8.0k	56.7m	310P	32C	6L	BA	UK	5426998
2	JAMES NEWMAN	1194t	63	8.0k	56.7m	310P	32C	6L	BA	UK	5411905
3	JOHN BURNS	1194t	63	8.0k	56.7m	310P	32C	6L	BA	UK	5416010

ERNEST BEVIN, JAMES NEWMAN, JOHN BURNS Built by Robb Caledon Shipbuilders Ltd, Dundee, UK for the *London County Council* who operated the service when the vessels were new. In 1965 ownership was transferred to the *Greater London Council*. Following the abolition of the *GLC* in April 1986, ownership was transferred to the *Department of Transport* and in 2001 to *Transport for London*. The *London Borough of Greenwich* operated the service on their behalf. In 2008 the operation of the service was transferred to Serco. An alternative loading is 6 x 18m articulated lorries and 14 cars; lorries of this length are too high for the nearby northbound Blackwall Tunnel.

Clew Bay Queen *(Brian Maxted)*

SECTION 2 – Minor Ferry Operators

Pauline Russ *(J.J. Jager)*

SECTION 3 - GB & IRELAND - FREIGHT ONLY FERRIES

CLDN/COBELFRET FERRIES

THE COMPANIES *Compagnie Luxembourgouise de Navigation SA (CLdN)* is a Luxemburg company. *Cobelfret Ferries NV* is a Belgian private sector company, a subsidiary of *Cobelfret NV* of Antwerp. The two companies operate as a single network with a single fleet.

MANAGEMENT **C.RO Agencies NV (Zeebrugge)** Tom De Wannemacker, **CLdN Ro-Ro SA (Luxembourg)** Caroline Dubois, **Cobelfret Waterways SA (Vlissingen)** Geert Bogaerts, **CLdN ro-ro Agencies Ltd (UK)** Martin Thompson.

ADDRESSES *Belgium* Sneeuwbeslaan 14, 2610 Antwerp, Belgium, *Luxembourg* CLdN ro-ro SA, 3-7 rue Schiller, 2519 Luxembourg, Luxembourg, *UK - Purfleet* CCLdN ro-ro Agencies Ltd, Long Reach House, London Road, Purfleet, Essex RM19 1RP UK, *UK - Killingholme* C.RO Ports Killingholme Ltd, Clough Lane, North Killingholme, Immingham DN40 3JS, UK, *Irish Republic* CLdN ro-ro Agencies AB, Port Centre, 2nd Floor, Alexandra Road, Dublin Port, Dublin 1 Republic of Ireland.

TELEPHONE Administration & Reservations *Belgium* + 32 (0)3 829 9100, *Luxembourg* + 352 (0)26 44 66 1, *UK (Purfleet, Ipswich & Killingholme)* + 44 (0)1708 865522, *Irish Republic* + 353 (0)1 856 1608.

FAX Administration & Reservations *Belgium* + 32 (0)3 829 45 07, *UK (Purfleet & Killingholme)* + 44 (0)1708 866418, *Luxembourg* + 352(0)26 44 66 299, *Irish Republic* + 353 (0)1 704 0164.

INTERNET Email postbox@cldn.com dir.antwerp@cobelfret.com Websites www.cldn.com www.cobelfret.com *(English)*

ROUTES OPERATED *Cobelfret Ferries* Services Zeebrugge - Purfleet (9 hrs; *ADELINE, CELANDINE, MAZARINE CLASS, VALENTINE, VICTORINE*; 2/3 per day), Zeebrugge - Killingholme (13 hrs; *PAULINE, YASMINE*; 6 per week), *CLdN* Rotterdam - Purfleet (14 hrs 30 mins; *MAZARINE CLASS*); 6 per week), Rotterdam - Killingholme (14 hrs; *OPALINE CLASS* and *MAZARINE CLASS*; 6 per week), Zeebrugge - Esbjerg (24hrs; *WILHELMINE, CLEMENTINE, VALENTINE, VICTORINE*; 1 per week), Zeebrugge - Dublin (36 hrs; *MAZARINE CLASS* and *OPALINE CLASS*; 2 per week), Rotterdam - Dublin (38 hrs;), *MAZARINE CLASS* and *OPALINE CLASS*; 2 per week), Rotterdam - Leixoes (Portugal) (69-79 hrs; *CATHERINE*; 1 per week), Zeebrugge - Gothenburg (32-33 hrs; *CELANDINE, CELESTINE, SOMERSET*; 6 per week). MAZARINE CLASS = MAZARINE, PALATINE, PEREGRINE and VESPERTINE; OPALINE CLASS = AMANDINE and OPALINE. *CLdN Container service* Rotterdam - Dublin (43/47 hrs;); *ARX* ; 1 per week).

Contract Services for Ford Motor Company Vlissingen - Dagenham (11 hrs; *CYMBELINE, MELUSINE, UNDINE*; 2 per day).

1	ADELINE	21020t	12	15.8k	150.0m	12P	-	170T	A	MT	9539092
2	AMANDINE	33960t	11	18.5k	195.4m	12P	-	270T	A	LU	9424869
3	CATHERINE	21287t	02	18.0k	182.2m	12P	-	200T	A2	BE	9209453
4	CELANDINE	23987t	00	17.9k	162.5m	12P	630C	157T	A	BE	9183984
5	CELESTINE	23986t	96	17.8k	162.5m	24P	630C	157T	A	BE	9125372
6	CLEMENTINE	23986t	97	17.8k	162.5m	24P	630C	157T	A	BE	9125384
7	CYMBELINE	11866t	92	17.0k	147.4m	8P	350C	100T	A2	LU	9007764
8	MAZARINE	25593t	09	18.5k	195.4m	12P	-	180T	A	LU	9376696
9	MELUSINE	23987t	99	17.8k	162.5m	12P	630C	157T	A	BE	9166637
10	OPALINE	33960t	10	18.5k	195.4m	12P	-	270T	A	MT	9424869
11	PALATINE	25593t	09	18.5k	195.4m	12P	-	180T	A	LU	9376701
12	PAULINE	49166t	06	21.7k	200.0m	12P	656C	258T	A	LU	9324473
13	PEREGRINE	25235t	10	18.5k	195.4m	12P	-	180T	A	MT	9376725
14	SOMERSET	21005t	00	18.0k	183.4m	12P	-	180T	A	BE	9188221
15	UNDINE	11854t	91	15.0k	147.4m	8P	350C	100T	A2	LU	9006112

16	VALENTINE	23987t	99	18.0k	162.5m	12P	630C	157T	A	BE	9166625
17	VESPERTINE	25235t	10	18.5k	195.4m	12P	-	180T	A	LU	9376713
18	VICTORINE	23987t	00	17.8k	162.5m	12P	630C	157T	A	BE	9184029
19	WILHELMINE	21020t	12	15.8k	150.0m	12P	-	170T	A	LU	9539080
20	WILLIAMSBORG	23235t	03	17.1k	193.0m	12P	-	180T	A	MT	9234094
21	YASMINE	49166t	07	21.7k	200.0m	12P	656C	258T	A	LU	9337353

ADELINE Built by the Kyokuyo Shipyard, Shimonoseki, Japan. After competition, a additional deck and sponsons were retro-fitted at the Chengxi Shipyard, Jiangyin, China. In November 2012 chartered to *RMR Shipping* to operate between Western Europe and West Africa. In January 2013 sub-chartered to *Castor Shipping* of Bulgaria. In March undertook another trip to West Africa and then returned to the Zeebrugge - Purfleet route in April. In November inaugurated a new ro-ro service from Rotterdam to Leixoes (Portugal). In March 2014 returned to the Zeebrugge -Purfleet route.

AMANDINE Built by Flensburger Schiffbau-Gesellschaft, Flensburg, Germany. Operates mainly between Rotterdam and Killingholme   and Rotterdam/Zeebrugge and Dublin.

CATHERINE Built as the ROMIRA by Zhonghua Shipyard, Zhonghua, China for *Dag Engström Rederi* of Sweden. For six months engaged on a number of short-term charters, including *Cobelfret Ferries* who used her on both the Rotterdam - Immingham and Zeebrugge - Purfleet routes. In September 2002 purchased by *Cobelfret Ferries* and, in November 2002, renamed the CATHERINE and placed on the Rotterdam - Immingham service. In Spring 2003 chartered to the *US Defense Department* to convey materials to the Persian Gulf. Returned in late summer and operated thereafter on the Rotterdam - Immingham service. In January 2009 chartered to *CoTuNav* of Tunisia. In February 2010 returned to *Cobelfret* service and operated on the Rotterdam - Purfleet service. In March 2010 again chartered to *CoTuNav*. In March 2011 chartered to *RMR Shipping* to operate between Western Europe and Antwerp, Eemshaven, Harwich and Dublin to Lagos (Nigeria). In May 2011 returned to *Cobelfret Ferries* and used on the Zeebrugge - Gothenburg service until January 2013 when she began operating on the Purfleet route during the week and the Gothenburg route at weekend (one round trip). From April 2013 operated full-time on the Purfleet service. In March 2014 transferred to the Rotterdam - Leixoes route.

CELANDINE, VALENTINE, VICTORINE Built by Kawasaki Heavy Industries, Sakaide, Japan for *Cobelfret*. The CELANDINE was originally to be called the CATHERINE and the VICTORINE the CELANDINE. The names were changed before delivery. Generally used on the Zeebrugge - Purfleet route. In May 2011 the CELANDINE was chartered to *RMR Shipping*.

CELESTINE Built by Kawasaki Heavy Industries, Sakaide, Japan as the CELESTINE. In 1996 chartered to the *British MoD* and renamed the SEA CRUSADER. She was originally expected to return to *Cobelfret Ferries* in early 2003 and resume the name CELESTINE; however, the charter was extended because of the Iraq war. Returned in September 2003 and placed on the Zeebrugge - Immingham service. In November 2006 moved to the Zeebrugge - Purfleet route. In November 2008 moved to the Ostend - Dartford service. In April 2009 the route became Ostend - Purfleet. In April 2010 chartered to *RMR Shipping*.

CLEMENTINE Built by Kawasaki Heavy Industries, Sakaide, Japan for *Cobelfret Ferries*. Mainly used on the Zeebrugge - Immingham service. In 2007 moved to the Zeebrugge - Purfleet route. In March 2013 chartered to *RMR Shipping*. In July 2013 chartered to *DFDS Seaways* and placed on the Immingham - Cuxhaven service. In November 2014 returned to *Cobelfret Ferries*. In January 2015 she retuned to charter with *DFDS Seaways* for four weeks.

CLIPPER POINT Built by Astilleros de Huelva SA, Huelva, Spain for *Seatruck Ferries*. In May 2012 chartered to *DFDS Seaways* and placed on the Immingham-Cuxhaven route. In April 2013 chartered to the organisers of the 'SATA Rally Azores 2013' car rally to take cars from Portugal to the Azores. In May began operating for *DFDS Seaways* in the Baltic. In October transferred to the Immingham - Cuxhaven route. In November 2014 the charter ended and she was placed on the Zeebrugge - Purfleet service.

CYMBELINE, UNDINE Built by Dalian Shipyard, Dalian, China for *Cobelfret Ferries*. Currently mainly used on the Dagenham - Vlissingen route. They were occasionally used on a weekend Southampton

- Vlissingen service but this ceased in 2012 following the closure of the Southampton Ford Transit factory. Occasional weekend trips are made to Middlesbrough (Teesport).

MAZARINE, PALATINE, PEREGRINE, VESPERTINE Built by Flensburger Schiffbau-Gesellschaft, Flensburg, Germany.

MELUSINE Built by Kawasaki Heavy Industries, Sakaide, Japan for *Cobelfret*. Similar to the CLEMENTINE. Currently used on Zeebrugge - Purfleet or Rotterdam - Purfleet.

OPALINE Built by Flensburger Schiffbau-Gesellschaft, Flensburg, Germany. Operates mainly between Rotterdam and Killingholme and Rotterdam and Dublin.

PAULINE, YASMINE Built by Flensburger Schiffbau-Gesellschaft, Flensburg, Germany to operate on the Zeebrugge - Killingholme route.

SOMERSET Built as the SPAARNEBORG by Flender Werft AG, Lübeck, Germany for *Wagenborg* of The Netherlands and time-chartered to *Stora-Enso* to operate between Zeebrugge and Gothenburg in conjunction with *Cobelfret Ferries*. She also operated between Tilbury and Gothenburg during 2010. In August 2011 chartered to the *Canadian MoD* to operate between Montreal and Cyprus in connection with the Libyan 'no fly zone'. On return in November she was laid up in Zeebrugge and in January 2012 moved to Gothenburg. In August 2012 chartered to *LD Lines* to operate between Marseilles and Tunis. In March 2013 returned to the *Stora Enso/ Cobelfret Ferries* Zeebrugge - Gothenburg service. In November 2014 the arrangement between *Stora Enso* and *Cobelfret Ferries* ended and she was chartered to *SOL Continent Line* who took over the operation of the service, operating between Finland, Germany, Belgium and the UK. In January 2015 sold to *CLdN* and renamed the SOMERSET. Generally operates between Zeebrugge and Gothenburg.

WILHELMINE Built by the Kyokuyo Shipyard, Shimonoseki, Japan for *CLdN*. After completion, a additional deck and sponsons were retro-fitted at the Chengxi Shipyard, Jiangyin, China. Initially used on the Zeebrugge - Purfleet service. In January 2013 chartered to *P&O Ferries* to operate between Tilbury and Zeebrugge. After three weeks moved to the Middlesbrough - Rotterdam service. In November 2014 the charter ended and she was placed on the Zeebrugge - Purfleet service. She returned to *P&O Ferries* for five weeks during the refit period in January and February 2015 and again operated Middlesbrough - Rotterdam.

WILLIAMSBORG Built as the BEACHY HEAD by Flensburger Schiffbau-Gesellschaft, Flensburg, Germany for *AWSR Shipping*. On delivery, chartered to *Transfennica* and operated between Hanko (Finland) and Lübeck (Germany). In July 2006 chartered to *Stora Enso* and placed on the Kotka - Gothenburg route. In late August transferred to the Antwerp - Gothenburg service. In 2007 chartered to *Transfennica*. In January 2009 chartered to *Finnlines* and normally used on the Helsinki - Aarhus route. In January 2012 chartered to *North Sea RoRo*. In March 2013 the service ceased and she was chartered to *DFDS Seaways*. In April 2014 sold to *C Bulk NV* of Belgium, an associated company of *CLdN/Cobelfret Ferries* and renamed the WILLIAMSBORG. In July she was chartered to *Nordana Line A/S* of Denmark operating from Mediterranean ports to the USA and Latin America.

CLdN also operates the container ship ARX (6901t, 2005, 707 TEU, IMO 9328625, Maltese flag (ex LUPUS 1 2005, ex C2C LUPUS 2007, ex C2C ASTRALIS 2010).

CLdN also own the CAPUCINE and SEVERINE, on charter to *Stena Line*.

FINNLINES

THE COMPANY *Finnlines PLC* is a Finnish private sector company. Services to the UK are marketed by *Finnlines UK Ltd*, a British private sector company. From 1st January 2001, *Finncarriers* was merged into the parent company, trading as *Finnlines Cargo Service*.

MANAGEMENT President & CEO Emanuele Grimaldi, **Head of Group Marketing North Sea ro-ro** Staffan Herlin.

ADDRESS *Finland* PO Box 197, 00181 Helsinki, Finland, **UK** Finnlines UK Ltd, Finhumber House, Queen Elizabeth Dock, Hedon Road, HULL HU9 5PB.

TELEPHONE Administration & Reservations *Finland* + 358 (0)10 343 50, **UK** + 44 (0)1482 377 655.

Wilhelmine (*Cees de Bijl*)

Opaline (*Matt Davies*)

Severine and Wilhelmine (*Rob de Visser*)

Finnsun (*J.J. Jager*)

FAX *Administration Finland* +358 (0)10 343 5200, *UK* +44 (0)1482 787 229.

INTERNET *Email Finland* info.fi@finnlines.com *UK* info.uk@finnlines.com *Website* www.finnlines.com (English, Finnish, German, Polish, Swedish)

ROUTES OPERATED Irregular service from St Petersburg, Helsinki, Rauma and Kotka to Hull, Immingham, Amsterdam, Antwerp and Bilbao. For details see website. In view of the fact that ships are liable to be transferred between routes, the following is a list of all Finnlines Cargo Service ro-ro vessels, including those which currently do not serve the UK. Ro-pax vessels on Baltic services are listed in Section 6.

1	BALTICA	21224t	90	19.0k	157.7m	0P	-	163T	A	MT	8813154
2	FINNBREEZE	28002t	11	20.0k	184.8m	12P	600C	200T	A	FI	9468889
3	FINNHAWK	11530t	01	20.0k	162.2m	12P	-	140T	A	FI	9207895
4	FINNKRAFT	11530t	00	20.0k	162.2m	12P	-	140T	A	FI	9207883
5	FINNMERCHANT	23235t	03	21.0k	193.0m	12P	-	180T	A	FI	9234082
6	FINNMILL	25732t	02	20.0k	184.8m	12P	-	190T	A	FI	9212656
7	FINNPULP	25732t	02	20.0k	184.8m	12P	-	190T	A	FI	9212644
8	FINNSEA	28002t	11	21.0k	184.8m	12P	600C	200T	A	FI	9468891
9	FINNSKY	28002t	12	21.0k	184.8m	12P	600C	200T	A	FI	9468906
10	FINNSUN	28002t	12	21.0k	184.8m	12P	600C	200T	A	FI	9468918
11	FINNTIDE	28002t	12	21.0k	184.8m	12P	600C	200T	A	FI	9468920
12	FINNWAVE	28002t	12	21.0k	184.8m	12P	600C	200T	A	FI	9468932
13	MISANA	14100t	07	20.0k	163.9m	12P	-	150T	A	FI	9348936
14	MISIDA	14100t	07	20.0k	163.9m	12P	-	150T	A	FI	9348948

BALTICA Built by Hyundai Heavy Industries, Ulsan, South Korea as the AHLERS BALTIC for *Ahlers Line* and chartered to *Finncarriers*. In 1995 acquired by *Poseidon Schiffahrt AG* of Germany and renamed the TRANSBALTICA. She continued to be chartered to *Finncarriers* and was acquired by them when they purchased *Poseidon Schiffahrt AG* (now *Finnlines Deutschland AG*) in 1997. In 2003 sold to Norwegian interests and chartered back; She was renamed the BALTICA. In recent years she operated on the Helsinki - St Petersburg - Hamina - Helsinki - Zeebrugge - Tilbury – Amsterdam – Antwerp - service with the MERCHANT. During 2007 she operated Helsinki - Turku – Antwerp on a one-week cycle. In January 2008 moved to Baltic services. In April 2011 chartered to *Power Line* to operate between Helsinki and Travemünde. In January 2013 returned to *Finnlines*.

FINNBREEZE, FINNSEA, FINNSKY, FINNSUN, FINNTIDE, FINNWAVE Built by Jinling Shipyard, Nanjing, China for *Finnlines*.

FINNHAWK Built by Jinling Shipyard, Nanjing, China for the *Macoma Shipping Group* and chartered to *Finnlines*. In April 2008 purchased by *Finnlines*. Currently operates used on service between Finland and The Netherlands, Belgium, the UK and Spain.

FINNKRAFT Built by Jinling Shipyard, Nanjing, China for the *Macoma Shipping Group* and chartered to *Finncarriers*. In April 2008 purchased by *Finnlines*. Currently operates on services between Finland and Germany.

FINNMERCHANT Built as the LONGSTONE by Flensburger Schiffbau-Gesellschaft, Flensburg, Germany for *AWSR Shipping* (later Foreland Shipping). Chartered to *Transfennica* and operated between Hanko (Finland) and Lübeck (Germany). In January 2009 chartered to *Finnlines* and placed on the Helsinki - Aarhus route. In January 2012 chartered to *North Sea RoRo*. In March 2013 the operation ceased and the charter was taken over by *DFDS Seaways* and she was placed on the Immingham - Cuxhaven route. In May took over the Zeebrugge - Rosyth route. In October 2013 sold to *C Bulk NV* of Belgium, an associated company of *CLdN/Cobelfret Ferries*. In April 2014 charter to *DFDS* ended and she was chartered to an Australian operator. In November 2014 renamed the DORSET. In December 2014 the charter ended and she returned to *CLdN*. In early January 2015 placed on the Zeebrugge - Purfleet service. Later in the month sold to *Finnlines* and renamed the FINNMERCHANT.

FINNMILL, FINNPULP Built by Jinling Shipyard, Nanjing, China for the *Macoma Shipping Group* and chartered to *Finnlines*. In 2008 purchased by *Finnlines*. During Winter 2008/09 extra ramps were added at STX Europe Helsinki shipyard to enable ro-ro traffic to be conveyed on the weather deck.

MISANA, MISIDA Built by J J Sietas, Hamburg, Germany for *Godby Shipping AB* of Finland and time-chartered to *UPM-Kymmene* of Finland to operate between Finland, Spain and Portugal. In July 2013 charter taken over by *Finnlines*.

Finnlines are expected to take delivery of the CARRIER and TRADER in January 2016. They are currently on charter to *Transfennica*.

FORELAND SHIPPING

THE COMPANY *Foreland Shipping Limited* (formerly *AWSR Shipping Limited*) is a UK private sector company. The principal shareholder in *Foreland Shipping* is now *Hadley Shipping Group*; *Bibby Group* and *James Fisher plc* having sold their shares to *Hadley Shipping*.

MANAGEMENT **Chairman** Peter Morton, **Managing Director** Paul Trudgeon.

ADDRESS 117-119 Houndsditch, London EC3A 7BT.

TELEPHONE + 44 (0)20 7480 4140.

FAX + 44 (0)20 7280 8790.

INTERNET **Website** www.foreland-shipping.co.uk *(English)*

ROUTES OPERATED No routes are operated. Ships are for charter to the *UK Ministry of Defence* for their 'Strategic Sealift Capability'.

1	ANVIL POINT	23235t	03	17.1k	193.0m	12P	-	180T	A	UK	9248540
2	EDDYSTONE	23235t	02	17.1k	193.0m	12P	-	180T	A	UK	9234070
3	HARTLAND POINT	23235t	03	17.1k	193.0m	12P	-	180T	A	UK	9248538
4	HURST POINT	23235t	02	17.1k	193.0m	12P	-	180T	A	UK	9234068

ANVIL POINT, HARTLAND POINT Built by Harland & Wolff, Belfast, UK for *AWSR Shipping*.

EDDYSTONE, HURST POINT Built by Flensburger Schiffbau-Gesellschaft, Flensburg, Germany for *AWSR Shipping*.

MANN LINES

THE COMPANY *Mann Lines* are owned by *Mann & Son (London) Ltd* of Great Britain. They replaced in 2001 ArgoMann Ferry Service, a joint venture between *Argo Reederei* of Germany and *Mann & Son*.

MANAGEMENT **Managing Director** Bill Binks, **Commercial Manager** David Brooks.

ADDRESS Mann & Son (London) Ltd, The Naval House, Kings Quay Street, Harwich CO12 3JJ.

TELEPHONE **Administration & Reservations** *UK* + 44 (0)1255 245200, *Germany* + 49 (0)421 1638500, *Finland* + 358 (0)2 275 0000, *Estonia* + 372 (0)679 1450.

FAX **Administration & Reservations** *UK* + 44 (0)1255 245219, *Germany* + 49 (0)421 1638520, *Finland* + 358 (0)2 253 5905, *Estonia* + 372 (0)679 1455.

INTERNET **Email** enquiry@manngroup.co.uk **Website** www.mannlines.com *(English, Finnish, Estonian, German, Russian)*

ROUTES OPERATED Harwich (Navyard) - Cuxhaven - Paldiski - Turku - Bremerhaven (Germany) – Harwich *(STENA FORETELLER*; weekly).

1	STENA FORETELLER	24688t	02	22.0k	195.3m	12P	-	210T	A2	SE	9214666

STENA FORETELLER Built as the STENA FORETELLER by Dalian Shipyard Co Ltd, Dalian, China for *Stena RoRo*. Initially chartered to *Cetam* of France to operate between Marseilles and Tunis and renamed the CETAM MASSILIA. In November 2003 the charter ended and she resumed her original

Finnhawk *(J.J. Jager)*

Misida *(J.J. Jager)*

name. A number of short-term commercial and military charters followed until June 2006 when she was chartered to *StoraEnso* paper group to operate between Gothenburg and Finnish ports. In September 2009 she was chartered to *Rederi AB Transatlantic* who took over responsibility to operate all *StoraEnso's* Baltic services. In February 2012 she was chartered to *Transfennica*. In January 2015 chartered to *Mann Lines*.

SCA TRANSFOREST

THE COMPANY *SCA Transforest* is a Swedish company.

MANAGEMENT Managing Director (UK) Hugo Heij.

ADDRESS *Sweden* Box 805, 851 23, Sundsvall, Sweden, *UK* Interforest Terminal London Ltd, 44 Berth, Tilbury Dock, Essex RM18 7HP.

TELEPHONE Administration & Reservations *Sweden* + 46 (0)60 19 35 00, *UK* + 44 (0)1375 488500.

FAX Administration & Reservations *Sweden* + 46 (0)60-19 35 65, *UK* + 44 (0)1375 488503.

INTERNET Email *Sweden* info@transforest.sca.com *UK* interforest.london@sca.com

Website www.sca.com/transforest *(English)*

ROUTE OPERATED Umeå - Sundsvall - Tilbury - Rotterdam (Eemhaven) - Helsingborg - Umeå (8/9 day round trip; *OBBOLA, ORTVIKEN, ÖSTRAND*; 1 per week), Umeå - Sundsvall - Tilbury - Rotterdam (Eemhaven) - Oxelösund - Umeå (8/9 day round trip; *OBBOLA, ORTVIKEN, ÖSTRAND*; 1 per week).

1	OBBOLA	20168t	96	16.0k	170.6m	0P	-	-	A	SE	9087350
2	ORTVIKEN	20154t	97	16.0k	170.4m	0P	-	-	A	SE	9087374
3	ÖSTRAND	20171t	96	16.0k	170.6m	0P	-	-	A	SE	9087362

OBBOLA, ORTVIKEN, ÖSTRAND Built by Astilleros Españoles, Seville, Spain for *Gorthon Lines* and chartered to *SCA Transforest*. They are designed for the handling of forest products in non-wheeled 'cassettes' but can also accommodate ro-ro trailers; however, no trailer capacity is quoted. The ORTVIKEN was lengthened during Autumn 2000 and the OBBOLA and ÖSTRAND were lengthened during 2001. In June 2001 purchased by *SCA Transforest*.

SEA-CARGO

THE COMPANY *Sea-Cargo AS* of Norway is a subsidiary of *SeaTrans DS* of Norway.

MANAGEMENT Managing Director Ole Saevild, Director Business Development Erik A Paulsen, General Manager (Immingham) Mark Brighton, General Manager (Aberdeen) Ian Shewan.

ADDRESS *Norway* Wernersholmvegen 5, 5232 Paradis, Norway, *Immingham* Sea-Cargo UK, West Riverside Road, Immingham Dock, Immingham DN40 2NT, *Aberdeen* Sea-Cargo Aberdeen Ltd, Matthews Quay, Aberdeen Harbour, Aberdeen, AB11 5PG.

TELEPHONE Administration & Bookings *Bergen* + 47 55 10 84 84, *Immingham* + 44 (0)1469 577119, *Aberdeen* + 44 (0)1224 596481.

FAX Administration & Reservations *Bergen* + 47 85 02 82 16, *Immingham* 44 (0)1469 577708, *Aberdeen* + 44 (0)1224 582360.

INTERNET Email mail@sea-cargo.no Website www.sea-cargo.no *(English)*

ROUTES OPERATED *Sea-Cargo* operate a network of services from West Norway to Amsterdam, Aberdeen, Immingham and Esbjerg. The schedule varies from week to week and is shown on the company website. The MARFRET NIOLON and NORRLAND are generally used on the twice-weekly Immingham - Tanager, Haugesund, Bergen and Odda service and the SEA-CARGO EXPRESS on the weekly Aberdeen - Tanager, Haugesund, Bergen, Florø, Aalesund, Kristiansund, Trondheim and Molde service.

Ortviken *(J.J. Jager)*

Obbola *(J.J. Jager)*

1	MARFRET NIOLON	7935t	91	16.5k	123.0m	12P	-	75T	A	LU	8912388
2	NORRLAND	5562t	90	14.5k	107.5m	0P	-	28T	A	AG	8818764
3	SC AHTELA	8610t	91	14.8k	139.5m	12P	-	92T	AS	MT	8911736
4	SC ASTREA	9528t	91	13.5k	129.1m	0p	-	58T	A	BS	8917895
5	SC CONNECTOR	12251t	97	15.0k	154.5m	12P	-	124T	AS	MT	9131993
6	SEA-CARGO EXPRESS	6693t	12	16.0k	117.4m	0P	-	35T	A	MT	9358060
7	TRANS CARRIER	9953t	94	14.5k	145.2m	0P	-	94T	AS	BS	9007879

MARFRET NIOLON Built as the BORE NORDIA by Solheimsviken A/S, Bergen, Norway for *Oy Rettig AB* of Finland. Operated on *Bore Line* their service to Harwich. In 1992 chartered to *Fnncarriers*. In 1997 renamed the FINNSEAL. In 2003 renamed the BORE NORDIA and chartered to *Transfennica*. In November 2011 sold to Attica Enterprise of Greece and in January 2012 renamed the NORDIA. There then followed a number of short term charters to several companies, including *Sea-Cargo*. In March 2007 sold to *Compagnie Maritime Marfret* of France. In October renamed the MARFRET NIOLON. Operated for them in the Mediterranean until July 2014 when she was chartered to *Traghetti Delle Isole Compagnia Di Navigazione* of Italy. In

November 2014 chartered to *Sea-Cargo*.

NORRLAND Built by J J Sietas KG, Hamburg, Germany for *Trailer Link* of Sweden. Chartered to *Sea-Cargo*.

SC AHTELA Built as the AHTELA by Brodogradiliste "Sava", Macvanska Mitrovica, Yugoslavia, completed by Fosen Mekaniske Verksteder, Rissa, Norway for *Rederi AB Gustav Erikson* of Finland. Chartered to *Transfennica*. In 1995 chartered to *DFDS Tor Line*. In 1996 chartered to *Finncarriers Oy* of Finland and in 1997 renamed the FINNOAK. In 2007 sold to *Hollming Oy* of Finland and in 2008 the charter ended and she was renamed the AHTELA. Chartered to *Navirail* of Estonia to operate between Helsinki and Muuga (Estonia). Between February and May 2011 chartered to *Sea-Cargo* to operate between Esbjerg (Denmark) and Egersund (Norway). In October 2012 purchased by *Sea-Cargo* and renamed the SC AHTELA.

SC ASTREA Built as the ASTREA by Tangen Verft Kragerø A/S, Kragerø, Norway for *Finncarriers* of Finland. Operated between Finland and Spain - Portugal via Antwerp. In 2006 chartered to *Danish MoD*. In 2007 chartered to *Sea-Cargo*. In August 2011 purchased by *Sea-Cargo* and renamed the SC ASTREA. Currently chartered out.

SC CONNECTOR Built as the UNITED EXPRESS by Fosen Mekaniske Verksteder A/S, Rissa, Norway for *United Shipping* (a subsidiary of *Birka Shipping*) of Finland and chartered to *Transfennica*. During 2000 used on their Kemi - Oulu - Antwerp - Felixstowe service. In 2001 the route was transferred to *Finnlines* and the vessel used sub-chartered to them (charter later transferred to *Finnlines*). In 2002 *United Shipping* was renamed *Birka Cargo* and she was renamed the BIRKA EXPRESS. In 2008 the charter was extended a further four years. In June 2013 renamed the EXPRESS. In November 2013 chartered to *Transfennica*. In April 2014 sold to *Sea-Cargo* but initially continued to operate for *Transfennica*. During winter 2015 re-engined and modified to allow to side loading. In February 2015 renamed the SC CONNECTOR. Entered service in late April.

SEA-CARGO EXPRESS One of two vessels ordered in 2005 from Bharati Ratnagiri Ltd, Mumbai, India for *Sea-Cargo*. The order for the second ship was cancelled. Trailers are carried on the main deck only. Containers are carried on the weather deck and pallets on the lower decks. A crane is provided for the containers and a side door for pallets. She operates on the Aberdeen - Norway service.

TRANS CARRIER Built as the KORSNÄS LINK by Brodogradiliste Kraljevica, Kraljevica, Croatia for *SeaLink AB* of Sweden and due to be time-chartered to *Korsnäs AB*, a Swedish forest products company. However, due to the war in Croatia, delivery was seriously delayed and she was offered for sale. In 1994 sold to the *Swan Group* and renamed the SWAN HUNTER. She was placed on the charter market. In 1997 she was chartered to *Euroseabridge* and renamed the PARCHIM. In 1999 the charter ended and she resumed the name SWAN HUNTER. In 1999 she was sold to *SeaTrans* and renamed the TRANS CARRIER. She operated for *Sea-Cargo*. In 2005 chartered to *Finnlines* and used on the Finland to Spain/Portugal service. In 2006 returned to *Sea-Cargo*. In January and February 2009 lengthened by 18.9 metres in Poland.

SEATRUCK FERRIES

THE COMPANY *Seatruck Ferries Ltd* is a British private sector company. It is part of the *Clipper Group*.

MANAGEMENT **Chairman** Kristian Morch, **CEO** Alistair Eagles.

ADDRESSES *Heysham (HQ)* North Quay, Heysham Port, Heysham, Morecambe, Lancs LA3 2UH, *Warrenpoint* Seatruck House, The Ferry Terminal, Warrenpoint, County Down BT34 3JR, *Liverpool:* Seatruck Ferry Terminal, Brocklebank Dock, Port of Liverpool, L20 1DB, *Dublin:* Seatruck Dublin, Alexandra Road, Dublin 1 Irish Republic.

TELEPHONE **Administration** +44 (0)1524 855377, **Reservations** *Heysham* +44 (0)1524 853512. *Warrenpoint* +44 (0)28 754400, *Liverpool* + (0)151 9333660, *Dublin* + (0) 353 18230492.

FAX **Administration** +44 (0)28 4175 4545, **Reservations** *Warrenpoint* +44 (0)28 4177 3737, *Heysham* +44 (0)1524 853549.

INTERNET **Email** aje@seatruckgroup.co.uk **Websites** www.seatruckferries.com *(English)*

ROUTES OPERATED Heysham - Warrenpoint (9 hrs; *CLIPPER PENNANT, SEATRUCK PANORAMA*; 2 per day), Heysham - Dublin (9 hrs; *SEATRUCK PACE;* 1 per day), Liverpool - Dublin (9 hrs; *SEATRUCK POWER, SEATRUCK PROGRESS*; 1 or 2 per day).

1	CLIPPER PENNANT	14759t	09	22.0k	142.0m	12P	-	120T	A	CY	9372688
2	CLIPPER RANGER	7606t	98	17.0k	122.3m	12P	-	84T	A	IM	9119402
3	SEATRUCK PACE	14759t	09	22.0k	142.0m	12P	-	120T	A	CY	9350678
4	SEATRUCK PANORAMA	14759t	09	22.0k	142.0m	12P	-	120T	A	CY	9372676
5	SEATRUCK POWER	19722t	11	21.0k	142.0m	12P	-	151T	A	IM	9506215
6	SEATRUCK PROGRESS	19722t	11	21.0k	142.0m	12P	-	151T	A	IM	9506203

CLIPPER PENNANT Built by Astilleros Sevilla SA, Seville, Spain for *Seatruck Ferries*. In January 2013 chartered to *Stena RoRo*.

CLIPPER RANGER Built as the LEMBITU by Astilleros de Huelva SA, Huelva, Spain for the *Estonian Shipping Company*. On completion chartered to *P&O European Ferries (Irish Sea)* and placed on their Liverpool - Dublin route. In Autumn 1998 she was chartered to *Dart Line* and placed on the Dartford - Vlissingen route. In 1999 she was renamed the DART 7. In Autumn 1999 the charter was ended and she was chartered to *Cetam* of France, resumed the name LEMBITU and was used on services between Marseilles and Tunis. In 2000 she was chartered to *P&O European Ferries (Irish Sea)* and renamed the CELTIC SUN; she operated between Liverpool and Dublin. In 2001 the charter ended; she then reverted to the name LEMBITU and was chartered to *NorseMerchant Ferries* and placed on the Heysham - Dublin service. In late 2001 the charter ended and she returned to *ESCO* service in the Baltic. In 2003 chartered to *Scandlines AG* and placed on their Rostock - Helsinki - Muuga service. This service finished in December 2004 and she was chartered to *Channel Freight Ferries* in January 2005. In March 2005 chartered to *NorseMerchant Ferries* again and operated between Heysham and Belfast. Later purchased by *Elmira Shipping* of Greece and renamed the RR CHALLENGE. In June 2005 chartered to *Seatruck Ferries*. In October 2007 sold to *Attica Group* of Greece and renamed the CHALLENGE. She continued to be chartered to *Seatruck Ferries*. In January 2008 she was transferred to the Liverpool - Dublin route and in April sold to *Seatruck Ferries*. In July renamed the CLIPPER RANGER. In June 2009 replaced the SHIELD (now the HILDASAY) until the new CLIPPER PENNANT took over in October. In May 2010 inaugurated a new Heysham - Larne service. In October 2013 chartered to *Caledonian MacBrayne* to replace the MUIRNEAG. The charter ended in May 2015.

SEATRUCK PACE Built as the CLIPPER PACE by Astilleros Sevilla SA, Seville, Spain for *Seatruck Ferries*. In March 2012 renamed the SEATRUCK PACE. In January 2013 chartered to *Blue Water Shipping* of Denmark to carry wind turbine parts between Mostyn (Wales) and Esbjerg. Now operates Heysham - Dublin.

SEATRUCK PANORAMA Built by Astilleros de Huelva SA, Huelva Spain for *Seatruck Ferries*. Launched as the CLIPPER PENNANT and renamed the CLIPPER PANORAMA before delivery. In December 2011 renamed the SEATRUCK PANORAMA.

SEATRUCK POWER, SEATRUCK PROGRESS Built by Flensburger Schiffbau-Gesellschaft, Flensburg, Germany for *Seatruck Ferries*.

Seatruck Ferries also own the ARROW currently on charter to *Isle of Man Steam Packet Company*, HELLIAR and HILDASAY, currently on charter to *NorthLink Ferries*, the STENA PERFORMER and STENA PRECISION, currently on charter to *Stena Line* and the CLIPPER POINT, currently on charter to *DFDS Seaways*.

SOL CONTINENT LINE

THE COMPANY *SOL Continent Line* is a division of *Swedish Orient Line*, a Swedish private sector company.

MANAGEMENT **Managing Director** Ragnar Johansson, **General Manager** Jonas Wåhlin.

ADDRESSES Svenska Orient Linien AB, Klippan 1A, SE-414 51 Gothenburg, Sweden.

TELEPHONE + 46 (0)31-354 40 00.

FAX + 46 (0)31-354 40 07.

INTERNET **Email** info@sollines.se **Website** www.sollines.se/en/content/sol-continent-line

ROUTES OPERATED Gothenburg - Zeebrugge (34 hrs; *SCHIEBORG, SLINGEBORG*; 4 per week), Oulu-Kemi-Lübeck-Antwerp-Zeebrugge-Tilbury-Oulu (*TRANSPULP, TRANSTIMBER*; 1 per week).

1	SCHIEBORG	21005t	00	18.0k	183.4m	12P	-	180T	A	NL	9188233
2	SLINGEBORG	21005t	00	18.0k	183.4m	12P	-	180T	A	NL	9188245
3	TRANSPULP	23128t	06	16.0k	190.7m	12P	-	200T	A	SE	9343261
4	TRANSTIMBER	23128t	07	16.0k	190.7m	12P	-	200T	A	SE	9343273

SCHIEBORG, SLINGEBORG, Built by Flender Werft AG, Lübeck, Germany for *Wagenborg* of The Netherlands and time-chartered to *Stora-Enso* to operate on the *Stora Enso/Cobelfret Ferries* service between Zeebrugge and Gothenburg. In November 2014 the arrangement between *Stora Enso* and *Cobelfret Ferries* ended and they were chartered to *SOL Continent Line* who took over the operation of the service.

TRANSPULP Built by Aker Finnyards, Rauma, Finland for *Baltic Container Shipping* of the UK and chartered to *Rederi AB Transatlantic* of Sweden. Operated on service operated for Stora Enso Paper Group, mainly in the Baltic. In early 2011 transferred to the Gothenburg - Tilbury (once weekly) and Gothenburg - Zeebrugge (*CLdN* service) (once weekly) services. In January 2013 began operating twice weekly to Tilbury, replacing the SELANDIA SEAWAYS of *DFDS Seaways*. In January 2015 chartered to *SOL Continent Line* to operate between Finland and Western Europe.

TRANSTIMBER Built by Aker Finnyards, Rauma, Finland for *Baltic Container Shipping* of the UK and chartered to *Rederi AB Transatlantic* of Sweden. Operated on service operated for Stora Enso Paper Group, mainly in the Baltic. In January 2015 chartered to *SOL Continent Line* to operate between Finland and Western Europe.

FLOTA SUARDIAZ

THE COMPANY *Flota Suardiaz SL* is owned by *Grupo Suardiaz*, a Spanish private sector logistics company which operates divisions in ports, bunkering, warehousing, haulage, freight forwarding and shipping.

MANAGEMENT **Presidente** Don Juan Riva, **Director General** Alfredo Menendez Garcia.

ADDRESSES **Spain** Calle Ayala, 6 28001 Madrid, Spain, **UK** Suardiaz Shipping Ltd, Suardiaz House, 193 Shirley Road, Southampton SO15 3FG.

TELEPHONE **Spain** + 34 914 31 66 40, **UK** + 44 (0) 2380 211 981.

FAX **Spain** + 34 914 36 46 74, **UK** + 44 (0) 2380 335309.

Slingeborg (J.J. Jager)

Seatruck Pace (Matt Davies)

INTERNET **Email** infoweb@suardiaz.com, **Website** www.suardiaz.com (*English, Spanish*).

ROUTES OPERATED **Channel Line** (3 times per week) Sheerness – Zeebrugge, Grimsby – Zeebrugge. **North Sea Line** (weekly) Cuxhaven – Immingham, **Cantabrian Line** (weekly) Teesport – Cuxhaven – Zeebrugge - Southampton – Le Havre – Santander, **Atlantic Line** (weekly) Vlissingen – Zeebrugge – Southampton – Vigo – Setubal - Las Palmas – Tenerife – Casablanca – Barcelona – Sete – Barcelona – Casablanca – Setubal – Sheerness – Newcastle **Biscay Line** (3 per week) St Nazaire – Vigo, **Canaries Line** (weekly) Barcelona – Tarragona – Las Palmas - Tenerife **Algeria Line** Barcelona – Mostagenem (weekly).

Services listed carry unaccompanied ro-ro cargo together with large volumes of trade cars for vehicle manufacturers and distributors. The Cantabrian and Channel Line services are operated by SCSC (Suardiaz CAT Shipping Co) a joint venture with European Car distributor CAT. The Biscay Line is operated with European Union funding from the TEN-T Programme and supported by a car carrying contract to GEFCO. Vessels are regularly transferred between routes and are often chartered out for short periods to other operators and vehicle manufacturers. In view of this the following is a list of all vessels in the *Flota Suardiaz* fleet at the present time including those that do not currently serve the UK.

1	BOUZAS	15224t	02	18.5k	149.4m	12P	1265C	105T	A	ES	9249996
2	GALICIA	16361t	03	15.0k	149.4m	12P	1390C	110T	A	ES	9268409
3	GRAN CANARIA CAR	9600t	01	18.0k	132.5m	0P	1150C	42T	AS	ES	9218014
4	IVAN	8191t	96	14.6k	102.5m	0P	853C	73T	A	PT	9112040
5	L'AUDACE	15222t	99	18.5k	149.4m	12P	1233C	105T	A	ES	9187318
6	LA SURPRISE	15222t	00	18.5k	149.4m	12P	1233C	105T	A	ES	9198719
7	SUAR VIGO	16361t	03	18.5k	149.4m	12P	1356C	110T	A	ES	9250000
8	TENERIFE CAR	13122t	02	20.0k	149.4m	12P	1354C	54T	AS	ES	9249984

BOUZAS, GALICIA, L'AUDACE, LA SURPRISE, SUAR VIGO Built by Hijos de J. Barreras SA, Vigo, Portugal for *Flota Suardiaz* of Spain for use on services in the Mediterranean and to the Canaries, U.K. and Benelux. The vessels are highly flexible with a 12 driver capacity and three full height freight decks, each fitted with a mezzanine deck for cars, together with a further dedicated car deck. In addition to operating for *Flota Suardiaz* a number of vessels have spent periods on charter to UECC. In February 2014 L'AUDACE was chartered to *P&O Ferries* to operate between Hull and Zeebrugge.

GRAN CANARIA CAR Built as HARALD FLICK by Hijos de J. Barreras SA, Vigo, Portugal for *Naviera del Odiel*, one of the shareholders in Barreras and placed on 10 year charter to *Flota Suardiaz* of Spain for use on services in the Mediterranean and to the Canaries, U.K. and Benelux. Renamed GRAN CANARIA CAR before entering service. In 2008 ownership passed to *Navicar SA* a subsidiary of *Flota Suardiaz*. In addition to operating for *Flota Suardiaz* has been chartered to UECC on a number of occasions.

IVAN Built by Astilleros De Murueta, Vizcaya, Spain for *Adamastor - Sociedade de Navegação, Lda* a subsidiary of *Flota Suardiaz* for use on short sea services. In recent years she has been used on services between Sheerness, Grimsby and Calais.

TENERIFE CAR Built by Hijos de J. Barreras SA, Vigo, Portugal for *Navicar SA* a subsidiary of *Flota Suardiaz* for use on services in the Mediterranean and to the Canaries, U.K. and Benelux.

TRANSFENNICA

THE COMPANY *Transfennica Ltd* is a Finnish private sector company wholly owned by *Spliethoff Bevrachtingskantoor* of The Netherlands.

MANAGEMENT **Managing Director** Dirk P. Witteveen, **Sales Director (UK)** Andrew Clarke.

ADDRESSES *Finland* Eteläranta 12, 00130 Helsinki, Finland, *UK* Finland House, 47 Berth, Tilbury Port, Tilbury, Essex RM18 7EH.

TELEPHONE **Administration & Reservations** *Finland* + 358 (0)9 13262, *UK* + 44 (0)1375 363 900.

FAX Administration & Reservations *Finland* +358 (0)9 652377, *UK* +44 (0)1375 840 888.

INTERNET Email *Finland* info@transfennica.fi *UK* info.uk@transfennica.com (*English*)

Website www.transfennica.com (*English*)

ROUTES OPERATED Tilbury (twice weekly) to various destinations in Finland and Russia. Please see the website. All *Transfennica* ships are listed below as ships are sometimes moved between routes.

1	CARRIER	12251t	98	20.0k	154.5m	12P	-	124T	A2	FI	9132002
2	FRIEDRICH RUSS	10471t	99	20.0k	153.5m	12P	-	120T	A2	AG	9186429
3	GENCA	28301t	07	22.0k	205.0m	12P	-	200T	A2	NL	9307372
4	KRAFTCA	28301t	06	22.0k	205.0m	12P	-	200T	A2	NL	9307360
5	PAULINE RUSS	10488t	99	22.0k	153.5m	12P	-	120T	A2	AG	9198989
6	PLYCA	28301t	09	22.0k	205.0m	12P	-	200T	A2	NL	9345398
7	PULPCA	28301t	08	22.0k	205.0m	12P	-	200T	A2	NL	9345386
8	SEAGARD	10488t	99	21.0k	153.5m	12P	-	134T	A2	FI	9198977
9	STENA FORERUNNER	24688t	02	22.0k	195.3m	12P	-	210T	A2	SE	9214666
10	TIMCA	28301t	06	22.0k	205.0m	12P	-	200T	A2	NL	9307358
11	TRADER	12251t	98	20.0k	154.5m	12P	-	124T	A2	FI	9132014
12	TRICA	28301t	07	22.0k	205.0m	12P	-	200T	A2	NL	9307384

CARRIER Built as the UNITED CARRIER by Fosen Mekaniske Verksteder A/S, Rissa, Norway for *United Shipping* (a subsidiary of *Birka Shipping*) of Finland and chartered to *Transfennica*. During 2000 she was used on their Kemi - Oulu - Antwerp - Felixstowe service. In 2001 the route was transferred to *Finnlines* and the vessel used sub-chartered to them (charter later transferred to *Finnlines*). In 2002 *United Shipping* was renamed *Birka Cargo* and the ship was renamed the BIRKA CARRIER. In 2006 the service ceased. In 2008 the charter was extended a further four years. In January 2013 chartered to *Transfennica*. In June 2013 she was renamed the CARRIER. In January 2015 sold to *Finnlines*. She will be delivered in January 2016.

FRIEDRICH RUSS, PAULINE RUSS, Built by J J Sietas KG, Hamburg, Germany for *Ernst Russ* of Germany and chartered to *Transfennica*.

GENCA, KRAFTCA, PLYCA, PULPCA, TIMCA, TRICA Built by New Szczecin Shipyard (SSN), Szczecin, Poland for *Spliethoff Bevrachtingskantoor*, owners of *Transfennica*.

SEAGARD Built by J J Sietas KG, Hamburg, Germany for *Bror Husell Chartering* of Finland (later acquired by *Bore Shipowning* of Finland) and chartered to *Transfennica*.

STENA FORERUNNER Built by Dalian Shipyard Co Ltd, Dalian, China for *Stena RoRo* and chartered to *Transfennica*.

TRADER Built as the UNITED TRADER by Fosen Mekaniske Verksteder A/S, Rissa, Norway for *United Shipping* (a subsidiary of *Birka Shipping*) of Finland and chartered to *Transfennica*. During 2000 used on their Kemi - Oulu - Antwerp - Felixstowe service. In 2001 the route was transferred to *Finnlines* and the vessels used sub-chartered to them (charter later transferred to *Finnlines*). In 2002 *United Shipping* was renamed *Birka Cargo* and she was renamed the BIRKA TRADER. In 2006 the service ceased. In 2008 the charter was extended a further four years. In January 2013 chartered to *Transfennica*. In July 2013 renamed the TRADER. In January 2015 sold to *Finnlines*. She will be delivered in January 2016.

SECTION 3 – FREIGHT ONLY FERRIES

UECC

THE COMPANY United European Car Carriers AS is a Norwegian private sector company jointly owned in equal shares by Nippon Yusen Kabushiki Kaisha (NYK) of Japan and Wallenius Lines of Sweden. UECC consists of companies in Norway, Germany, Spain, France, Portugal and the UK. The fleet technical and ship management department is based in Grimsby (UK).

MANAGEMENT **Chief Executive Officer** Glenn Edvardsen **Sales Manager UK** Nick Clark.

ADDRESSES **Norway** Karenlyst Allè 57, 0277 Oslo, **UK** 17 St. Helen's Place, London EC3A 6DG and Units 5B & 5C Appian Way, Europa Park, Grimsby, DN31 2UT.

TELEPHONE **Norway** +47 21 00 98 00, **UK** +44 (0)207 628 2855 and +44 (0)1472 269429.

FAX **Norway** +47 21 00 98 01, **UK** +44 (0)207 628 2858.

INTERNET **Email** companymail@uecc.com, **Website** www.uecc.com (English).

ROUTES OPERATED **Bristol Service** Portbury - Pasajes (AUTOSUN; every 4 days), **Biscay Services** Santander – Pasajes – Zeebrugge – Southampton – Santander (AUTOSTAR; weekly), Santander – Pasajes – Rotterdam - Zeebrugge – Santander (AUTOSKY, AUTOPRIDE; twice weekly), Santander – Zeebrugge – Southampton – Le Havre – Santander (VIKING ODESSA; weekly), **Atlantic Service** Santander – Le Havre – Zeebrugge – Vigo – Santander (SPICA LEADER; weekly), Vigo – Sheerness – Zeebrugge – Vigo (BALTIC BREEZE; weekly), Vigo – Santander – Le Havre - Zeebrugge – Vigo (AGEAN BREEZE; weekly), **North Sea Service** Southampton – Zeebrugge – Malmo – Cuxhaven – Southampton (ASIAN BREEZE, weekly), Southampton – Cuxhaven – Immingham – Cuxhaven – Southampton (AUTORUNNER, weekly), **Norway Service** Bremerhaven – Oslo – Drammen – Walhamn – Oslo – Drammen - Bremerhaven (AUTOPROGRESS, twice weekly), Bremerhaven – Drammen – Cuxhaven – Immingham – Zeebrugge – Bremerhaven (AUTOPREMIER; weekly), **Baltic Service** Southampton – Zeebrugge – Gydnia –– Hanko – Ust Luga – St Petersburg – Uusikapunki – Bremerhaven – Southampton (AUTO BAY, AUTO BANK; weekly), Southampton – Bremerhaven – Ust Luga – Cuxhaven – Immingham – Bremerhaven – Southampton (AUTOPRESTIGE, fortnightly), **North – South Service** Bremerhaven - Zeebrugge - Portbury – Vigo – Malaga – Sagunto – Tarragona - Livorno - Piraeus - Derince - Yenikoy – Borusan - Vigo - Bremerhaven (OPAL LEADER, CORAL LEADER, EMERALD LEADER, JUPITER LEADER, VIKING CHANCE; weekly), **Intra Med Service** Vigo - Djen Djen – Tunis – Misurata – Gioia Tauro –Vigo (VARIOUS, weekly).

Services listed carry unaccompanied ro-ro cargo together with large volumes of trade cars and may call at additional ports for an inducement and regular additional ports include Cork, Dublin, Immingham, Liverpool, Sheerness, Portbury, Tilbury, and Newcastle. A number of short-sea contract sailings for vehicle manufacturers and distributors are also operated serving additional ports in Northern Europe. Vessels are regularly transferred between routes and contracts and the following is a list of all owned and long term chartered vessels in the UECC fleet at the current time, including those that do not presently serve the UK. Additionally the fleet is regularly supplemented by short term chartered vessels from Flota Suardiaz and Fret Cetam (the Louis Dreyfus Armateurs and Höegh Auto-liners Airbus joint venture) and with deep sea ocean-going ro-ro vessels from Eukor and parent companies NYK Line and Wallenius Lines. Chartered vessels at the time of preparation and considered out of the scope of this book were the CORAL LEADER, EMERALD LEADER, OPAL LEADER, SPICA LEADER, JUPITER LEADER, VIKING ODESSA and VIKING CHANCE.

1	AEGEAN BREEZE	27876t	83	18.0k	164.0m	0P	3242C	260T	QRS	SG	8202367
2	ARABIAN BREEZE	27876t	83	18.0k	164.0m	0P	3242C	260T	QRS	SG	8202355
3	ASIAN BREEZE	27876t	83	18.0k	164.0m	0P	3242C	260T	QRS	SG	8202381
4	AUTO BALTIC	18979t	96	20.0k	138.5m	12P	1452C	105T	A2	FI	9121998
5	AUTO BANK	19107t	96	20.0k	138.8m	12P	1610C	105T	A2	FI	9160774
6	AUTO BAY	19094t	96	20.0k	138.8m	12P	1610C	105T	A2	FI	9122007
7	AUTOPREMIER	11591t	97	20.0k	128.8m	0P	1220C	-	AS	MD	9131943
8	AUTOPRESTIGE	11596t	99	20.0k	128.8m	0P	1220C	-	AS	MD	9190157
9	AUTOPRIDE	11591t	97	20.0k	128.8m	0P	1220C	-	AS	MD	9131955
10	AUTOPROGRESS	11591t	98	20.0k	128.8m	0P	1220C	-	AS	MD	9131967

Carrier *(Cees de Bijl)*

Autorunner *(J.J.Jager)*

SECTION 3 – FREIGHT ONLY FERRIES

11	AUTORACER	9693t	94	20.0k	119.9m	0P	1060C	-	AS	MD	9079200
12	AUTORUNNER	9693t	94	20.0k	119.9m	0P	1060C	-	AS	MD	9079212
13	AUTOSKY	21010t	00	20.9k	140.0m	0P	2080C	-	AS	MD	9206774
14	AUTOSTAR	21010t	00	20.9k	140.0m	0P	2080C	-	AS	MD	9206786
15	AUTOSUN	21094t	00	20.9k	140.0m	0P	1220C	-	AS	MD	9227053
16	BALTIC BREEZE	29979t	83	17.5K	164.0m	0P	3242C	260T	QRS	SG	8312590

AEGEAN BREEZE, ARABIAN BREEZE, ASIAN BREEZE Built by Kurushima Dockyard, Onishi, Japan for *Fuji Shipping* of Tokyo. Sold in 1988 to *Amon Shipping*. In 1990 sold to *Wallenius Lines*, Singapore and later chartered to *UECC*. Of deep-sea ocean-going ro-ro design with quarter ramps, each was re-engined and heavily rebuilt in 2008 at COSCO Dalian Shipyard, China to extend lifespan and improve suitability for short sea operation.

AUTO BALTIC Built as the TRANSGARD by Umoe Sterkoder, Kristiansund, Norway for *Bror Husell Chartering* of Finland for long-term charter to *Transfennica* and used between Rauma and Antwerp and Hamina and Lübeck. Later chartered to *Finncarriers*. In 2005 she underwent conversion in Poland to add a garage on top of the original weather deck and was placed on long-term charter to *UECC* with options to purchase. Generally used on the Baltic or Iberian services. In 2007 renamed AUTO BALTIC.

AUTO BANK Built as the SERENADEN by Umoe Sterkoder AS, Kristiansund, Norway for *Rederi AB Engship* of Finland and chartered to *Transfennica*. In 2006 *Rederi AB Engship* was taken over by *Rettig Group Bore*. In 2007 converted at COSCO Shipyard, Nantong, China to add a garage on top of the weather deck, renamed AUTO BANK and placed on long-term charter to *UECC*. Generally used on the Baltic or Iberian services.

AUTO BAY Built as the HERALDEN by Umoe Sterkoder AS, Kristiansund, Norway for *Rederi AB Engship* of Finland and chartered to *Transfennica*. In 2006 *Rederi AB Engship* was taken over by *Rettig Group Bore*. In 2007 converted at COSCO Shipyard, Nantong, China to add a garage on top of the weather deck, renamed AUTO BAY and placed on long-term charter to *UECC*. Generally used on the Baltic or Iberian services.

AUTOPREMIER, AUTOPRESTIGE, AUTOPROGRESS, AUTOPRIDE Built by Frisian Shipyard, Harlingen, the Netherlands for *UECC*. Designated P-class, they are an enlarged version of the R-class and built to a 'Grimsby-Max' specification with greater capacity for ro-ro cargo. Generally used on scheduled sailings between Iberia or Germany and Norway, the Benelux and UK.

AUTORUNNER, AUTORACER. Built by Brattvaag Skipsverft, Brattvaag, Norway for *UECC*. Designated as R-class, they are normally used on scheduled sailings between Iberia or Germany and Norway, the Benelux and UK.

AUTOSKY, AUTOSTAR, AUTOSUN Built by Tsuneishi Zosen, Tadotsu, Japan for *UECC*. Designated S-class, they are a further enlargement of the P-class and R-class designs and are normally used on Biscay routes.

BALTIC BREEZE Built by Kurushima Dockyard, Onishi, Japan for *Fuji Shipping Co* of Tokyo. Sold in 1988 to *Amon Shipping*. Sold to *Wallenius Lines*, Singapore in 1990. Chartered to *Eukor* then to *UECC*. Of deep-sea ocean-going ro-ro design with quarter ramps, she was re-engined and heavily rebuilt in 2008 at COSCO Dalian Shipyard, China to extend lifespan and improve suitability for short sea operation.

Under Construction

| 17 | NEWBUILDING 1 | 43,200t | 16 | 18.6K | 181.0m | 0P | 3800C | - | QRS | - | - |
| 18 | NEWBUILDING 2 | 43,200t | 16 | 18.6K | 181.0m | 0P | 3800C | - | QRS | - | - |

NEWBUILDING 1, NEWBUILDING 2 Dual fuel LNG Ice Class 1A pure car and truck carriers with side and quarter under construction by Kawasaki Heavy Industries at NACKS shipyard, Nantong, China for *UECC* and due for delivery in the second half of 2016. Intended for use on Baltic services, the vessels will be refuelled by specialist barge in Zeebrugge.

SECTION 4 - GB & IRELAND - CHAIN, CABLE ETC FERRIES

CUMBRIA COUNTY COUNCIL

Address Resources Directorate, Highways Transportation and Fleet, County Offices, Kendal, Cumbria

LA9 4RQ **Tel** +44 (0)1539 713040, **Fax** +44 (0)1539 713035.

Internet Email peter.hosking@cumbria.gov.uk *(English)*

Website www.cumbria.gov.uk/roads-transport/highways-pavements/windermereferry.asp *(English)*

Route Bowness-on-Windermere - Far Sawrey.

1	MALLARD	-	90	-	25.9m	140P	18C	-	BA

MALLARD Chain ferry built by F L Steelcraft, Borth, Dyfed for *Cumbria County Council*.

DARTMOUTH - KINGSWEAR FLOATING BRIDGE CO LTD

Address Dart Marina, Sandquay Road, Dartmouth, Devon TQ6 9PH. **Tel** +44 (0)1803 839622.

Internet Website www.dartmouthhigherferry.com *(English)*

Route Dartmouth - Kingswear (Devon) across River Dart (higher route) (forms part of A379).

1	HIGHER FERRY	540t	09	-	52.7m	240P	32C	-	BA

HIGHER FERRY Built by Ravestein BV, Deest, The Netherlands under contract to Pendennis Shipyard, Falmouth, who fitted the vessel out between January and June 2009.

ISLE OF WIGHT COUNCIL (COWES FLOATING BRIDGE)

Address Ferry Office, Medina Road, Cowes, Isle of Wight PO31 7BX. **Tel** +44 (0)1983 293041.

Route West Cowes - East Cowes.

1	NO 5	-	76	-	33.5m	-	15C	-	BA

NO 5 Chain ferry built by Fairey Marine, East Cowes, UK for *Isle of Wight County Council*, now *Isle of Wight Council*.

KING HARRY FERRY AND CORNWALL FERRIES

Address 2 Ferry Cottages, Feock, Truro, Cornwall TR3 6QJ. **Tel** +44 (0)1872 861917.

Internet Email beverley@kingharry.net **Website** www.falriver.co.uk *(English)*

Route Philliegh - Feock (Cornwall) (across River Fal)

1	KING HARRY FERRY	500t	06	-	55.2m	150P	34C	-	BA	UK	9364370

KING HARRY FERRY Chain ferry built by Pendennis Shipyard, Falmouth (hull constructed at Ravestein Shipyard, Deest, The Netherlands) to replace the previous ferry.

REEDHAM FERRY

Address Reedham Ferry, Ferry Inn, Reedham, Norwich NR13 3HA. **Tel** +44 (0)1493 700999.

Internet Email info@reedhamferry.co.uk **Website** www.reedhamferry.co.uk *(English)*

Route Acle - Reedham - Norton (across River Yare, Norfolk).

1	REEDHAM FERRY	-	84	-	11.3m	20P	3C	-	BA		

REEDHAM FERRY Chain ferry built by Newsons, Oulton Broad, Lowestoft, UK for *Reedham Ferry*. Maximum vehicle weight: 12 tons.

SANDBANKS FERRY

Address *Company* Bournemouth-Swanage Motor Road and Ferry Company, Shell Bay, Studland, Swanage, Dorset BH19 3BA. **Tel** +44 (0)1929 450203, **Fax** +44 (0)1929 450498), *Ferry* Floating Bridge, Ferry Way, Sandbanks, Poole, Dorset BH13 7QN. **Tel** +44 (0)1929 450203.

Internet Email email@sandbanksferry.co.uk **Website** www.sandbanksferry.co.uk *(English)*

Route Sandbanks - Shell Bay (Dorset).

1	BRAMBLE BUSH BAY	625t	93	-	74.4m	400P	48C	-	BA	UK	9072070

BRAMBLE BUSH BAY Chain ferry, built by Richard Dunston (Hessle) Ltd, Hessle, UK for the *Bournemouth-Swanage Motor Road and Ferry Company*.

SOUTH HAMS DISTRICT COUNCIL

Address Lower Ferry Office, The Square, Kingswear, Dartmouth, Devon TQ6 0AA. **Tel** +44 (0)1803 861234.

Internet Website www.southhams.gov.uk/DartmouthLowerFerry *(English)*

Route Dartmouth - Kingswear (Devon) across River Dart (lower route).

1	THE TOM AVIS	-	94	-	33.5m	50P	8C	-	BA		
2	THE TOM CASEY	-	89	-	33.5m	50P	8C	-	BA		

THE TOM AVIS Float (propelled by tugs) built by c Toms & Sons, Fowey, UK for *South Hams District Council*.

THE TOM CASEY Float (propelled by tugs) built by Cosens, Portland, UK for *South Hams District Council*.

TORPOINT FERRY

Address 2 Ferry Street, Torpoint, Cornwall PL11 2AX. **Tel** +44 (0)1752 812233, **Fax** +44 (0)1752 816873.

Internet Website www.tamarcrossings.org.uk *(English)*

Route Devonport (Plymouth) - Torpoint (Cornwall) across the Tamar. The three ferries operate in parallel, each on her own 'track'. Pre-booking is not possible and the above numbers cannot be used for that purpose.

1	LYNHER II	748t	06	-	73.0m	350P	73C	-	BA	UK	9310941
2	PLYM II	748t	04	-	73.0m	350P	73C	-	BA	UK	9310927
3	TAMAR II	748t	05	-	73.0m	350P	73C	-	BA	UK	9310939

LYNHER II, PLYM II, TAMAR II Chain ferries built by Ferguson Shipbuilders Ltd, Port Glasgow, UK to replace 1960s-built ships. Unlike previous ferries, they are registered as 'Passenger/Ro-Ro Cargo' ships and thus have gross tonnage, nation of registry and, being over 100t, an IMO number.

WATERFORD CASTLE HOTEL

Address The Island, Waterford, Irish Republic. **Tel** +353 (0)51 878203.

Internet Email info@waterfordcastleresort.com **Website** www.waterfordcastleresort.com *(English)*

Route Grantstown - Little Island (in River Suir, County Waterford).

1•	LORELEY	110t	59	-	32.0m	57P	12C	-	BA		
2	MARY FITZGERALD	122t	72	10.0k	35.0m	100P	14C	-	BA	IR	8985531

LORELEY Chain ferry built as the LORELEY V by Ruthof, Mainz, Germany to operate between St Goarshausen and St Goar on the River Rhine. In 2004 replaced by a new vessel (the LORELEY VI) and became a reserve vessel In 2007, sold to the *Waterford Castle Hotel* and renamed the LORELEY and, in 2008 replaced the previous ferry. Self propelled and guided by cable. In August 2014 replaced by the MARY FITZGERALD and laid up.

MARY FITZGERALD Built as the STEDINGEN by Abeking & Rasmussen, Lemwerder, Germany for *Schnellastfähre Berne-Farge GmbH* (later *Fähren Bremen-Stedingen GmbH*) to operate across the River Weser (Vegesack - Lemwerder and Berne - Farge). In 2004 sold to the *Lough Foyle Ferry Company Ltd* and renamed the FOYLE RAMBLER. Generally used on the Buncrana - Rathmullan (Lough Swilly) service, which did not resume in summer 2014. In 2014 sold to *Waterford Castle Hotel* and renamed the MARY FITZGERALD. Modified to be cable guided.

SECTION 5 - GB & IRELAND - MAJOR PASSENGER-ONLY FERRIES

There are a surprisingly large number of passenger-only ferries operating in the British Isles, mainly operated by launches and small motor boats. There are, however, a few 'major' operators who operate only passenger vessels (of rather larger dimensions) and have not therefore been mentioned previously.

Aran Island Ferries BANRÍON NA FARRAIGE (117t, 27.4m, 1984, 188 passengers, IMO 8407709) (ex ARAN EXPRESS 2007), CEOL NA FARRAIGE$ (234t, 2001, 37.4m, 294 passengers, IMO 9246750), DRAÍOCHT NA FARRAIGE$ (318t, 1999, 35.4m, 294 passengers, IMO 9200897), GLÓR NA FARRAIGE (170t, 1985, 33.5m, 244 passenger, IMO 8522391) and SEA FLYER 2007), SEA SPRINTER (16t, 11.6m, 35 passengers). **Routes operated** Rossaveal (Co Galway) – Inishmor, Rossaveal - Inis Meáin, Rossaveal - Inisheer. **Tel** + 353 (0)91 568903 (572050 after 19.00), **Fax** + 353 (0)91 568538, **Email** info@aranislandferries.com **Website** www.aranislandferries.com *(English)*

Brixham Express BRIXHAM EXPRESS (2015, 31t, 15.0m, 98 passengers) **Route operated** Brixham - Torquay. **Tel** 07553 359596, **Website** www.brixhamexpress.com

Clyde Cruises (Clyde Marine Services Ltd) CHIEFTAIN (ex SEABUS, 2014) (54t, 2007, 19.5m, 100 passengers) CLYDE CLIPPER (125t, 2009, 27m, 250 passengers), CRUISER (ex POOLE SCENE, 2001, HYTHE HOTSPUR, 1995, SOUTHSEA QUEEN, 1978) (119t, 1974, 24.4m, 245 passengers),FENCER (18t, 1976, 11.0m, 33 passengers), ROVERS (48t, 1964, 19.8m, 120 passengers), THE SECOND SNARKS (45t, 1938, 22.9m, 120 passengers). **Routes operated** Glasgow city cruise, Caledonian Canal sailings, Oban from Dunstaffnage Marina, Aberdeen Harbour tours and cruises and private charters around the Clyde area. **Tel** + 44 (0)1475 721281, **Email** info@clydecruises.com **Website** www.clydecruises.com www.clyde-marine.co.uk *(English)*.

Clydelink ISLAND PRINCESS (1996, 13.7m, 96 passengers), **Route operated** Gourock - Kilcreggan (operated on behalf of *Strathclyde Partnership for Transport*) ISLAND TRADER (12 passengers), SILVER SWAN (12 passengers) **Route operated** Renfrew - Yoker (operated on behalf of *Strathclyde Partnership for Transport*). **Tel** 0871 705 0888, **Website** www.clydelink.co.uk *(English)*.

Dartmouth Steam Railway & Riverboat Company DARTMOUTH PRINCESS (22t, 1990, 18.3m, 156 passengers), KINGSWEAR PRINCESS (ex TWIN STAR II) (27t, 1978, 19.1m, 150 passengers) **Route operated** Dartmouth - Kingswear. CARLINA (5t, 8.5m, 12 passengers), CHAMPION (4t, 1952, 9.7m, 12 passengers), WARRIOR (3.5t, 1947, 9.7m, 12 passengers). **Route operated** Dartmouth – Dittisham. **Note:** Pleasure craft owned by this operator are also used for the ferry service on some occasions. **Tel** + 44 (0)1803 555872, **Email** bookings@dsrrb.co.uk **Website** www.dartmouthrailriver.co.uk *(English)*

Doolin2Aran Ferries DOOLIN DISCOVERY (2009, 15.2m, 72 passengers), JACK B (2005, 15.2m, 67 passengers), HAPPY HOOKER (77t, 1989, 19.8m, 96 passengers), MACDARA (2010, 8.5m, 12 passengers), ROSE OF ARAN (113t, 1976, 20.1m, 96 passengers. IMO 7527916). **Routes operated**

Bramble Bush Bay *(John Bryant)*

Doolin - Inisheer, Doolin - Inishmore, Doolin - Inishmaan. **Tel** +353 (0)65 707 5949, **Email** info@doolin2aranferries.ie **Website** www.doolin2aranferries.com *(English)*

Doolin Ferry (O'Brien Line) CAILIN OIR$ (1999, 15.2m, 72 passengers), QUEEN OF ARAN (113t, 1976, 20.1m, 96 passengers, IMO 7527928), TRANQUILITY (62t, 1988, 15.8m, 100 passengers). **Routes operated** Doolin - Inisheer, Doolin - Inishmaan, Doolin - Inishmore. Also cruises to Cliffs of Mohr. **Tel** +353 (0)65 707 5555, +353 (0)65 707 5618, **Email** info@doolinferry.com **Website** www.doolinferry.com *(English)*

Exe to Sea Cruises MY QUEEN (ex GONDOLIER QUEEN) (1929, 37t, 18m, 127 passengers), ORCOMBE (1954, 14.3m, 100 passengers), PRINCESS MARINA (1936, 15.8m, 60 passengers). **Route operated** Exmouth - Starcross. **Tel** +44 (0)1626 774770, **Email** info@exe2sea.co.uk **Website** www.exe2sea.co.uk *(English)*

Fleetwood - Knott End Ferry (operated by *Wyre Marine Services Ltd*) ##WYRE ROSE$ (2005, 32 passengers). **Route operated** Fleetwood - Knott End. **Route operated** Fleetwood - Knott End. **Tel** +44 (0)1253 871113, **Ferry mobile** +44 (0) 7793 270934, **Fax** +44 (0)1253 87 79 74 **Email** info@wyremarine.co.uk **Website** www.wyre.gov.uk (search for ferry) *(English)*

Gosport Ferry GOSPORT QUEEN (159t, 1966, 30.5m, 250 passengers, IMO 8633700), HARBOUR SPIRIT (293t, 2015, 32.8m, 297 passengers, IMO 9741669), PORTSMOUTH QUEEN (159t, 1966, 30.5m, 250 passengers, IMO 8633695), SPIRIT OF GOSPORT (300t, 2001, 32.6m, 300 passengers, IMO 8972089), SPIRIT OF PORTSMOUTH (377t, 2005, 32.6m, 300 passengers, IMO 9319894) **Route operated** Gosport - Portsmouth. **Tel** +44 (0)23 9252 4551, **Fax:** +44(0)23 9252 4802, **Email** admin@gosportferry.co.uk **Website** www.gosportferry.co.uk *(English)*

Gravesend - Tilbury Ferry (operated by the *Lower Thames & Medway Passenger Boat Co Ltd*) DUCHESS M (ex VESTA 1979) (71t, 1956, 23.8m, 124 passengers), PRINCESS POCAHONTAS (ex FREYA II 1989, LABOE I 1985, LABOE 1984) (180t, 1962, 29.9m, 207 passengers, IMO 5201271). The PRINCESS POCAHONTAS is an excursion vessel operating regularly to Greenwich, Westminster, Chelsea and Southend, also occasionally to Rochester and Whitstable but sometimes covers the ferry roster. **Route operated** Gravesend (Kent) - Tilbury (Essex), **Tel** +44 (0)1732 353448, **Direct Line to Ferry** +44 (0)7973 390124, **Email** enquiry@princess-pocahontas.com **Websites** www.princess-pocahontas.com *(English)* www.gravesham.gov.uk/__data/assets/pdf_file/0004/74965/Ferry Timetable SEPT2012.pdf *(English)*

Hamble - Warsash Ferry CLAIRE (2.1t, 1985, 7.3m, 12 passengers), EMILY (3.7t, 1990, 8.5m, 12 passengers), **Route operated** Hamble - Warsash (across Hamble River) . **Tel** +44 (0)23 8045 4512, **Mobile** +44 (0) 7720 438402 **Email** mike@hambleferry.co.uk, **Website** www.hambllferry.co.uk *(English)*

Hayling Ferry PRIDE OF HAYLING (1989, 11.9m, 63 passengers), TINA MARIE (12 passengers) **Route operated** Eastney – Hayling Island. Service currently suspended. Vessels are for sale. New operator may take over.

Hovertravel FREEDOM 90 (1990, 25.4m, 95 passengers, BHC AP1-88/100S hovercraft, converted from AP1-88/100 in 1999), ISLAND EXPRESS (ex FREJA VIKING, 2002) (1985, 25.4m, 95 passengers, BHC AP1-88/100S hovercraft, converted from BHC AP1-88/100 in 2001). **Under Construction:** NEWBUILDING 1 (2016, 22.4m, 80 passengers, NEWBUILDING 2 (2016, 40.0k, 22.4m, 80 passengers, Griffon Hovercraft 12000TD/AP), **Route operated** Southsea - Ryde. **Tel** +44 (0)8434 878887, **Fax** +44 (0)1983 562216, **Email** info@hovertravel.com **Website** www.hovertravel.com *(English)*

Hythe Ferry (White Horse Ferries) GREAT EXPECTATIONS (66t, 1992, 21.3m, 162 passengers - catamaran), URIAH HEEP (25.6t, 1999, 60 passengers (tri-maran)), **Tel.** *Head Office* +44 (0)1793 618566, *Local Office* +44 (0)23 8084 0722, **Email** post@hytheferry.co.uk **Website** www.hytheferry.co.uk *(English)*

Isle of Sark Shipping Company BON MARIN DE SERK (118t, 1983, 20.7m, 131 passengers, IMO 8303056), SARK BELLE (ex BOURNEMOUTH BELLE 2011) (50t, 1979, 26.2m, 180 passengers), SARK VENTURE (133t, 1986, 21.3m, 122 passengers, IMO 8891986), SARK VIKING (Cargo Vessel) (104t, 2007, 21.2m, 12 passengers, IMO 8648858). **Route operated** St Peter Port (Guernsey) - Sark. **Tel**

Lynher II (*John Hendy*)

Freedom 90 (*Miles Cowsill*)

Spirit of Gosport (*Miles Cowsill*)

Royal Iris of the Mersey (*Miles Cowsill*)

+44 (0) 1481 724059, **Fax** +44 (0) 1481 713999, **Email** info@sarkshippingcompany.com **Website** www.sarkshippingcompany.com *(English)*

John O'Groats Ferries PENTLAND VENTURE (186t, 1987, 29.6m, 250 passengers, IMO 8834122). **Route operated** John O'Groats – Burwick (Orkney). **Tel** +44 (0)1955 611353, **Email** Office@jogferry.co.uk **Website** www.jogferry.co.uk *(English)*

Kintyre Express KINTYRE EXPRESS II (5.75t, 2011, 11.0m, 12 passengers), KINTYRE EXPRESS III (5.75t, 2012, 11.0m, 12 passengers), KINTYRE EXPRESS IV\$ (5.75t, 2012, 11.0m, 12 passengers). **Routes operated** Campbeltown - Ballycastle, Port Ellen (Islay) - Ballycastle,. **Tel** +44 (0) 1586 555895, **Email** info@kintyreexpress.com **Website** www.kintyreexpress.com *(English)*

Lundy Company OLDENBURG (294t, 1958, 43.6m, 267 passengers, IMO 5262146). **Routes operated** Bideford - Lundy Island, Ilfracombe - Lundy Island. Also North Devon coastal cruises and River Torridge cruises. **Tel** +44 (0)1237 470074, **Fax** +44 (0)1237 477779, **Email** info@lundyisland.co.uk **Website** www.lundyisland.co.uk *(English)*

Manche Iles Express (trading name of Société Morbihannaise de Navigation) ##GRANVILLE\$ (ex BORNHOLM EXPRESS 2014) (325t, 2006, 41.0m, 245 passengers, IMO 9356476 - catamaran), VICTOR HUGO (ex SALTEN 2003) (387t, 1997, 35.0m, 195 passengers, IMO 9157806 - catamaran). **Route operated** Granville – Jersey - Sark - Guernsey, Portbail or Carteret – Jersey, Guernsey and Sark, Diélette - Alderney - Guernsey. **Tel** +33 0825 131 050, **Fax** +33 02 33 90 03 49, **Website** www.manche-iles-express.com *(French, English)*

MBNA Thames Clippers (trading name of Collins River Enterprises Ltd) AURORA CLIPPER (181t, 2007, 37.8m, 27.5k, 220 passengers, IMO 9451824), CYCLONE CLIPPER (181t, 2007, 37.8m, 27.5k, 220 passengers, IMO 9451880), HURRICANE CLIPPER (181t, 2002, 37.8m, 27.5k, 220 passengers, IMO 9249702), METEOR CLIPPER (181t, 2007, 37.8m, 27.5k, 220 passengers, IMO 9451812), MONSOON CLIPPER (181t, 2007, 37.8m, 27.5k, 220 passengers, IMO 9451795), MOON CLIPPER (ex DOWN RUNNER 2005) (98t, 2001, 32.0m, 25.0k, 138 passengers, IMO 9245586), SKY CLIPPER (ex VERITATUM 1995, SD10 2000) (60t, 1992, 25.0m, 62 passengers), STAR CLIPPER (ex CONRAD CHELSEA HARBOUR SD9 2000) (60t, 1992, 25.0m, 62 passengers), STORM CLIPPER\$ (ex DHL WORLDWIDE EXPRESS 1995, SD11 2000) (60t, 1992, 25.0m, 62 passengers), SUN CLIPPER (ex ANTRIM RUNNER 2005) (98t, 2001, 32.0m, 25.0k, 138 passengers, IMO 9232292), TORNADO CLIPPER (181t, 2007, 37.8m, 27.5k, 220 passengers, IMO 9451783), TWIN STAR (45t, 1974, 19.2m, 120 passengers),TYPHOON CLIPPER (181t, 2007, 37.8m, 27.5k, 220 passengers, IMO 9451771, NEWBUILDING (2015, 34.0m, 154 seats) The 'Typhoon', 'Tornado', 'Cyclone' and 'Monsoon', 'Aurora' and 'Meteor' Clippers were designed by AIMTEK and built by Brisbane Ship Constructions in Australia in 2007. 'Newbuilding' was designed by One2three Naval Architects and built by Aluminium Boats, Brisbane, Australia. **Routes operated** Embankment - Waterloo - Blackfriars – Bankside - London Bridge - Tower - Canary Wharf – Greenland - Masthouse Terrace - Greenwich – North Greenwich – Woolwich, Bankside – Millbank - St George (Tate to Tate Service), Putney - Wandsworth - Chelsea Harbour - Cardogan - Embankment - Blackfriars, Canary Wharf - Rotherhithe Hilton Docklands Hotel (TWIN STAR). **Tel** +44 (0)870 781 5049, **Fax** +44 (0)20 7001 2222, **Email** sean.collins@thamesclippers.com **Website** www.thamesclippers.com (English).

Mersey Ferries ROYAL DAFFODIL (ex OVERCHURCH 1999) (751t, 1962, 46.6m, 860 passengers, IMO 4900868) (laid up), ROYAL IRIS OF THE MERSEY (ex MOUNTWOOD 2002) (464t, 1960, 46.3m, 750 passengers, IMO 8633712), SNOWDROP (ex WOODCHURCH 2004) (670t, 1960, 46.6m, 750 passengers, IMO 8633724). **Routes operated** Liverpool (Pier Head) - Birkenhead (Woodside), Liverpool - Wallasey (Seacombe) with regular cruises from Liverpool and Seacombe to Salford along the Manchester Ship Canal. **Tel** *Admin* +44 (0)151 639 0609, *Reservations* +44 (0)151 330 1444, **Fax** +44 (0)151 639 0578, **Email** info@merseyferries.co.uk **Website** www.merseyferries.co.uk *(English)*

Mudeford Ferry (Derham Marine) FERRY DAME (4t, 1989, 9.1m, 48 passengers), JOSEPHINE (10.5t, 1997, 10.7m, 70 passengers - catamaran), JOSEPHINE II (10.5t, 2013, 11.0m, 86 passengers - catamaran). **Route operated** Mudeford Quay - Mudeford Sandbank. **Tel** +44 (0)7968 334441 **Email** information@mudefordferry.co.uk **Website** www.mudefordferry.co.uk *(English)*

SECTION 5 – MAJOR PASSENGER ONLY FERRIES

Nexus (trading name of Tyne & Wear Integrated Transport Authority) PRIDE OF THE TYNE (222t, 1993, 24.0m, 240 passengers, IMO 9062166), SPIRIT OF THE TYNE (174t, 2006, 25.0m, 200 passengers). **Route operated** North Shields - South Shields. Also cruises South Shields - Newcastle. **Tel** + 44 (0)191 2020747, **Email** customerservices@nexus.org **Website** www.nexus.org.uk/ferry (*English*)

Sherkin Island Ferry MYSTIC WATERS (100t, 1971, 19.8m, 99 passengers, IOM 8943038), ##YOKER SWAN$ (65t, 1984, 21.9m, 50 passengers). **Route operated** Baltimore (Co Cork) - Sherkin Island. **Tel** + 353 (0)87 244 7828, **Email** info@sherkinferry.com **Website** www.sherkinferry.com

Travel Trident HERM TRIDENT V (79t, 1989, 25.9m, 250 passengers), TRIDENT VI (79t, 1992, 22.3m, 250 passengers). **Route operated** St Peter Port (Guernsey) - Herm. **Tel** + 44 (0)1481 721379, **Fax** + 44 (0)1481 700226, **Email** peterwilcox@cwgsy.net **Website** www.traveltrident.com (*English*)

Waverley Excursions WAVERLEY (693t, 1947, 73.2m, 925 passengers, IMO 5386954). **Routes operated** Excursions all round British Isles. However, regular cruises in the Clyde, Bristol Channel, South Coast and Thames provide a service which can be used for transport purposes and therefore she is in a sense a ferry. She is the only seagoing paddle steamer in the world. **Tel** + 44 (0)845 130 4647, **Fax** + 44 (0)141 248 2150, **Email** info@waverleyexcursions.co.uk **Website** www.waverleyexcursions.co.uk (*English*)

Western Isles Cruises Ltd WESTERN ISLES (46t, 1960, 19.5m, 81 passengers). **Route Operated** Mallaig - Inverie (Knoydart) - Tarbet. **Tel** + 44 (0)1687 462233, **Email** info@westernislescruises.co.uk, **Website** www.westernislescruises.co.uk (*English*)

Western Lady Ferry Service WESTERN LADY VI (ex TORBAY PRINCESS ex DEVON PRINCESS II) (50t, 1981, 19.2m, 173 passengers), WESTERN LADY VII (ex TORBAY PRINCESS II, ex BRIXHAM BELLE II, ex DEVON PRINCESS III) (46t, 1984, 19.8m, 177 passengers). **Route Operated** Torquay - Brixham. **Tel** + 44 (0)1803 293797, **Website** www.westernladyferry.com (*English*) Note: The service is now part of *Dartmouth Steam Railway & Riverboat Company* but is marketed separately.

White Funnel BALMORAL (735t, 1949, 62.2m, 800 passengers, IMO 5034927) Excursions in Bristol Channel and North West (range may be extended in 2016). Regular cruises in the Bristol Channel provide a service which can be used for transport purposes and therefore she is in a sense a ferry. **Tel** + 44 (0)117 325 6200 **Email** balmoral@whitefunnel.co.uk **Website** www.whitefunnel.co.uk

Duchess M (*John Hendy*)

King Harry Ferry *(Andrew Cooke)*

Waverley *(John Hendy)*

Galaxy (Silja Line)

SCANDINAVIAN AND NORTHERN EUROPE REVIEW - 2014/15

The following geographical review again takes the form of a voyage along the coast of The Netherlands and Germany, round the southern tip of Norway, down the Kattegat, through the Great Belt and into the Baltic then up to the Gulf of Finland and Gulf of Bothnia. Please note that because this review covers an eighteen month period, there will be some duplication with the review in *Ferries 2015*.

FRISIAN ISLANDS

EVT, a private sector rival to Rederij Doeksen, who introduced the 55 car *Spathoek* onto the Harlingen - Terschelling route in 2012, ceased operations in April 2014 following the intervention of the Dutch Government. Doeksen took over EVT and its vessel and EVT received €9 million in compensation. They are expected to order new tonnage during 2015. Dutch Company TESO and German company Rederi Norden Frisia both ordered new tonnage. Rederi AG Ems converted their *Ostfriesland* to dual fuel (diesel and LNG).

NORWEGIAN DOMESTIC

In late 2014 Hurtigruten was sold to Silk Bidco, a British funds management company.

Following the continuation of their franchise to continue to operate the Moss - Horten service until 2026, Bastø Fossen ordered three larger ferries from the Cemre Shipyard, Yalova, Turkey. However, the five ship service will continue to operate.

SKAGERRAK & KATTEGAT

Fjord Lines' second newbuilding, the *Bergensfjord*, was delivered in February 2014 and entered service in March. Having learned lessons from the introduction of her sister, the *Stavangerfjord*, her introduction proved much smoother. The introduction of the second vessel enabled a daily service to Langesund to be operated. The previous *Bergensfjord* had been withdrawn at Christmas 2013 and sent to the STX Finland shipyard at Rauma for conversion to a day ferry suitable for the short Sandefjord - Strömstad crossing. Renamed *Oslofjord*, she entered service in June 2014.

Despite reports that Color Line was looking at new tonnage, the company continued to operate the *Bohus* of 1971 on their Sandefjord - Strömstad service, with no sign of a replacement on the horizon.

Stena Line did not operate the HSS 900 *Stena Carisma* between Gothenburg and Frederikshavn during summer 2014 and there are no plans to operate her in 2015. During winter 2015, one of the *Stena Germanica's* engines was converted for methanol fuel during the course of a long refit at Gdansk. Arrangements were made for the rapid conversion of the other three engines should the trial prove successful.

DANISH DOMESTIC

The Samsø Municipality took control of the Færgen operated Hou - Sælvig route in January 2015. Their new ferry, ordered from Remontowa Shipbuilding in Gdansk, Poland, was not ready in time and the *Ane Læsø* was chartered from Færgeselskabet Læsø. The *Samsø* eventually entered service in March 2015. The *Ane Læsø* will continue to serve as reserve vessel for the route when available.

The Færgen vessel previously used on the route, the *Kanhave*, was moved to the Kalundborg - Samsø service, with the terminal moving from Koby Kås to Ballen. The introduction of a faster vessel and a shorter crossing enabled the transit time to be reduced by 15 minutes. The vessel previously on that route, the *Kyholm*, was then moved to the Fynshav (Als) - Bøjden route and renamed the *Fynshav*. In May 2015 the Samsø was renamed the *Prinsesse Isabella* after the eight year old grand-daughter of the Danish queen.

Finlandia *(Matthew Punter)*

Frigg Sydfyen *(Peter Therkildsen)*

SOUTH BALTIC

In early 2015 the Helsingborg - Helsingør service, operated jointly by Stena Line and Scandlines was sold to the Australia based private equity company First State Investments. It continues to be marketed as Scandlines.

On 11th March 2015, Scandlines Puttgarden - Rødby vessel *Prinsesse Benedikte* was damaged at the Remontowa shipyard in Gdansk whilst undergoing a refit. The 1976 built *Holger Dankse*, normally used only for hazardous cargoes undertook additional trips and the Helsingborg - Helsingør vessel *Mercandia VIII* was brought in to assist with freight carryings. The *Prinsesse Benedikte* was expected to return to service in late June.

In March 2014 Scandlines purchased, at a knock down price, the *Copenhagen* and *Berlin*, the two ships built for them by Volkswerft Stralsund, Stralsund, Germany and rejected as being too heavy for the Gedser - Rostock route (earlier plans to have two LNG vessels built by STX Europe in Finland were dropped). The two vessels, one of which had undertaken sea trials, were sent to Blohm + Voss Shipyards, Hamburg, to be lightened by removing some of the upper superstructure and, in the case of the *Copenhagen*, completion of mechanical and electrical work. However, after a few weeks they were moved again the Fayard Shipyard at Odense, Denmark where the work then started. They are expected now to enter service in late 2015.

In May Stena Line's Trelleborg-Sassnitz route ceased to convey rail wagons and all rail traffic between Germany and Sweden was diverted to the Rostock - Trelleborg route. The company took the 1981-built *Trelleborg* out of service from October 2014 until May 2015, reducing the route to a single daily sailing each way.

TT-Line started a new service from Trelleborg to Swinoujscie in Poland in January 2014. Operated by the ro-pax *Nils Dacke*, the once daily service represents further competition for Polferries rather aged fleet and one wonders how much longer they can continue. In December, the *Robin Hood* was moved to the route but renamed the *Nils Dacke*. The previous *Nils Dacke* returned to the Travemünde - Trelleborg service and adopted the name *Robin Hood*.

In December 2014 Polferries' purchased the Indonesian built *Euroferry Brindisi* (formely the *Finnarrow*) from the Grimaldi Group of Italy to replace the 1980 built *Scandinavia*. In turn the *Scandinavia* was sold to Ventouris Ferries of Greece, for delivery in early May 2015. Late completion of the refurbishment of the new vessel, renamed the *Mazovia*, meant that the Swinoujscie - Ystad then became a single ship operation until mid June when the new ship entered service on that route. The *Wawel* was moved to the Gdansk - Nynäshamn route following the departure of the *Scandinavia* in May The Polish government has placed the state owned company for sale.

During 2013 announcements were made that a new operator, Gotlandsbäten, would start an unsubsidised summer-only service from Västervik on the Swedish mainline to the Visby on the Swedish holiday island of Gotland in summer 2014. Initially the new service was linked to Caledonian MacBrayne's *Isle of Mull*, but in the event the chosen vessel was the 1986 built Greek ferry *Princess T* (originally the *Queen Diamond* in Japan), to be renamed the *Västervik*. However, despite the work supposedly carried out on this vessel in Greece, she did not leave the Mediterranean and after the start date had been put back several times, it was announced that the service would not start until 2015 and with a different ship. It was later announced that the new service would start in 2016. Meanwhile the franchise to operate all-year services to the island from 1st February 2017 until 1st February 2027, with the possibility of extension, was awarded to the incumbent operator, Destination Gotland who ordered a new ship from China.

CROSS BALTIC

Finnlines withdrew the *Transrussia* from their Lübeck - St Petersburg service in early 2014. She reverted to her original name of *Finnhansa* and was placed on the Kotka - Rostock - Lübeck service. The service continued on a once weekly basis using one of the Travemünde - Malmö vessels - the *Finnclipper*, *Finnpartner* and *Finntrader* on a three week cycle - ie two weeks on the Malmö service and then a round trip to St Petersburg.

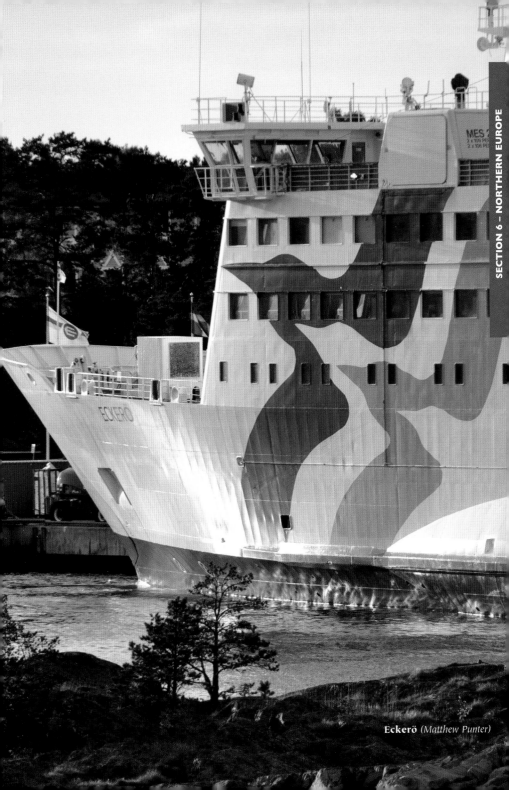

Eckerö (*Matthew Punter*)

Peter Pan *(John Bryant)*

Prinsesse Isabella *(Peter Therkildsen)*

In April 2014 DFDS's *Finlandia Seaways* was replaced by the *Anglia Seaways* on the service between Kiel and St Petersburg and in May the service was once again reduced to a single crossing per week, operated by the *Anglia Seaways*, with the *Botnia Seaways* deployed on a Kiel - Klaipéda roster, supplementing the service provided by the passenger ferries. In July it was all change again with the *Botnia Seaways* transferring to the Russian route and the *Anglia Seaways* inaugurating a new Travemünde - Klaipéda route. This new service only lasted until September, when the *Anglia Seaways* left the Baltic and returned to more familiar waters on the Vlaardingen - Immingham service, providing additional capacity.

NORTH BALTIC

At the start of 2014, Tallink/Silja Line replaced the *Silja Europa* on the Turku - Stockholm route with the smaller but 15 years younger *Baltic Princess*. The *Silja Europa* took over the Helsinki - Tallinn cruise roster. In August the *Silja Europa* was chartered to Australian interests as an accommodation vessel and she was replaced by the *Baltic Queen*. She, in turn was replaced on the Stockholm - Tallinn service by the *Romantika*, which was moved from the Stockholm - Riga route. This route reverted to being a single ship operation with alternate day departures.

In March 2015 Tallink signed a contract with Meyer Turku for a new LNG powered ship for the Tallinn - Helsinki shuttle. The company disposed of the *Regina Baltica* and *Delta Spirit Lodge* (formerly the *Silja Festival*). They have an option on a second vessel.

From mid June until the end of August the overnight Viking Line ship from Stockholm, alternately the *Mariella* or *Gabriella*, undertook a round trip to from Helsinki to Tallinn during the day to provide extra capacity on the route.

Eckerö Line introduced the *Finlandia* in January 2014. Formerly the *Moby Freedom*, she replaced both the *Nordlandia* and freight ferry *Translandia*.

Navirail, who operate between Paldiski in Estonia and Hanko in Finland, upgraded their service in January 2014 by chartering the 320 passenger *Liverpool Seaways* from DFDS Seaways. This lasted until January 2015, when the *Finnsailor*, previously deployed on Finnlines' Kapellskär - Paldiski service was again chartered. In February Navirail purchased the vessel and renamed her the *Sailor*. Meanwhile, Finnlines service became a two ship operation.

In early October 2014 DFDS deployed the former Harwich - Esbjerg vessel *Sirena Seaways* on their Paldiski - Kapellskär service, replacing the *Patria Seaways*. This lasted until January 2014, when the *Liverpool Seaways* came off charter to Navirail and was placed on the route. The *Sirena Seaways* then spent most of the winter providing relief coverage in the Southern Baltic whilst other ships were undergoing refits until moving to Gdansk in April for preparations for her charter to Brittany Ferries as the *Baie de Seine*.

St Peter Line's Stockholm and Helsinki to St Petersburg service was suspended during February 2014 when the ferries, the *Princess Maria* and *SPL Princess Anastasia*, went to the Black Sea to act as hotel vessels for the Winter Olympics at Sochi in Russia.

The Port of Tallinn has won the contract to operate to the western islands of Saaremaa, Muhu and Hiiumaa and has ordered four new ferries. Existing operator Saaremaa Laevakompanii may continued to operate some of the services on a commercial basis but is also planning to place two of its newest vessels on a service in Germany between Cuxhaven and Brunsbüttel. Under the ElbLink banner.

Nick Widdows

Marstal *(Peter Therkildsen)*

Superspeed 1 *(Miles Cowsill)*

6 - NORTHERN EUROPE

ÆRØ FÆRGERNE

THE COMPANY *Ærø Færgerne* is a Danish company, owned by the municipality of Ærø.

MANAGEMENT Managing Director Keld Moller, Marketing Coordinator Jeanette Eriksen.

ADDRESS Vestergade 1, 5970 Ærøskøbing, Denmark.

TELEPHONE Administration & Reservations + 45 62 52 40 00.

FAX Administration & Reservations + 45 62 52 20 88.

INTERNET Email info@aeroe-ferry.dk Website www.aeroe-ferry.dk *(Danish, English, German)*

ROUTE OPERATED Ærøskøbing (Ærø) - Svendborg (Fyn) (1hr 15mins; *ÆRØSKØBING, MARSTAL;* every 1/2 hours), Søby (Ærø) - Faaborg (Fyn) (1hr; *SKJOLDNÆS;* 3 per day), Søby (Ærø) - Fynshav (Als) (1hr 10mins; *SKJOLDNÆS;* 3 per day).

1	ÆRØSKØBING	1617t	99	12.0k	49.0m	395P	42C	L	BA	DK	9199086
2	MARSTAL	1617t	99	12.0k	49.0m	395P	42C	L	BA	DK	9199074
3	SKJOLDNÆS	986t	79	11.0k	47.1m	290P	36C	L	BA	DK	7925649

ÆRØSKØBING, MARSTAL Built by EOS, Esbjerg, Denmark for *Ærø Færgerne.*

SKJOLDNÆS Built as the SAM-SINE by Søren Larsen & Sønner Skibsværft A/S, Nykøbing Mors, Denmark for *Hou-Sælvig Ruten Aps* of Denmark. Operated between Hou (Jutland) and Sælvig (Samsø). In 1995 she was taken over by *Samsø Linien.* In 2001 she was lengthened by Ørskov Christensen's Staalskibsværft, Frederikshavn, Denmark. In 2009 sold to *Ærø Færgerne* and renamed the SKJOLDNÆS.

BASTØ FOSEN

THE COMPANY *Bastø Fosen* is a Norwegian private sector company, a subsidiary of *Torghatten ASA* - Brønnøysund.

MANAGEMENT Managing Director May Kristin Salberg.

ADDRESS PO Box 94, 3191 Horten, Norway.

TELEPHONE Administration + 47 33 03 17 40, Reservations + 47 33 03 17 40 (buses only).

FAX Administration + 47 33 03 17 49, Reservations + 47 33 03 17 49 (buses only).

INTERNET Email bastohorten@fosen.no Website www.basto-fosen.no *(Norwegian)*

ROUTE OPERATED Moss - Horten (across Oslofjord, Norway) (30 mins; *BASTØ I, BASTØ II, BASTØ III, BASTØ IV, BASTØ V* up to every 15 mins).

1	BASTØ I	5505t	97	14.0k	109.0m	550P	200C	18L	BA	NO	9144081
2	BASTØ II	5505t	97	14.0k	109.0m	550P	200C	18L	BA	NO	9144093
3	BASTØ III	7310t	05	18.0k	116.2m	540P	212C	18L	BA	NO	9299408
4	BASTØ IV	2835t	86	13.5k	80.1m	456P	140C	12L	BA	NO	8512114
5	BASTØ V	3397t	90	16.0k	92.0m	650P	155C	-	BA	NO	8917340

BASTØ I, BASTØ II Built by Fosen Mekaniske Verksteder, Frengen, Norway for *Bastø Fosen.*

BASTØ III Built by Stocznia Remontowa, Gdansk, Poland for *Bastø Fosen.*

BASTØ IV Built as the AUSTRHEIM by Trønderverftet A/S, Hommelvik, Norway for *A/S Bergen-Nordhordland Rutelag (BNR),* operating between Steinestø and Knarvik. In 1993 chartered to *Rogaland Trafikkselskap A/S* and operated between Stavanger and Tau. In 1995 sold to *Hardanger Sunnhordlandske Dampskibsselskap (HSD)* of Norway and renamed the BJØRNEFJORD. Operated between Valevåg and Skjersholmane. In 2001 sold to *Boknafjorden Ferjeselskap A/S* and renamed the

BOKNAFJORD. Later transferred to *Båtbygg A/S* and operated between Mortaviken and Arsvågen. In 2002 transferred to *Rogaland Trafikkselskap Ferjer A/S* and in 2003 transferred to *Stavangerska Ferjer A/S*. In 2008 and 2009 she was briefly chartered to a number of operators and in 2008 sold to *Tide Sjø AS*. In December 2010 she was sold to Bastø *Fosen* and renamed the BASTØ IV.

BASTØ V Built as the NORDKAPPHORN by *Trønderverftet A/S*, Hommelvik, Norway for Finnmark Fylkesrederi og Ruteselskap AS of Norway. In 1992 chartered to *Rogaland Trafikkselskap A/S* and renamed the RENNESØY. In January 2012 sold to *Torghatten Nord A/S* and renamed the TRANØY. In September 2012 sold to *Bastø Fosen* and renamed the BASTØ V.

Under Construction

6	NEWBUILDING 1	-	16	16.0k	142.9m	600P	200C	30L	BA	NO	-
7	NEWBUILDING 2	-	17	16.0k	142.9m	600P	200C	30L	BA	NO	-
8	NEWBUILDING 3	-	17	16.0k	142.9m	600P	200C	30L	BA	NO	-

NEWBUILDING 1, NEWBUILDING 2, NEWBUILDING 3 Under construction by Cemre Shipyard, Yalova, Turkey. They will replace three older ships and a five ship service will continue to be operated.

COLOR LINE

THE COMPANY *Color Line ASA* is a Norwegian private sector stock-listed limited company. The company merged with *Larvik Scandi Line* of Norway (which owned *Larvik Line* and *Scandi Line*) in 1996. In 1997 the operations of *Larvik Line* were incorporated into *Color Line; Scandi Line* continued as a separate subsidiary until 1999, when it was also incorporated into *Color Line*. The marketing name *Color Scandi Line* was dropped at the end of 2000.

MANAGEMENT Managing Director Trond Kleivdal.

ADDRESS *Commercial* Postboks 1422 Vika, 0115 Oslo, Norway, *Technical Management* Color Line Marine AS, PO Box 2090, 3210 Sandefjord, Norway.

TELEPHONE Administration & Reservations + 49 40 381096 9113

INTERNET Website www.colorline.com *(English, Danish, German, Norwegian, Swedish,)*

ROUTES OPERATED Conventional Ferries Oslo (Norway) - Kiel (Germany) (19 hrs 30 mins; *COLOR FANTASY, COLOR MAGIC;* 1 per day), Kristiansand (Norway) - Hirtshals (3 hrs 15 mins; *SUPERSPEED 1;* 4 per day), Larvik (Norway) - Hirtshals (Denmark) (3 hrs 45 mins; *SUPERSPEED 2;* up to 2 per day), Sandefjord (Norway) - Strömstad (Sweden) (2 hrs 30 mins; *BOHUS, COLOR VIKING;* up to 4 per day).

1	BOHUS	9149t	71	20.5k	123.4m	1165P	240C	34T	BA	NO	7037806
2	COLOR FANTASY	75027t	04	22.3k	224.0m	2750P	750C	90T	BA	NO	9278234
3	COLOR MAGIC	75100t	07	22.3k	223.7m	2750P	550C	90T	BA	NO	9349863
4	COLOR VIKING	19763t	85	16.4k	134.0m	2000P	320C	40T	BA2	NO	8317942
5	SUPERSPEED 1	36822t	08	27.0k	211.3m	2250P	525C	121T	BA2	NO	9374519
6	SUPERSPEED 2	34231t	08	27.0k	211.3m	1800P	525C	121T	BA2	NO	9378682

BOHUS Built as the PRINSESSAN DESIREE by Aalborg Værft A/S, Aalborg, Denmark for *Rederi AB Göteborg-Frederikshavn Linjen* of Sweden (trading as *Sessan Linjen*) for their service between Gothenburg and Frederikshavn. In 1981 the company was taken over by *Stena Line* and she became surplus to requirements. During 1981 she had a number of charters including *B&I Line* of Ireland and *Sealink UK*. In 1982 she was chartered to *Sally Line* to operate as second vessel on the Ramsgate - Dunkerque service between June and September. She bore the name 'VIKING 2' in large letters on her hull although she was never officially renamed. In September 1982 she returned to *Stena Line* and in 1983 she was transferred to subsidiary company *Varberg-Grenaa Line* for their service between Varberg (Sweden) and Grenaa (Denmark), renamed the EUROPAFÄRJAN. In 1985 she was renamed the EUROPAFÄRJAN II. In 1986, following a reorganisation within *Stena Line*, ownership was transferred to subsidiary company *Lion Ferry AB* and she was named the LION PRINCESS. In 1993 she

Color Magic (*Miles Cowsill*)

Gotland (*Miles Cowsill*)

was sold to *Scandi Line* and renamed the BOHUS. In 1999 *Scandi Line* operations were integrated into *Color Line*.

COLOR FANTASY Built by Kværner Masa-Yards, Turku, Finland for *Color Line* to replace the PRINSESSE RAGNHILD on the Oslo – Kiel service.

COLOR MAGIC Built by Aker Yards, Turku, Finland (hull construction) and Rauma, Finland (fitting out), for the Oslo - Kiel route.

COLOR VIKING Built as the PEDER PAARS by Nakskov Skibsværft A/S, Nakskov, Denmark for *DSB (Danish State Railways)* for their service between Kalundborg (Sealand) and Århus (Jutland). In 1990 purchased by *Stena Line* of Sweden for delivery in 1991. In that year renamed the STENA INVICTA and entered service on the *Sealink Stena Line* Dover - Calais service. She was withdrawn from the route in February 1998, before the formation of *P&O Stena Line*, but ownership was transferred to that company. In Summer 1998, she was chartered to *Silja Line* to operate between Vaasa and Umeå under the marketing name 'WASA JUBILEE'. In Autumn 1998 she was laid up at Zeebrugge. She remained there until Autumn 1999 when she was chartered to *Stena Line* to operate between Holyhead and Dublin. In 2000 she was chartered to *Color Line*, renamed the COLOR VIKING and in April entered service on the Sandefjord - Strömstad service. In 2002 purchased by *Color Line*.

SUPERSPEED 1, SUPERSPEED 2 Built by Aker Yards, Rauma, Finland for the Kristiansand - Hirtshals and Larvik - Hirtshals routes. In January 2011, the SUPERSPEED 1 was modified to provide additional facilities and increase passenger capacity.

DESTINATION GOTLAND

THE COMPANY *Destination Gotland AB* is a Swedish private sector company owned by *Rederi AB Gotland*.

MANAGEMENT Managing Director Christer Bruzelius, Marketing Manager Per-Erling Evensen.

ADDRESS PO Box 1234, 621 23 Visby, Gotland, Sweden.

TELEPHONE Administration +46 (0)498-20 18 00, Reservations +46 (0)771-22 33 00.

FAX Administration & Reservations +46 (0)498-20 13 90.

INTERNET Email info@destinationgotland.se Website www.destinationgotland.se *(Swedish, English, Finnish, German)*

ROUTES OPERATED Fast Conventional Ferries Visby (Gotland) - Nynäshamn (Swedish mainland) (3 hrs 15 mins; *GOTLAND, VISBY*; 1/2 per day), Visby - Oskarshamn (Swedish mainland) (2 hrs 55 mins; *GOTLAND, VISBY*; 1/4 per day). Fast Ferries (Summer only) Visby - Nynäshamn (3 hrs 15 mins; *GOTLANDIA II*; up to 3 per day), Visby - Oskarshamn (Swedish mainland) (2 hrs 55 mins; *GOTLANDIA*; 1 per day (selected)).

1	GOTLAND	29746t	03	28.5k	195.8m	1500P	500C	118T	BAS2	SE	9223796
2»	GOTLANDIA	5632t	99	35.0k	112.5m	700P	140C	-	A	SE	9171163
3»	GOTLANDIA II	6554t	06	36.0k	122.0m	780P	160C	-	A	SE	9328015
4	VISBY	29746t	03	28.5k	195.8m	1500P	500C	118T	BAS2	SE	9223784

GOTLAND, VISBY Built by Guangzhou Shipyard International, Guangzhou, China for *Rederi AB Gotland* for use on *Destination Gotland* services.

GOTLANDIA Alstom Leroux Corsair 11500 monohull vessel built as the GOTLAND at Lorient, France for *Rederi AB Gotland* and chartered to *Destination Gotland*. In 2003 renamed the GOTLANDIA. In 2006 laid up. In 2007 inaugurated a new route between Visby and Grankullavik (Öland). In 2014 will operate between Visby and Oskarshamn.

GOTLANDIA II Fincantieri SF700 monohull fast ferry built at Riva Trigoso, Italy for *Rederi AB Gotland* for use by *Destination Gotland*.

Under Construction

| 5 | NEWBUILDING 1 | 48000t | 17 | - | 200.0m | 1650P | - | 110L | BAS2 SE | - |

NEWBUILDING Under construction by Guangzhou Shipyard International, Guangzhou, China for *Rederi AB Gotland* for use on *Destination Gotland* services. To be LNG powered.

DFDS SEAWAYS

THE COMPANY DFDS *Seaways* is a division of *DFDS A/S*, a Danish private sector company.

MANAGEMENT CEO DFDS A/S Niels Smedegaard, **Head of Shipping Division** Peder Gellert Pedersen, **Head of Baltic Sea Business Area** Anders Refsgaard, **Head of Passenger Business Area** Kim Heiberg.

ADDRESS *Copenhagen* Sundkrogsgade 11, 2100 Copenhagen Ø, Denmark.

TELEPHONE Administration +45 33 42 33 42, **Reservations** *Denmark* +45 78 79 55 36, *Germany* +49 (0)40-389037, *Lithuania* +370 46 393616, *Sweden* +46 454 33680

FAX Administration +45 33 42 33 41. INTERNET Administration incoming@dfdsseaways.dk, Reservations *Denmark* incoming@dfdsseaways.dk *Germany* service.de@dfds.com *Lithuania* booking.lt@dfds.com, *Sweden* pax@dfds.com

Website www.dfdsseaways.com (*English, Danish, Dutch, German, Italian, Japanese, Norwegian, Polish, Swedish*)

ROUTES OPERATED *Passengers services* Copenhagen - Oslo (Norway) (16 hrs 30 mins; *CROWN SEAWAYS, PEARL SEAWAYS*; 1 per day), Klaipéda (Lithuania) - Kiel (Germany) (21 hrs; *OPTIMA SEAWAYS, VICTORIA SEAWAYS*; 6 per week), Klaipéda - Karlshamn (Sweden) (14 hrs; *ATHENA SEAWAYS, REGINA SEAWAYS*; 7 per week), Paldiski (Estonia) - Kapellskär (Sweden) (10 hrs; *LIVERPOOL SEAWAYS*; 1 per day) (joint with *Baltic Scandinavia Line*), **Freight only services** Fredericia - Copenhagen - Klaipéda (call at Aarhus once per week) (*CORONA SEAWAYS*; 2 per week), Kiel - Klaipéda - Ust Luga - St Petersburg, (*BOTNIA SEAWAYS*; 1 per week).

See Section 1 for services operating to Britain.

1	ATHENA SEAWAYS	24950t	07	23.0k	199.1m	500P	-	190T	A	LT	9350680
2F	BOTNIA SEAWAYS	11530t	00	20.0k	162.2m	12P	-	140T	A	LT	9192129
3F	CORONA SEAWAYS	25609t	08	20.0k	184.8m	12P	-	250T	AS	UK	9357597
4	CROWN SEAWAYS	35498t	94	22.0k	169.4m	1940P	450C	50T	BA	DK	8917613
5•	KAUNAS SEAWAYS	25606t	89	16.3k	190.9m	262P	460C	93Tr	A2	LT	8311924
6	LIVERPOOL SEAWAYS	21856t	97	20.0k	186.0m	320P	100C	135T	A	LT	9136034
7	OPTIMA SEAWAYS	25206t	99	21.5k	186.3m	327P	164C	150T	A	LT	9188427
8	PATRIA SEAWAYS	18332t	92	17.0k	154.0m	242P	-	114T	BA2	LT	8917390
9	PEARL SEAWAYS	40039t	89	21.0k	178.4m	2090P	350C	70T	BA	DK	8701674
10	REGINA SEAWAYS	25518t	10	24.0k	199.1m	600P	-	190T	A	LT	9458535
11	VICTORIA SEAWAYS	24950t	09	23.0k	199.1m	600P	-	190T	A	LT	9350721
12	VILNIUS SEAWAYS	22341t	87	16.3k	190.9m	132P	460C	112Tr	A2	LT	8311900

ATHENA SEAWAYS Built as the CORAGGIO by Nuovi Cantieri Apuani, Marina di Carrara, Italy. First of an order of eight vessels for *Grimaldi Holdings* of Italy. Used on *Grimaldi Lines* Mediterranean services. In September 2010, bare-boat chartered to *Stena Line* to operate between Hook of Holland and Killingholme. In November 2011 replaced by the new STENA TRANSIT and returned to Mediterranean service. In December 2013 renamed the ATHENA SEAWAYS, chartered to DFDS *Seaways* and replaced the LIVERPOOL SEAWAYS on the Klaipéda - Kiel service. In June 2014 moved to the Klaipéda - Karlshamn route.

BOTNIA SEAWAYS Built as the FINNMASTER by Jinling Shipyard, Nanjing, China for the *Macoma Shipping Group* and chartered to *Finncarriers*. In 2008 sold to *DFDS Lisco* and in January 2009 delivered, chartered to *DFDS Tor Line* and renamed the TOR BOTNIA. Operated on the Immingham - Rotterdam route until December 2010. In January 2011 moved to the Kiel - St Petersburg route. In January 2013 renamed the BOTNIA SEAWAYS.

Pearl Seaways (*Miles Cowsill*)

Liverpool Seaways (*Matthew Punter*)

CORONA SEAWAYS Built as the TOR CORONA by Jinling Shipyard, Nanjing, China for *Macoma Shipping Ltd* of the UK and time-chartered to *DFDS Tor Line* for ten years. Used on the Fredericia – Copenhagen - Klaipėda service. In April 2012 renamed the CORONA SEAWAYS.

CROWN SEAWAYS Launched as the THOMAS MANN by Brodogradevna Industrija, Split, Croatia for *Euroway AB* for their Lübeck - Travemünde - Malmö service. However, political problems led to serious delays and, before delivery, the service had ceased. She was purchased by *DFDS*, renamed the CROWN OF SCANDINAVIA and introduced onto the Copenhagen - Oslo service. In January 2013 renamed the CROWN SEAWAYS.

LIVERPOOL SEAWAYS Built as the LAGAN VIKING by CN Visentini, Donada, Italy for *Levantina Trasporti* of Italy and chartered by *Norse Irish Ferries*, operating between Liverpool and Belfast. In 1999 the charter was taken over by *Merchant Ferries*. Purchased by *NorseMerchant Ferries* in 2001. In 2002 the service transferred to Twelve Quays River Terminal, Birkenhead. In January 2005 renamed the LIVERPOOL VIKING and in December moved to the Birkenhead – Dublin route. In August 2010 renamed the LIVERPOOL SEAWAYS. In February 2011 moved to the Klaipėda - Karlshamn service. In January 2014 chartered to *NaviRail*. In January 2015 returned to *DFDS* and placed on the Paldiski - Kapellskär service.

KAUNAS SEAWAYS Train ferry built as the KAUNAS by VEB Mathias-Thesen-Werft, Wismar, Germany (DDR) for *Lisco* of the former Soviet Union and operated between Klaipėda and Mukran in Germany (DDR). She was part of a series of vessels built to link the USSR and Germany (DDR), avoiding Poland. In 1994/95 she was modified to offer passenger facilities and placed on the Klaipėda – Kiel service. In 2003 transferred to the Klaipėda – Karlshamn route. Early in 2004 chartered to *DFDS Tor Line* to operate between Lübeck and Riga. In 2005 returned to the Klaipėda – Karlshamn route. In May 2009 replaced by the LISCO OPTIMA and laid up. In October 2009 placed on the Travemünde - Riga route; this route ceased in January 2010 and she was laid up again. In May 2010 chartered to *Scandlines* and placed on a new Travemünde - Liepaja (Latvia) service. In December 2010 returned to *DFDS Seaways*. In March 2011 chartered to *Baltic Scandinavian Line* to operate between Paldiski (Estonia) and Kapellskär. In May returned to *DFDS Seaways* and inaugurated a new service between Kiel and Ust Luga (Russia). In May 2012 she was renamed the KAUNAS SEAWAYS and in June transferred to the Klaipėda - Sassnitz route. At the end of September 2013 this route closed and in October she was transferred to the Paldiski - Kapellskär service. Now laid up.

OPTIMA SEAWAYS Ro-pax vessel built as the ALYSSA by C N Visentini di Visentini Francesco & C Donada, Italy for *Levantina Trasporti* of Italy for charter. Initially chartered to *CoTuNav* of Tunisia for service between Marseilles, Genoa and Tunis and in 2000 to *Trasmediterranea* of Spain for service between Barcelona and Palma de Mallorca. In 2001 chartered to *Stena Line Scandinavia AB*, renamed the SVEALAND and placed as second vessel on the *Scandlines AB* freight-only Trelleborg - Travemünde service. In 2003 sub-chartered to *Scandlines AG* and placed on the Kiel - Klaipėda route, replacing the ASK and PETERSBURG. In 2004 sold to *Rederia AB Hornet*, a *Stena* company. In late 2005 the *Scandlines* Kiel - Klaipėda service ended. In early 2006 she was chartered to *TT-Line* to cover for the rebuilding of the engines of their four newest vessels. Later sold to *DFDS*, renamed the LISCO OPTIMA and returned to the Kiel - Klaipėda route in Spring 2006. In May 2009 moved to the Klaipėda – Karlshamn route and in February 2011 moved to the Klaipėda - Kiel route but in September moved back. In April 2012 renamed the OPTIMA SEAWAYS. In June 2014 moved to the Klaipėda - Kiel route.

PATRIA SEAWAYS Ro-pax vessel built as the STENA TRAVELLER by Fosen Mekaniske Verksteder, Trondheim, Norway for *Stena RoRo*. After a short period with *Stena Line* on the Hook of Holland - Harwich service, she was chartered to *Sealink Stena Line* for their Southampton - Cherbourg route, initially for 28 weeks. At the end of the 1992 summer season she was chartered to *TT-Line* to operate between Travemünde and Trelleborg and was renamed the TT-TRAVELLER. In late 1995, she returned to *Stena Line*, resumed the name STENA TRAVELLER and inaugurated a new service between Holyhead and Dublin. In Autumn 1996 she was replaced by the STENA CHALLENGER (18523t, 1991). In early 1997 she was again chartered to *TT-Line* and renamed the TT-TRAVELLER. She operated on the Rostock - Trelleborg route. During Winter 1999/2000 her passenger capacity was increased to 250 and passenger facilities renovated. In early 2002 the charter ended and she was renamed the STENA TRAVELLER, chartered to *Stena Line* and placed on their Karlskrona - Gdynia service. This charter ended in May 2003 and she was sold to *Lisco Baltic Service* and renamed the LISCO PATRIA.

Placed on the Klaipéda - Karlshamn service. In January 2006 transferred to the Klaipéda - Kiel service to replace the *Scandlines* vessel SVEALAND following that company's withdrawal from the joint route. In Spring 2006 returned to the Klaipéda – Karlshamn route. In May 2011 chartered to *Baltic Scandinavia Lines* and placed on their Paldiski - Kapellskär service. In September 2011 a controlling interest in this service was acquired by *DFDS Seaways*. In January 2012 renamed the PATRIA SEAWAYS. In September 2014 replaced by the *Sirena Seaways* and became a relief vessel. In April 2015 chartered as a windfarm accommodation vessel off Esbjerg.

PEARL SEAWAYS Built as the ATHENA by Wärtsilä Marine, Turku, Finland for *Rederi AB Slite* of Sweden (part of *Viking Line*) and used on 24-hour cruises from Stockholm to Mariehamn (Åland). In 1993 the company went into liquidation and she was sold to *Star Cruises* of Malaysia for cruises in the Far East. She was renamed the STAR AQUARIUS. Later that year she was renamed the LANGKAPURI STAR AQUARIUS. In February 2001 sold to *DFDS* and renamed the AQUARIUS. After rebuilding, she was renamed the PEARL OF SCANDINAVIA and introduced onto the Copenhagen - Oslo service. In January 2011 renamed the PEARL SEAWAYS.

REGINA SEAWAYS Built as the ENERGIA by Nuovi Cantieri Apuani, Marina di Carrara, Italy for *Grimaldi Holdings* of Italy. In August 2011 chartered to DFDS Seaways and moved to Klaipéda for modifications. In September 2011 renamed the REGINA SEAWAYS and placed on the Klaipéda - Kiel service. In January 2014 moved to the Klaipéda - Karlshamn service.

VICTORIA SEAWAYS Built by Nuovi Cantieri Apuani, Marina di Carrara, Italy. Launched as the FORZA. Fifth of an order of eight vessels for *Grimaldi Holdings* of Italy. Whilst under construction, sold to *DFDS Tor Line*. On delivery renamed the LISCO MAXIMA. In March/April 2012 renamed the VICTORIA SEAWAYS. Operates between Kiel and Klaipéda.

VILNIUS SEAWAYS Train ferry as KAUNAS SEAWAYS. Built as the VILNIUS. In 1993 rebuilt in Liverpool to convert from a 12 passenger freight vessel to a 120 passenger ro-pax vessel. Operated on the Klaipéda - Kiel service until June 2003. Later chartered to *DFDS Tor Line* to operate between Lübeck and Riga. In Summer 2006 transferred to the *DFDS Lisco* Klaipéda - Sassnitz route. In January 2011 renamed the VILNIUS SEAWAYS. In June 2012 she was transferred to the Kiel - Ust Luga service. In June 2013 she was chartered to *Ukrferry* of the Ukraine for service in the Black Sea.

REDERIJ DOEKSEN

THE COMPANY *BV Rederij G. Doeksen en Zn BV* is a Dutch private sector company. Ferries are operated by subsidiary *Terschellinger Stoomboot Maatschappij*, trading as *Rederij Doeksen*.

MANAGEMENT **Managing Director** P J M Melles, **Manager Operations** R. de Vries, **Controller** R. Herrema, **Manager Hospitality, FO & CC** Dirk Spoor, **Manager Personnel & Organization** A. Idzinga

ADDRESS Waddenpromenade 5, 8861 NT Harlingen, The Netherlands.

TELEPHONE *In The Netherlands* 088 – 9000 888, *From abroad* + 31 562 442 002.

FAX + 31 (0)517 413303.

INTERNET **Email** info@rederij-doeksen.nl **Website** www.rederij-doeksen.nl *(Dutch, English, German))* **Facebook** www.facebook.com/rederijdoeksen **Twitter** www.twitter.com/rederijdoeksen

ROUTES OPERATED **Conventional Ferries** Harlingen (The Netherlands) - Terschelling (Frisian Islands) (2 hrs; *FRIESLAND, MIDSLAND)* (up to 6 per day), Harlingen - Vlieland (Frisian Islands) (1 hr 45 mins; *VLIELAND*; 3 per day). **Fast Passenger Ferries** Harlingen - Terschelling (45 mins; *KOEGELWIECK, TIGER*; 3 to 6 per day), Harlingen - Vlieland (45 mins; *KOEGELWIECK, TIGER*; 2 per day), Vlieland - Terschelling (30 mins; *KOEGELWIECK, TIGER*; 2 per day). **Freight Ferry** Harlingen - Terschelling (2 hrs; *NOORD-NEDERLAND)*, Harlingen - Vlieland (1hr 45 mins; *NOORD-NEDERLAND)*.

1	FRIESLAND	3583t	89	14.0k	69.0m	1100P	122C	12L	BA	NL	8801058
2»p	KOEGELWIECK	439t	92	33.0k	35.5m	315P	0C	0L	-	NL	9035527

3	MIDSLAND	1812t	74	15.5k	77.9m	700P	55C	6L	BA	NL	7393066
4F	NOORD-NEDERLAND	361t	02	14.0k	48.0m	12P	-	9L	BA	NL	9269611
5•	SPATHOEK	1743t	88	12.0k	67.4m	975P	55C	-	BA	NL	8800975
5»p	TIGER	660t	02	37.0k	52.0m	414P	0C	0L	BA	NL	9179191
6	VLIELAND	2726t	05	15.0k	64.1m	1950P	58C	4L	BA	NL	9303716

FRIESLAND Built by Van der Giessen-de Noord, Krimpen aan den IJssel, Rotterdam, The Netherlands for *Rederij Doeksen*. Used on the Harlingen - Terschelling route.

KOEGELWIECK Harding 35m catamaran built at Rosendal, Norway for *Rederij Doeksen* to operate between Harlingen and Terschelling, Harlingen and Vlieland and Terschelling and Vlieland.

MIDSLAND Built as the RHEINLAND by Werftunion GmbH & Co, Cassens-Werft, Emden, Germany for *AG Ems* of Germany. In 1993 purchased by *Rederij Doeksen* and renamed the MIDSLAND. Used mainly on the Harlingen - Terschelling route but also used on the Harlingen - Vlieland service. She is now a reserve vessel.

NOORD-NEDERLAND Catamaran built by ASB, Harwood, New South Wales, Australia for *Rederij Doeksen*. Used on freight services from Harlingen to Terschelling and Vlieland.

SPATHOEK Built by Husumer Schiffswerft, Husum, Germany as the SCHLESWIG-HOLSTEIN for *Wyker Dampfschiffs-Reederei Föhr-Amrum GmbH* of Germany. She operated between Föhr and Amrum. In March 2011 sold to *EVT* and renamed the SPATHOEK. In March 2012 began operating between Harlingen and Terschelling. In April 2014 acquired by *Rederij Doeksen* following that company's acquisition of *EVT*. In October 2014 withdrawn and laid up for sale.

TIGER Catamaran built as the SUPERCAT 2002 by FBMA Babcock Marine, Cebu, Philippines for *SuperCat* of the Philippines. In 2007 purchased by *Rederij Doeksen* and renamed the TIGER. Operates from Harlingen to Terschelling and Vlieland.

VLIELAND Catamaran built by FBMA Babcock Marine, Cebu, Philippines for *Rederij Doeksen* to operate between Harlingen and Vlieland.

REDERI AB ECKERÖ

THE COMPANY *Rederi AB Eckerö* is an Åland Islands company. It operates two ferry companies, a cruise operation from Stockholm (*Birka Cruises*), a ro-ro time chartering company (*Eckerö Shipping*) and a bus company on Åland (*Williams*).

ADDRESS PB 158, AX-22101 Mariehamn, Åland, Finland.

TELEPHONE Administration + 358 (0)18 28 030.

FAX Administration + 358 (0)18 12 011.

INTERNET Email info@rederiabeckero.ax Website www.rederiabeckero.ax (*Swedish*)

ECKERÖ LINE

THE COMPANY *Eckerö Line Ab Oy* is a Finnish company, 100% owned by *Rederi Ab Eckerö* of Åland, Finland. Until January 1998, the company was called *Eestin-Linjat*.

MANAGEMENT Managing Director Irja Hanelius, Marketing Director Ida Toikka-Everi.

ADDRESS PO Box 307, 00181 Helsinki, Finland.

TELEPHONE Administration & Reservations + 358 9 (0)2288 544.

FAX Administration & Reservations + 358 (0)9 2288 550.

INTERNET Email info@eckeroline.fi Website www.eckeroline.fi (*Swedish, Finnish, English*)

ROUTE OPERATED Passenger Service Helsinki (Länsisatama) - Tallinn (Estonia) (2 hrs 30 mins; FINLANDIA; up to 2 per day).

1	FINLANDIA	36093t	01	27.0k	175.0m	1880P	665C	116T	BA	FI	9214379

FINLANDIA Built as the MOBY FREEDOM by Daewoo Shipbuilding & Heavy Machinery Ltd., Okpo, South Korea for *Moby SpA (Moby Line)* of Italy. Operated on their Genoa/Civitavecchia/Livorno - Olbia routes. In March 2012 sold to *Eckerö Line*, and renamed the FREEDOM. Refitted at Landskrona and, in June, renamed the FINLANDIA. She entered service on 31st December 2012.

ECKERÖ LINJEN

THE COMPANY *Eckerö Linjen* is an Åland Islands company 100% owned by *Rederi AB Eckerö*.

MANAGEMENT Managing Director Tomas Karlsson, Marketing Manager Maria Hellman.

ADDRESS Torggatan 2, Box 158, AX-22100 Mariehamn, Åland.

TELEPHONE Administration + 358 (0)18 28 000, Reservations + 358 (0)18 28 300.

FAX Administration + 358 (0)18 28 380. Reservations + 358 (0)18 28 230.

INTERNET Email info@eckerolinjen.ax Website www.eckerolinjen.se *(Swedish, Finnish, English)*

ROUTE OPERATED Eckerö (Åland) - Grisslehamn (Sweden) (2 hrs; *ECKERÖ*; 3 per day).

1	ECKERÖ	12358t	79	19.5k	121.1m	1500P	265C	34T	BA	SE	7633155

ECKERÖ Built as the JENS KOFOED by Aalborg Værft A/S, Aalborg, Denmark for *Bornholmstrafikken*. Used on the Rønne - Copenhagen, Rønne - Ystad and (until December 2002) Rønne - Sassnitz services. Rønne - Copenhagen service became Rønne – Køge in September 2004. In October 2004 sold to *Eckerö Linjen* for delivery in May 2005. Renamed the ECKERÖ and substantially rebuilt before entering service in early 2006. In January 2009 transferred from the Finnish to the Swedish flag.

AG EMS

THE COMPANY *AG Ems* is a German public sector company.

MANAGEMENT Managing Director & Chief Executive B W Brons, Marine Superintendent Knut Gerdes, Operations Manager Hans-Jörd Oltmanns.

ADDRESS Am Aussenhafen, Postfach 1154, 26691 Emden, Germany.

TELEPHONE Administration & Reservations + 49 (0)1805-180182.

INTERNET Email info@ag-ems.de Website www.ag-ems.de *(German)* www.borkumlijn.nl *(Dutch)* www.helgolandlinie.de *(German)*

ROUTES OPERATED Conventional Ferries Emden (Germany) - Borkum (German Frisian Islands) (2 hrs; *MÜNSTERLAND, OSTFRIESLAND*; up to 4 per day), Eemshaven (The Netherlands) - Borkum (55 mins; *GRONINGERLAND*; up to 4 per day), Wilhelmshaven - Heligoland (3 hrs; *HELGOLAND*; 1 per day) (Operated by subsidiary *Reederei Cassen Eils* - tourist cars not conveyed). Fast Ferries Emden - Borkum (1 hr; *NORDLICHT* up to 4 per day), Eemshaven - Borkum (30 mins; *NORDLICHT*; 1 per week in summer).

1	GRONINGERLAND	1070t	91	12.0k	44.4m	621P	30C	-	BA	DE	9002465
2	HELGOLAND	1812t	72	15.5k	77.9m	1200P	65C	10L	BA	DE	7217004
3	MÜNSTERLAND	1859t	86	15.5k	78.7m	1200P	70C	10L	BA	DE	8601989
4p»	NORDLICHT	435t	89	33.0k	38.8m	272P	0C	0L	-	DE	8816015
5	OSTFRIESLAND	1859t	85	15.5k	78.7m	1200P	70C	10L	BA	DE	8324622
6p	WAPPEN VON BORKUM	287t	76	11.5k	42.8m	358P	0C	0L	-	DE	7525918

GRONINGERLAND Built by Husumer Schiffswerft, Husum, Germany as the HILLIGENLEI for *Wyker Dampfschiffs-Reederei Föhr-Amrum GmbH* of Germany. Operated Schlüttsiel - Halligen – Wittdün (North Frisian Islands). In 2004 laid up. In late 2005 sold to *AG Ems*. In 2006 renamed the GRONINGERLAND and placed on the Eemshaven – Borkum route.

Finlandia (*Matthew Punter*)

HELGOLAND Built by as the WESTFALEN C Cassens Schiffswerft, Emden, Germany for *AG Ems*. Rebuilt in 1994. In 2006 renamed the HELGOLAND and inaugurated a new Wilhelmshaven - Heligoland service for subsidiary *Helgoland Linie*.

MÜNSTERLAND, OSTFRIESLAND Built by Martin Jansen GmbH & Co KG Schiffswerft, Leer, Germany for *AG Ems*.

NORDLICHT Fjellstrand 38m passenger-only catamaran built at Mandal, Norway for *AG Ems*.

WAPPEN VON BORKUM Built as the HANNOVER by Schiffswerft Schlömer GmbH & Co KG, Oldersum, Germany for *Friesland Fahrlinie* of Germany. In 1979 sold to *AG Ems* and renamed the STADT BORKUM. In 1988 sold to *ST-Line* of Finland, operating day trips from Rauma and renamed the PRINCESS ISABELLA. In 1994 returned to *AG Ems* and renamed the WAPPEN VON BORKUM.

FÆRGEN

THE COMPANIES *Danske Færger A/S* trading as *Færgen (previously Nordic Ferry Services A/S)* is a Danish mixed public and private sector company.

MANAGEMENT CEO John Steen-Mikkelsen.

ADDRESSES Dampskibskajen 3, 3700 Rønne, Denmark.

TELEPHONE **Administration & Reservations** + 45 70 23 15 15. (Reservations not possible on FanøFærgen).

INTERNET Website www.faergen.com *(Danish, German, English)*

ROUTES OPERATED

AlsFærgen Fynshav (Als) - Bøjden (Fyn) (50 mins; *FRIGG SYDFYEN, FYNSHAV*; hourly (summer) two-hourly (winter)), *BornholmerFærgen* **Conventional Ferries** Rønne (Bornholm, Denmark) - Køge (6 hrs 30 mins; *HAMMERODDE*; 1 per day, *April-October only:* Rønne – Sassnitz (Germany) (3 hrs 30 mins; *POVL ANKER*; 1 per day). **Fast Ferry** Rønne - Ystad (Sweden) (1 hr 20 mins; *LEONORA CHRISTINA, VILLUM CLAUSEN*; **Peak season:** departure every 2 hours. **Low season:** 3 trips a day), *FanøFærgen* Esbjerg (Jutland) - Nordby (Fanø) (12 mins; *FENJA, MENJA, SØNDERHO*; every 20-40 mins), *LangelandsFærgen* Spodsbjerg (Langeland) - Tårs (Lolland) (40 mins; *LANGELAND, LOLLAND*; hourly), *SamsøFærgen* Kalundborg - Ballen (Samsø) (1 hr 15 min; *KANHAVE*; up to 4 per day).

1	FENJA	751t	98	11.5k	49.9m	396P	34C	4L	BA	DK	9189378
2	FRIGG SYDFYEN	1676t	84	13.5k	70.1m	338P	50C	8L	BA	DK	8222824
3	FYNSHAV	3380t	98	14.5k	69.2m	450P	96C	8L	BA	DK	9183025
4	HAMMERODDE	13906t	05	18.5k	124.9m	400P	342C	106T	A	DK	9323699
5	KANHAVE	4250t	08	16.0k	91.4m	600P	122C	30L	BA	DK	9548562
6	LANGELAND	4500t	12	16.0k	99.9m	600P	122C	36L	BA	DK	9596428
7»	LEONORA CHRISTINA	8235t	11	40.0k	112.6m	1400P	359C	-	BA	DK	9557848
8	LOLLAND	4500t	12	16.0k	99.9m	600P	122C	36L	BA	DK	9594690
9	MENJA	751t	98	11.5k	49.9m	396P	34C	4L	BA	DK	9189380
10	POVL ANKER	12131t	78	19.5k	121.0m	1500P	262C	26T	BA	DK	7633143
11p	SØNDERHO	93t	62	10.0k	26.3m	163P	0C	0L	-	DK	
12»	VILLUM CLAUSEN	6402t	00	40.0k	86.6m	1055P	200C	-	BA	DK	9216250

FENJA Built by Morsø Værft A/S, Nykøbing Mors, Denmark for *Scandlines Sydfyenske A/S* for the Esbjerg - Nordby service.

FRIGG SYDFYEN Built by Svendborg Skibsværft A/S, Svendborg, Denmark for *Sydfyenske Dampskibsselskab (SFDS)* of Denmark for the service between Spodsbjerg and Tårs. In June 2012 moved to the Fynshav - Bøjden route.

FYNSHAV Built as the KYHOLM by Ørskov Staalskibsværft, Frederikshavn, Denmark for *Samsø Linien* of Denmark. In October 2008 chartered to *Nordic Ferry Services* and in July 2009 sold to them. Used

Eckerö (*Matthew Punter*)

Leonora Christina (*John Bryant*)

Fynshav *(Peter Therkildsen)*

Finntrader *(John Bryant)*

on the Kalundborg - Koby Kås service. In March 2015 renamed the FYNSHAV and moved to the Fynshav - Bøjden service.

HAMMERODDE Built by Merwede Shipyard, Hardinxveld-Giessendam, The Netherlands for *Bornholmstrafikken*. In Winter 2010 an additional vehicle deck was added for freight and some additional cabins.

KANHAVE Built by Frantzis Shipyard, Perama, Greece. Used on the Hou - Sælvig route. In January 2015 transferred to the Kalundborg - Koby Kås (Samsø) service. Later in January 2015 the Samsø terminal was moved to Ballen.

LANGELAND Built by Sietas Werft, Hamburg, Germany for the Spodsbjerg - Tårs route.

LEONORA CHRISTINA Austal Auto-Express 113 catamaran built at Fremantle, Australia for *Færgen*. Used on the Rønne - Ystad route.

LOLLAND Built by Sietas Werft, Hamburg, Germany. She was launched as the SAMSØ and it was intended that she would be operated on the Hou - Sælvig service, being owned by *Samsø Linien* and operated by *Færgen*. However, these plans were dropped and in February 2012 she was renamed the LOLLAND. After delivery in March 2012 she was, in April, placed on the Spodsbjerg - Tårs route.

MENJA Built by Morsø Værft A/S, Nykøbing Mors, Denmark for *Scandlines Sydfyenske A/S* for the Esbjerg - Nordby service.

POVL ANKER Built by Aalborg Værft A/S, Denmark for *Bornholmstrafikken*. Used on the Rønne - Copenhagen (until September 2004), Rønne - Køge (October 2004-date), Rønne - Ystad and Rønne - Sassnitz services. In recent years she has operated between Rønne and Sassnitz and Rønne and Ystad in the peak summer period.

SØNDERHO Passenger-only ferry built by Esbjerg Jernstøberi & Maskinfabrik A/S, Esbjerg, Denmark for *Post & Telegrafvæsenet* (Danish Post Office). In 1977 taken over by *DSB*. Used on extra peak sailings and late night and early morning sailings between Esbjerg and Nordby.

VILLUM CLAUSEN Austal Auto-Express 86 catamaran built at Fremantle, Australia for *Bornholmstrafikken*. Used on the Rønne - Ystad service. Car capacity increased in 2005.

FINNLINES

THE COMPANY *Finnlines plc* is a Finnish private sector company. The Italian company *Grimaldi Compagnia de Navigazione SpA* has a controlling interest. It operates four passenger brands: *Finnlines HansaLink, Finnlines NordöLink* and *FinnLink* and *TransRussiaExpress*.

MANAGEMENT President and CEO Uwe Bakosch, Vice-President Mrs Seija Turunen.

ADDRESS PO Box 197, 00180 Helsinki, Finland.

TELEPHONE Administration + 358 (0)10 343 50, Reservations + 358 (0)9 231 43 100.

FAX Administration + 358 (0)10 343 5200.

INTERNET *Finnlines* Email info.fi@finnlines.com Website *Finnlines* www.finnlines.com (*English, Finnish, German, Polish, Swedish*)

ROUTES OPERATED *Finnlines Hansalink branded routes* Helsinki - Travemünde (27 hrs; FINNLADY, FINNMAID, FINNSTAR; 7 per week), Helsinki - Rostock (32 hrs; FINNHANSA; 1 per week).

Finnlines NordöLink branded route Malmö - Travemünde (9 hrs; FINNCLIPPER, FINNPARTNER, FINNTRADER, NORDLINK; up to 4 per day).

FinnLink branded route Naantali (Finland) - Långnäs - Kapellskär (Sweden) (6 hrs; FINNEAGLE, FINNFELLOW, up to 2 per day).

TranRussia Express branded route Lübeck - Travemünde - Sassnitz - Ventspils - St Petersburg (60 hours; FINNCLIPPER or FINNPARTNER or FINNTRADER; 1 per week),

1	FINNCLIPPER	29841t	99	22.0k	188.3m	440P	-	210T	BA2	SE	9137997

2	FINNEAGLE	29841t	99	22.0k	188.3m	440P	-	185T	BA2	FI	9138006
3	FINNFELLOW	33769t	00	22.0k	188.3m	452P	-	220T	BA	FI	9145164
4	FINNLADY	45923t	07	25.0k	216.0m	500P	-	300T	BA2	FI	9336268
5	FINNMAID	45923t	06	25.0k	216.0m	500P	-	300T	BA2	FI	9319466
6	FINNPARTNER	32534t	94	21.3k	183.0m	270P	-	236T	A2	SE	9010163
7	FINNSTAR	45923t	06	25.0k	216.0m	500P	-	300T	BA2	FI	9319442
8	FINNTRADER	32534t	95	21.3k	183.0m	270P	-	220T	BA2	SE	9017769
9	NORDLINK	45923t	07	25.0k	216.0m	500P	-	300T	BA2	SE	9336256

FINNCLIPPER 'Ro-pax' ferry built by Astilleros Españoles, Cadiz, Spain. Ordered by Stena RoRo of Sweden and launched as the STENA SEAPACER 1. In 1998 sold, before delivery, to Finnlines and renamed the FINNCLIPPER. Entered service on the Helsinki - Travemünde route in 1999. During Winter 1999/2000 she was converted to double-deck loading. In 2003 transferred to FinnLink. In 2007 an additional freight deck was added. Currently operating on the Travemünde - Malmö and Lübeck - St Petersburg services.

FINNEAGLE 'Ro-pax' vessel built by Astilleros Españoles, Cadiz, Spain. Ordered by Stena RoRo of Sweden and launched as the STENA SEAPACER 2. In 1998 sold, before delivery, to Finnlines and renamed the FINNEAGLE. Although expected to join her sister the FINNCLIPPER on the Helsinki - Travemünde route, on delivery in November 1999 she entered service with FinnLink. During Winter 1999/2000 she was modified for two-deck loading. She has operated on both the FinnLink and Finnlines NordöLink services.

FINNFELLOW 'Ro-pax' ferry built as the STENA BRITANNICA by Astilleros Españoles, Cadiz, Spain for Stena RoRo and chartered to Stena Line BV to operate between Hook of Holland and Harwich. In 2003 replaced by a new STENA BRITANNICA, sold to Finnlines, renamed the FINNFELLOW and placed on the Helsinki – Travemünde route. In 2004 transferred to FinnLink.

FINNLADY, FINNMAID Built by Fincantieri-Cantieri Navali Italiani SpA, Ancona, Italy to operate between Helsinki and Travemünde.

FINNPARTNER 'Ro-pax' vessel built by Stocznia Gdanska SA, Gdansk, Poland for Finnlines Oy of Finland to provide a daily service conveying both freight and a limited number of cars and passengers on the previously freight-only route between Helsinki and Travemünde. In February 2007 replaced by the FINNLADY and placed on the Turku - Travemünde freight service; in May sent to the Remontowa Shipyard in Gdansk for rebuilding to increase passenger capacity and allow for two-deck through loading. Currently operating on the Travemünde - Malmö and Lübeck - St Petersburg services.

FINNSTAR Built by Fincantieri-Cantieri Navali Italiani SpA, Castellamare, Italy to operate between Helsinki and Travemünde.

FINNTRADER 'Ro-pax' vessel built by Stocznia Gdanska SA, Gdansk, Poland for Finnlines Oy of Finland to provide a daily service conveying both freight and a limited number of cars and passengers on the previously freight-only route between Helsinki and Travemünde. In 2006/07 rebuilt to increase passenger capacity and allow for two-deck through loading. In 2007 transferred to the Malmö - Travemünde route. Currently operating on the Travemünde - Malmö and Lübeck - St Petersburg services.

NORDLINK Built by Fincantieri-Cantieri Navali Italiani SpA, Castellamare, Italy for Finnlines to operate for Finnlines NordöLink between Travemünde and Malmö. Currently operating on the Travemünde - Malmö service.

Bergensfjord *(Matthew Punter)*

Nordkapp *(John Byant)*

Full speed ahead – on green gas

Fjord Line is leading the way through its commitment to
the market's most environmentally friendly fuel.

The new cruise ferries MS Stavangerfjord and MS Bergensfjord
are the first ships of such a large size to run on solely natural gas
(LNG), allowing our passengers to choose the greenest sea route
between Norway and the EU.

THE ENVIRONMENTAL BENEFITS INCLUDE:

92 % reduction in NOx emissions.
23 % reduction in greenhouse gas emissions.
98 % reduction in particle emissions.
100 % reduction in sulfur emissions.

fjordline.com

FJORD LINE

THE COMPANY *Fjord Line* is a Norwegian company. During 2007 most of the shares of the company were purchased by *Frode and Ole Teigen*. The company bought and merged with *Master Ferries* during December 2007 and all operations are branded as *Fjord Line*.

MANAGEMENT CEO Rickard Ternblom, **Sales and Marketing Director** Eva Sørås Mellgren, **CFO** Svein Ege, **Director Fjord Line Denmark** Gert Balling, **Technical & Nautical Director** Morten Larsen.

ADDRESS PO Box 513, 4379 Egersund, Norway.

TELEPHONE Administration + 47 55 54 87 00, **Reservations** + 47 51 46 40 99.

INTERNET Email info@fjordline.com **Website** www.fjordline.com (*English, Danish, German, Dutch, Polish, Norwegian,*)

ROUTE OPERATED Conventional Ferry Bergen (Norway) – Stavanger - Hirtshals (Denmark) (17 hrs; *BERGENSFJORD, STAVANGERFJORD*; daily), Langesund (Norway) - Hirtshals (4 hrs 30 mins; *BERGENSFJORD, STAVANGERFJORD*, daily), Sandefjord (Norway) - Strömstad (Sweden) (2 hrs 30 mins; *OSLOFJORD*; 2 per day), **Fast Ferry** *May-August* Kristiansand (Norway) - Hirtshals (Denmark) (2 hrs 15 min; *FJORD CAT*; up to 3 per day).

1	BERGENSFJORD	31678t	13	21.5k	170.0m	1500P	600C	90T	BA	DK	9586617
2»	FJORD CAT	5619t	98	43.0k	91.3m	663P	220C	-	A	DK	9176060
3	OSLOFJORD	16794t	93	19.0k	134.4m	882P	350C	44T	BA	DK	9058995
4	STAVANGERFJORD	31678t	13	21.5k	170.0m	1500P	600C	90T	BA	DK	9586605

BERGENSFJORD, STAVANGERFJORD Built by Bergen Group Fosen AS, Rissa, Norway for *Fjord Line*. They operate on LNG.

FJORD CAT Incat 91-metre catamaran, built speculatively at Hobart, Tasmania, Australia. In Spring 1998, following *Incat's* acquisition of a 50% share in *Scandlines Cat-Link A/S*, she was chartered by *Nordic Catamaran Ferries K/S* to that company, operating between Århus and Kalundborg and named the CAT-LINK V. She is the current holder of the Hales Trophy for fastest crossing of the Atlantic during her delivery voyage between the USA and Falmouth, UK (although this claim is disputed because it was not a genuine commercial service). In 1999 the charter was transferred to *Mols-Linien*, she was renamed the MADS MOLS and operated between Århus and Odden. Charter ended in July 2005. Laid up and renamed the INCAT 049. In 2006 sold to *Gabriel Scott Rederi (Master Ferries)* and renamed the MASTER CAT. In December 2008 purchased by *Fjord Line* renamed the FJORD CAT. Did not operate in 2009 but service resumed in 2010.

OSLOFJORD Built by Fosen Mekaniske Verksteder, Rissa, Norway for *Rutelaget Askøy-Bergen* as the BERGEN and used on the *Fjord Line* Bergen - Egersund - Hanstholm service. In April 2003 chartered to *DFDS Seaways*, renamed the DUCHESS OF SCANDINAVIA and, after modifications, introduced onto the Harwich - Cuxhaven service. In 2004 sold to *Bergensfjord KS* of Norway and chartered to *DFDS Seaways*. In 2005 sub-chartered to *Fjord Line* for 5 months (with DFDS officers and deck-crew) and renamed the ATLANTIC TRAVELLER. In 2006 chartered directly to *Fjord Line*. In March 2008 purchased by *Fjord Line* and renamed the BERGENSFJORD. In January 2014 renamed the OSLOFJORD, rebuilt as a day ferry by STX Finland, Rauma, Finland and, in June 2014, inaugurated a new service between Sandefjord and Strömstad.

HURTIGRUTEN

THE COMPANY *Hurtigruten ASA* is a Norwegian private sector company. The service was originally provided by a consortium of companies. By 2006, through mergers and withdrawal from the operation, there were just two companies - *Troms Fylkes D/S* and *Ofotens og Vesteraalens D/S* and in that year *Hurtigruten ASA* was formed.

MANAGEMENT Chairman Trygve Hegnar, **Managing Director** Daniel Skjeldam.

ADDRESS Hurtigruten ASA, Postboks 6144, 9291 Tromsø, Norway.

TELEPHONE Administration + 47 970 57 030, Reservations *Norway* + 47 810 03 030,
UK + 44 (0)203 627 8249.

INTERNET Email firmapost@hurtigruten.com uk.sales@hurtigruten.com

Websites www.hurtigruten.co.uk *(English)* www.hurtigruten.no *(Norwegian)* www.hurtigruten.de
(German) www.hurtigruten.fr *(French)* www.hurtigruten.us *(US English)*

ROUTE OPERATED 'Hurtigruten' sail every day throughout the year from Bergen and calls at 34
ports up to Kirkenes and takes you along one of the world's most exciting coast lines, where you will
find yourself close to nature, people and traditions. Daily departures throughout the year. The round
trip takes just under 11 days.

1	FINNMARKEN	15539t	02	18.0k	138.5m	1000P	47C	0L	S	NO	9231951
2P	FRAM	11647t	07	18.0k	110.0m	500P	0C	0L	S	NO	9370018
3	KONG HARALD	11204t	93	18.0k	121.8m	691P	45C	0L	S	NO	9039119
4	LOFOTEN	2621t	64	16.0k	87.4m	410P	0C	0L	C	NO	5424562
5	MIDNATSOL	16151t	03	18.0k	135.7m	1000P	45C	0L	S	NO	9247728
6	NORDKAPP	11386t	96	18.0k	123.3m	691P	45C	0L	S	NO	9107772
7	NORDLYS	11204t	94	18.0k	121.8m	691P	45C	0L	S	NO	9048914
8	NORDNORGE	11384t	97	18.0k	123.3m	691P	45C	0L	S	NO	9107784
9	POLARLYS	11341t	96	18.0k	123.0m	737P	35C	0L	S	NO	9107796
10	RICHARD WITH	11205t	93	18.0k	121.8m	691P	45C	0L	S	NO	9040429
11	TROLLFJORD	16140t	02	18.0k	135.7m	822P	45C	0L	S	NO	9233258
12	VESTERÅLEN	6262t	83	18.0k	108.6m	560P	35C	0L	S	NO	8019368

FINNMARKEN Built by Kværner Kleven Skeppsvarv, Ulsteinvik, Norway for *Ofotens og Vesteraalens
D/S*. In October 2009 chartered as a support vessel for the Gorgon Project (natural gas) in Western
Australia. In November 2011 returned to *Hurtigruten* and, in February 2012, returned to service.

FRAM Built by Fincantieri-Cantieri Navali Italiani SpA at Trieste for *Hurtigruten Group ASA* (ordered
by OVDS). Since 2007 she has operated cruises around Greenland and Svalbad during the summer
period and in South America during the winter and this has been the pattern since. She is named after
Fridtjof Nansen's expedition ship Fram and has ice class 1A/1B.

KONG HARALD Built by Volkswerft, Stralsund, Germany for *Troms Fylkes D/S*.

LOFOTEN Built by A/S Aker Mekaniske Verksted, Oslo, Norway for *Vesteraalens D/S*. In 1988 she was
sold to *Finnmark Fylkesrederi og Ruteselskap*. In 1996 she was sold to *Ofotens og Vesteraalens D/S*. In
2002 she was replaced by the FINNMARKEN but she then operated summer cruises and in the winter
months substituted for the NORDNORGE when that vessel was sailing in the Chilean Fjords and
Antarctica. Since 2008 she has operated on the main Hurtigruten roster.

MIDNATSOL Built by Fosen Mekaniske Verksteder, Rissa, Norway for *Troms Fylkes D/S*.

NORDKAPP Built by Kværner Kleven Skeppsvarv, Ulsteinvik, Norway for *Ofotens og Vesteraalens D/S*.
During the winters of 2005/06 and 2006/07 she operated cruises in South America but following the
delivery of the FRAM she now remains on the Hurtigruten throughout the year.

NORDLYS Built by Volkswerft, Stralsund, Germany for *Troms Fylkes D/S*. In 2002 sold to *Kilberg
Shipping KS* of Norway and leased back on 15 year bareboat charter with options to repurchase. She
was laid up during winter 2008/09 until required to replace the damaged RICHARD WITH from the
end of January. She now operates full-time on the Hurtigruten roster.

NORDNORGE Built by Kværner Kleven, Ulsteinvik, Norway for *Ofotens og Vesteraalens D/S*. During
winters 2002/03 - 2007/08 she operated cruises in South America. During most of Winter 2008/09
she was used as an accommodation vessel for a liquefied natural gas field. Laid up at Bremerhaven
during winter 2009/10.

POLARLYS Built by Ulstein Verft A/S, Ulsteinvik, Norway for *Troms Fylkes D/S*.

RICHARD WITH Built by Volkswerft, Stralsund, Norway for *Ofotens og Vesteraalens D/S*. In 2002 sold to *Kystruten KS*, of Norway and leased back on 15 year bareboat charter with options to re-purchase.

TROLLFJORD Built by Fosen Mekaniske Verksteder, Rissa, Norway for *Troms Fylkes D/S*.

VESTERÅLEN Built by Kaarbös Mekaniske Verksted A/S, Harstad, Norway for *Vesteraalens D/S*. From 1987 owned by *Ofotens og Vesteraalens D/S* and from 2006 by *Hurtigruten Group ASA*.

FÆRGESELSKABET LÆSØ

THE COMPANY *Færgeselskabet Læsø K/S* is a Danish public sector company, 50% owned by by the county of North Jutland and 50% by the municipality of Læsø.

MANAGEMENT Managing Director Lars Ricks, Marketing Manager Bente Faurholt.

ADDRESS Havnepladsen 1, Vesterø Havn, 9940 Læsø, Denmark.

TELEPHONE Administration & Reservations + 45 98 49 90 22

FAX Administration + 45 98 49 95 22.

INTERNET Email info@laesoe-line.dk Website www.laesoe-line.dk *(Danish, English, German)*

ROUTE OPERATED Læsø - Frederikshavn (Jutland) (1 hr 30 mins; *ANE LÆSØ, MARGRETE LÆSØ*; up 7 per day).

1	ANE LÆSØ	2208t	95	12.0k	53.8m	440P	72C	-	BA	DK	9107370
2	MARGRETE LÆSØ	3668t	97	13.5k	68.5m	586P	76C	12L	BA	DK	9139438t

ANE LÆSØ Built as the VESBORG by Ørskov Stålskibsværft, Ørskov, Denmark for *Samsø Linien*. In March2012 sold to *Læsø Færgen*. Rebuilt by Soby Yard, Aerø, Denmark and renamed the ANE LÆSØ. Between September 2014 and February 2015 she operated on the Hou - Sælvig (Samsø) service which had been taken over by *Samsø Rederi* before their new SAMSØ was delivered. She will continue to act as reserve vessel on this route.

MARGRETE LÆSØ Built as the LÆSØ FÆRGEN by A/S Norsdsøværftet, Ringkøbing, Denmark for *Andelsfærgeselskabet Læsø* of Denmark. In June 1997 renamed the MARGRETE LÆSØ. In July 1999 transferred to *Færgeselskabet Læsø*.

LINDA LINE

Lindaliini AS (trading as *Linda Line*) is an Estonian Company owned by three Estonian investors - Enn Rohula (26.8%), Urmas Sardis & Janek Veeber (73.2%).

MANAGEMENT CEO Enn Rohula.

ADDRESS Ädala 4A, Tallinn 10614, Estonia.

TELEPHONE Administration + 372 6999 340 Reservations + 372 6999 331.

FAX Administration + 372 6999 341.

INTERNET Email info@lindaline.ee Website www.lindaline.ee *(Estonian, Finnish, English Russian)*

ROUTE OPERATED Tallinn (Estonia) – Helsinki (Finland) (1hr 40 mins, *KAROLIN, MERILIN*; up 6 to per day (April – December) depending on winter ice conditions).

1P	KAROLIN	636t	00	40.0k	42.0m	402P	0C	0L	EE	9124433
2P	MERILIN	963t	99	37.0k	52.0m	450P	0C	0L	EE	9194256

KAROLIN Construction began 1995 at Austal Ships Pty Ltd (Hendersons) initially as the OCEANFAST FERRIES NO 16 and later the CARAIBE-JET but not completed until 2000. In 2000 sold to *AG Ems of Germany* as the POLARSTERN for services between from Emden and Frisian Island of Borkum and Helgoland (summer only). In 2009 sold to *Lindaliini AS* and renamed the KAROLIN.

MERILIN Built 1999 by Austal Freemantle for AG Reederei Norden-Frisa, Germany, for services between Norddeich and Norderney (German Frisian Islands). Originally named the NO 1 (1999) but upon entering service immediately renamed CAT 1. In 2007 bought by *Lindaliini AS* and renamed the MERILIN.

MOLS-LINIEN

THE COMPANY *Mols-Linien A/S* is a Danish private sector company; previously a subsidiary of *J Lauritzen A/S*, it was sold in 1988 to *DIFKO No LXII (Dansk Investeringsfond)*. Since 1994 shares in the company have been traded on the Stock Exchange. In January 1999 a 40% share in the company was acquired by *Scandlines Danmark A/S*. Their *Scandlines Cat-Link* Århus - Kalundborg service became part of *Mols-Linien* in February 1999 and the service was switched from Kalundborg to Odden in April 1999. The *Scandlines* share in the company was acquired by the *Clipper Group* in 2007.

MANAGEMENT **Managing Director** Preben Wolff, **Marketing Manager** Mikkel Hybel.

ADDRESS Sverigesgade 6, 8000 Aarhus C, Denmark.

TELEPHONE **Administration** + 45 89 52 52 00, **Reservations** + 45 70 10 14 18 (press 1).

FAX **Administration** + 45 89 52 53 93.

INTERNET Email mols-linien@mols-linien.dk Website www.mols-linien.dk *(Danish, English, German)*

ROUTES OPERATED Århus - Odden (Sealand) (1 hr 5 mins; *KATEXPRESS 1, KATEXPRESS 2, MAX MOLS*; up to 7 per day), Ebeltoft (Jutland) - Odden (45 mins; *KATEXPRESS 1, KATEXPRESS 2, MAX MOLS*; up to 4 per day).

1»	KATEXPRESS 1	10841	09	40.0k	112.6m	1200P	417C	34L	A	DK	9501590
2»	KATEXPRESS 2	10841	13	40.0k	112.6m	1000P	417C	34L	A	DK	9561356
3»	MAX MOLS	5617t	98	43.0k	91.3m	800P	220C	-	A	DK	9176058

KATEXPRESS 1 Incat 112m catamaran built by Incat Tasmania Pty Ltd for *MGC Chartering* of the Irish Republic. Launched as the INCAT 066. On completion, sold to for *MGC Chartering* of the Irish Republic and renamed the MGC 66. In April 2009 chartered to *LD Lines*, renamed the NORMAN ARROW and, in June, placed on the Dover - Boulogne route. In November 2009 withdrawn and laid up for the winter. In April 2010 began operating on the Portsmouth Le Havre - route. In March 2012 chartered to *Mols-Linien* and renamed the KATEXPRESS 1 (Note: in upper and lower case spelt 'KatExpress 1'). Entered service in May 2012.

KATEXPRESS 2 Incat 112m catamaran built by Incat Tasmania Pty Ltd. Launched as the INCAT 067. In March 2013 chartered to *Mols-Linien* and renamed the KATEXPRESS 2 for ten years with a purchase option. (Note: in upper and lower case spelt 'KatExpress 2'). Entered service in May 2013.

MAX MOLS Incat 91-metre catamaran, built speculatively at Hobart, Tasmania, Australia. In Spring 1998, following *Incat's* acquisition of a 50% share in *Scandlines Cat-Link A/S*, she was sold to that company and named the CAT-LINK IV. In 1999 purchased by *Mols-Linien* and renamed the MAX MOLS. In 2000 chartered to *Marine Atlantic* of Canada to operate between Port aux Basques (Newfoundland) and North Sydney (Nova Scotia). Returned to *Mols-Linien* in Autumn 2000. In Summer 2002 chartered to *Riga Sea Lines* to operate between Riga and Nynäshamn. Returned to *Mols-Linien* in Autumn 2002. In 2004 chartered to *P&O Ferries* to operate between Portsmouth and Caen. Operated under the marketing name 'Caen Express'. In November 2004 returned to *Mols-Linien* and placed on the Århus – Odden route to enhance the service as second vessel.

Lofoten (*John Bryant*)

Baltivia (*John Bryant*)

NAVIRAIL

THE COMPANY *Navirail* is an Estonian company.

MANAGEMENT Managing Director Igor Zimin, Marketing Manager Jelena Andilevko.

ADDRESS Liimi 1, 10621 Tallinn, Estonia.

TELEPHONE Administration +372 666 16 81, Reservations +372 66 616 83.

FAX Administration & Reservations +372 66 616 59.

INTERNET Email navirail@navirail.com Websites www.navirail.com *(English, Estonian, Finnish, Polish, Russian)*

ROUTE OPERATED Paldiski Northern Port (Estonia) - Hanko (Finland) (3 hrs; *SAILOR*; 2 per day).

1	SAILOR	20921t	87	19.0k	157.6m	119P	50C	82L	A2	EE	8401444

SAILOR Built as the FINNSAILOR by Gdansk Shipyard, Gdansk, Poland for *Finnlines* of Finland for freight service between Finland and Germany. In 1996 converted to ro-pax format to inaugurate a new passenger/freight service between Helsinki and Norrköping (Sweden) for subsidiary *FinnLink*. In 1997 this service was transferred to the Kapellskär - Naantali route and passengers (other than lorry drivers) ceased to be conveyed. In 2000 she was chartered to *Nordö-Link* to operate between Travemünde and Malmö. In 2002 she returned to *FinnLink*. In 2004 transferred to *Nordö-Link*. In 2007 returned to *FinnLink* as fourth ship. In early 2009 transferred to *Finnlines'* freight service operating between Helsinki, Turku and Travemünde but in April transferred back. In March 2011 moved back to *Finnlines NordöLink*. In November 2013 chartered to *Navirail* of Estonia to operate between Paldiski and Hanko. In January 2014 returned to *Finnlines* and placed on the Naantali - Kapellskär route. In January 2015 time chartered again to *Navirail*. In February 2015 demise chartered to *Navirail* and renamed the SAILOR.

REEDEREI NORDEN-FRISIA

THE COMPANY *Aktiengesellschaft Reederei Norden-Frisia* is a German public sector company.

MANAGEMENT President/CEO C U Stegmann, Managing Director/CFO Prok. Graw, Technical Manager Prok. H Stolle.

ADDRESS Postfach 1262, 26534 Norderney, Germany.

TELEPHONE *Administration* +49 (0)4931 987 0.

FAX *Administration* +49 (0)4931 987 1131.

INTERNET *Email* info@reederei-frisia.de *Website* www.reederei-frisia.de *(German)*

ROUTES OPERATED Car Ferries & Passenger Ferries Norddeich (Germany) - Norderney (German Frisian Islands) (1 hr; *FRISIA I, FRISIA IV, FRISIA VI*; up to 15 per day), Norddeich - Juist (German Frisian Islands) (1 hr 20 mins; *FRISIA II, FRISIA V, FRISIA VII*; up to 15 per day). Excursion Vessels *(FRISIA IX, FRISIA X, RÜM HART, WAPPEN VON NORDENEY*; varies).

1	FRISIA I	1020t	70	12.3k	63.7m	1500P	53C	-	BA	DE	7018604
2	FRISIA II	1125t	78	12.0k	63.3m	1340P	53C	-	BA	DE	7723974
3	FRISIA IV	1574t	02	12.0k	71.7m	1342P	60C	-	BA	DE	9246839
4	FRISIA V	1007t	65	11.0k	63.8m	1442P	53C	-	BA	DE	8827181
5	FRISIA VI	768t	68	12.0k	54.9m	1096P	35C	-	BA	DE	8827179
6F	FRISIA VII	363t	84	12.0k	53.0m	12P	30C	-	BA	DE	8891807
7p	FRISIA IX	571t	80	11.0k	57.0m	785P	0C	-	-	DE	7924310
8p	FRISIA X	187t	72	12.0k	36.3m	290P	0C	-	-	DE	7222308
9p	RÜM HART	105t	69	12.0k	35.4m	940P	0C	-	-	DE	8137237
10p	WAPPEN VON NORDENEY	154t	67	14.0k	31.1m	200P	0C	-	-	DE	7935395

FRISIA I, FRISIA II, FRISIA V, FRISIA VI Built by Jos L Meyer Werft, Papenburg, Germany for *Reederei Norden-Frisia*. Passenger capacities relate to the summer season. Capacity is reduced during the winter.

FRISIA IV Built by Schiffswerft und Maschinenfabrik Cassens GmbH, Emden, Germany for *Reederei Norden-Frisia* to replace the FRISIA VIII.

FRISIA VII Built by Schlömer Werft, Oldersum, Germany for *Reederei Norden-Frisia*. Conveys ro-ro freight to Norderney and Juist.

FRISIA IX, FRISIA X Built by Schiffswerft Julius Diedrich GmbH & Co. KG, Oldersum, Germany for *Reederei Norden-Frisia*. The FRISIA IX was built to convey 9 cars at the bow end but is now used in passenger-only mode. These ships are generally used for excursions.

RÜM HART Built by Julius Diedrich Schiffswerft, Odersum, Germany as the BALTRUM IV for *Baltrum-Linie* of Germany. In November 1982 sold to *Wyker Dampfschiffs-Reederei* and renamed the RÜM HART. In March 2014 sold to *Reederei Norden-Frisia*.

WAPPEN VON NORDENEY Built by Cassens-Werft, Emden, Germany for *Reederei Norden-Frisia*. Used for excursions.

Under Construction

11	FRISIA III	1574t	15	12.0k	71.7m	1342P	60C	-	BA	DE

FRISIA III Under construction by Cassen-Werft, Emden, Germany.

POLFERRIES

THE COMPANY *Polferries* is the trading name of *Polska Zegluga Baltycka SA (Polish Baltic Shipping Company)*, a Polish state-owned company.

MANAGEMENT **Financial Director and Board Member** Piotr Redmerski.

ADDRESS ul Portowa 41, 78-100 Kolobrzeg, Poland.

TELEPHONE **Administration** +48 94 35 52 103, +48 94 35 52 102, **Reservations** +48 801 003 171.

INTERNET **Email** info@polferries.pl **Website** www.polferries.pl *(Polish, Danish, English, German, Swedish)*

ROUTES OPERATED Swinoujscie - Ystad (7 hrs; BALTIVIA, MAZOVIA; 2 per day), Gdansk - Nynäshamn (Sweden) (18 hrs; WAWEL; 3 per week).

1	BALTIVIA	17790t	81	19.0k	146.9m	250P	30C	80L	BA	BS	7931997
2	MAZOVIA	25996t	96	21.0k	168.0m	200P	-	154T	BA2	BS	9010814
3	WAWEL	25318t	80	19.0k	163.9m	900P	550C	75L	A2	BS	7814462

BALTIVIA Built as the SAGA STAR by Fartygsentreprenader AB, Kalmar, Sweden for *TT-Saga-Line* and, from 1982, used on freight services between Travemünde and Trelleborg/Malmö. (Originally ordered by *Rederi AB Svea* as the SAGALAND). In 1989 sold to *Cie Meridionale* of France, renamed the GIROLATA and used on SNCM (later CMR) services in the Mediterranean. In 1993 she was chartered back to *TT-Line*, resumed her original name and was used on the Travemünde - Trelleborg service. Following delivery of the ROBIN HOOD and the NILS DACKE in 1995, she was transferred to the Rostock - Trelleborg route. In July 1997 she was purchased by *TT-Line* and in 1998 passenger facilities were completely renovated to full ro-pax format; following the delivery of the TOM SAWYER she was transferred back to the Travemünde - Trelleborg route, operating additional freight sailings. Briefly transferred back to Rostock - Trelleborg when the charter of the TT-TRAVELLER ended. Withdrawn in 2002, sold to *Transmanche Ferries* and renamed the DIEPPE. In 2006 replaced by the SEVEN SISTERS, sold to *Polferries*, renamed the BALTIVIA and, in 2007, placed on the Gdansk - Nynäshamn route. In February 2013 transferred to the Swinoujscie – Ystad service.

MAZOVIA Built as the GOTLAND by Pt Dok Kodja Bahri, Kodja, Indonesia for *Rederi AB Gotland* for charter. In 1997 briefly chartered to *Tor Line* and then to *Nordic Trucker Line*, to operate between Oxelösund and St Petersburg (a ro-ro freight service). In June 1997 she was chartered to *SeaWind Line*, enabling a twice-daily passenger service to be operated. In late 1997 she was sold to *Finnlines* and renamed the FINNARROW. She started operating twice weekly between Helsinki and Travemünde. During Summer 1998 she was transferred to *FinnLink*; a bow door was fitted and she was modified to allow for two-level loading. In 2003 transferred to *Nordö Link*. In 2005 returned to *FinnLink*. In 2006 transferred to *Finnlines Nordö Link* again. In 2007 chartered to *Stena Line* to operate between Karlskrona and Gdynia. In December 2011 transferred to the Hook of Holland - Killingholme route. In March 2011 returned to *Finnlines* and placed on the Travemünde - Malmö service. In October 2011 transferred to *FinnLink*. Between January and March 2013 chartered to *Stena Line* to cover Irish Sea routes during the refit period but withdrawn from service prematurely following an accident. In April 2013 chartered to *Grimaldi Line* of Italy for five years and renamed the EUROFERRY BRINDISI. In October 2014 sold to the *Grimaldi Group* of Italy. In November sold to *Polferries* and renamed the MAZOVIA. Entered service in June 2015 on the Swinoujscie - Ystad service.

WAWEL Built as the SCANDINAVIA by Kockums Varvet AB, Malmö, Sweden for *Rederi AB Nordö* of Sweden. After service in the Mediterranean for *UMEF*, she was, in 1981, sold to *SOMAT* of Bulgaria, renamed the TZAREVETZ and used on *Medlink* services between Bulgaria and the Middle East, later on other routes. In 1986 she was chartered to *Callitzis* of Greece for a service between Italy and Greece. In 1988 she was sold to *Sealink*, re-registered in The Bahamas and renamed the FIESTA. She was then chartered to *OT Africa Line*. During Autumn 1989 she was rebuilt at Bremerhaven to convert her for passenger use and in March 1990 she was renamed the FANTASIA and placed on the Dover - Calais service. Later in 1990 she was renamed the STENA FANTASIA. In 1998 transferred to *P&O Stena Line*. In 1999 she was renamed the P&OSL CANTERBURY. In 2002 renamed the PO CANTERBURY. In Spring 2003 replaced by the PRIDE OF CANTERBURY and laid up at Dunkerque. Later in the year sold to *GA Ferries* and renamed the ALKMINI A. In 2004 moved to Greece and, after a partial rebuild (including the welding up of the bow door) placed on the Igoumenitsa – Brindisi route. Later in 2004 sold to *Polferries* and renamed the WAWEL; rebuilt to increase the number of cabins. In 2005 placed on the Swinoujscie – Ystad service. In May 2015 transferred to the Gdansk - Nynäshamn route.

SAAREMAA LAEVAKOMPANII

THE COMPANY *Saaremaa Laevakompanii AS* is an Estonian shipping company, founded in 1992. Subsidiary company is *OÜ Väinamere Liinid*, founded in 2005. Brand name "Tuule Laevad" (meaning Wind Ships) brings together different ferry services and is a part of Tuule Grupp identity which was created in 2007.

MANAGEMENT General Director Tõnis Rihvk.

ADDRESS Kohtu 1, 93819 Kuressaare, Estonia.

TELEPHONE Administration + 372 452 4350, Reservations *from Estonia* + 372 14204, *from abroad* + 372 452 4444.

INTERNET Email *customer service* info@tuulelaevad.ee, *administration* slk@laevakompanii.ee *ElbLink* mail@Elb-Link.com Website www.tuulelaevad.ee *(Estonian, English)* elblink.com (German)

ROUTES OPERATED Vehicle Ferries Kuivastu - Virtsu (30 mins, *IONAS, REGULA*, up to 34 per day), Heltermaa (Hiiumaa) – Rohuküla (1 hr 30 mins; *HIIUMA, ST OLA*; up to 11 per day), Triigi – Sõru (1 hr 5 mins; *KÕRGELAID*; up to 8 per day), Summer Only Roomassaare – Ringsu (2 hrs 10 mins, *RUNÖ*,), Ringsu - Pärnu (3 hrs 10 mins, *RUNÖ*,), Munalaid – Ringsu (2 hrs 45 mins, *RUNÖ*). Elb-Link service: Cuxhaven - Brunsbüttel (across River Elbe, Germany) *(MUHUMAA, SAAREMAA)*. Note: The contract to operate the Kuivastu - Virtsu and Heltermaa (Hiiumaa) – Rohuküla services has been awarded to the *Port of Tallin* with effect from October 2016 and four new ferries are under construction.

1P	AEGNA	101t	79	18.0k	24.9 m	93P	0C	0L	-	EE	8874366
2	HARILAID	1028t	85	9.9k	49.9m	120P	35C	5L	BA	EE	8727367

3	HIIUMAA	5233t	11	15.0k	97.9m	600P	150C	20L	BA2	EE	9481805
4	IONAS	4296t	89	14.0k	95.0m	400P	85C	16L	BA	CY	8611659
5	KÖRGELAID	1028t	87	9.9k	49.9m	190P	35C	5L	BA	EE	8725577
6	MUHUMAA	5233t	10	15.0k	97.9m	600P	150C	12L	BA	EE	9474060
7	REGULA	3774t	71	14.5k	71.2m	580P	105C	20L	BA2	EE	7051058
8	RUNÖ	169t	12	20.0k-	23.9m	60P	2C	0L	A	EE	9643336
9	SAAREMAA	5900t	10	15.0k	97.9m	600P	150C	12L	BA	EE	9474072
10	ST OLA	4833t	71	14.50k	85.9m	480P	120C	14L	BA	EE	7109609

AEGNA Built as the RÅSA by Fjellstrand, Omastrand, Norway for Helgeland Trafikkselskap of Norway. In 2003 sold to Jan og Torleif Charter DA. In 2005 sold to Saaremaa Laevakompanii and renamed the AEGNA. Inaugurated a passenger-only service between Saaremaa and Ruhnu and Pärnu. This no longer operates and she is now laid up.

HARILAID, KÖRGELAID Built by Riga Shiprepair Yard, Riga, Latvia (USSR) for ESCO of Estonia. In 1994 transferred to Saaremaa Laevakompanii. The HARILAID is now a spare vessel.

HIIUMAA, MUHUMAA, SAAREMAA Built by Fiskerstrand Verft A/S, Aalesund, Norway for Saaremaa Laevakompanii. In summer 2015 the MUHUMAA and SAAREMAA were transferred to the new ElbLink service.

IONAS Built as the SUPERFLEX HOTEL by North East Shipbuilders Ltd, Sunderland, England for VR Shipping Aps of Denmark. Operated in the Öresund. In 1992 chartered to Scarlett Line of Sweden and in 1993 renamed the FREJA SCARLETT. In 1995 sold to ISNASA-Islena de Navegacion SA of Spain and renamed the MIGUEL HERNANDEZ. Operated on the Straits of Gilbraltar. In 2003 sold to Enermar Trasporti Isole Sarde SrL of Italy and renamed the BUDELLI. Operated between Palau and La Maddalena. In 2005 sold to RFI SpA of Italy and operated between Villa San Giovanni and Messina (Sicily). In April 2012 sold to Corfu Superflex I Ltd of the Marshall Islands and renamed the IONAS. In May 2014 chartered to Kerch Ferry State Shipping of Russia and operated on the Black Sea. In May 2015 chartered to Saaremaa Laevakompanii. Operates on the Kuivastu - Virtsu service.

REGULA Built by Jos L Meyer, Papenburg, Germany for Stockholms Rederi AB Svea of Sweden for the service between Helsingborg and Helsingør operated by Linjebuss International AB (a subsidiary company). In 1980 she was sold to Scandinavian Ferry Lines. During Winter 1984/85 she was rebuilt to increase vehicle and passenger capacity. In 1991 ownership was transferred to SweFerry and operations to ScandLines on the Helsingborg - Helsingør service. Ownership later transferred to Scandlines AB. In 1997 sold to Saaremaa Laevakompanii.

RUNÖ Built by Baltic Workboats AS, Nasva, Saaremaa, Estonia for the Government of Estonia. Chartered to Saaremaa Laevakompanii.

ST OLA Built as the SVEA SCARLETT for by Jos L Meyer, Papenburg, Germany Stockholms Rederi AB Svea of Sweden and used on the SL (Skandinavisk Linjetrafik) service between Copenhagen (Tuborg Havn) and Landskrona (Sweden). In 1980 she was sold to Scandinavian Ferry Lines of Sweden and Dampskibsselskabet Øresund A/S of Denmark (jointly owned). Initially she continued to serve Landskrona but later that year the Swedish terminal became Malmö. In 1981 she operated on the Helsingborg - Helsingør service for a short while, after which she was withdrawn and laid up. In 1982 she was sold to Eckerö Linjen of Finland, renamed the ECKERÖ and used on services between Grisslehamn (Sweden) and Eckerö (Åland Islands). In 1991 she was sold to P&O Scottish Ferries and renamed the ST OLA. In March 1992 she replaced the previous ST OLA (1345t, 1974) on the Scrabster - Stromness service. In September 2002 withdrawn and sold to Saaremaa Laevakompanii. In 2011 laid up. Re-entered service in summer 2015 on the Heltermaa – Rohuküla service.

SAMSØ REDERI

THE COMPANY Samsø Rederi is the trading name of Samsø Linien A/S, a Danish public sector company owned by the Samsø Municipality.

MANAGEMENT Managing Director Carsten Kruse.

ADDRESS Søtofte 10, 8305 Samsø, Denmark.

TELEPHONE Administration and Reservations + 45 7022 5900.

INTERNET Email tilsamsoe@samsoe.dk Website www.tilsamsoe.dk (Danish, German, English).

ROUTE OPERATED Sælvig (Samsø) - Hou (Jutland) (1 hr; PRINCESSE ISABELLA; up to 7 per day).

1	PRINSESSE ISABELLA	5478t	15	9.9k	100.0m	600P	160C	16T	BA	DK	9692806

PRINSESSE ISABELLA Built as the SAMSØ by Stocznia Remontowa, Gdansk, Poland. Entered service in March 2015. In June 2014 renamed the PRINSESSE ISABELLA.

SASSNITZ - UST LUGA FERRY

THE COMPANY The Sassnitz - Ust Luga Ferry is operated by Black Sea Ferry in partnership with Russian Railways and AnRuss Trans. Trans-Exim act as agents.

ADDRESS Trans-Exim, 45 Suvorova street, Kaliningrad, Russia.

TELEPHONE Administration + 7 (4012) 66 04 70, Reservations + 7 (4012) 66 04 73.

FAX Administration & Reservations + 7 (4012) 66 04 76.

INTERNET Email infotransexim.ru Website transexim.ru/en/ferry-schedule (English, Russian)

ROUTE OPERATED Ust Luga (Russia) - Baltiysk (Kaliningrad, Russia) - Sassnitz (Germany) (PETERSBURG; 1 per week).

1	PETERSBURG	25353t	86	16.0k	190.8m	144P	329C	110T	A2	RU	8311883

PETERSBURG Built Mathias Thesen Werft, Wismar, East Germany as the MUKRAN for DSR of Germany (DDR) to operate between Mukran (Sassnitz) and Klaipéda, a joint service with Lisco of Lithuania. In 1994 the service was taken over by Euroseabridge. In 1995 she was rebuilt to introduce road vehicle and additional passenger capacity and was renamed the PETERSBURG. In 2001 she was transferred to the Kiel - Klaipéda service, replacing the sister vessel GREIFSWALD whose charter was ended. In April 2003, the service became part of Scandlines and she was transferred to transferred to the Karlshamn - Liepaja (Latvia) route. In 2009, the charter ended and she returned to her owners. In October 2010 she was sold to Baltic Fleet LLC of Russia and the following month placed on a service between Baltiysk (Kaliningrad) and Ust Luga. In June 2012 she inaugurated a new service between Sassnitz and Ust Luga via Baltiysk.

SCANDLINES

THE COMPANY In 2007, the owners of Scandlines AG, the Danish Ministry of Transport and Energy and Deutsche Bahn AG, decided to sell their shares. The new owner was a consortium of the 3i Group (UK), Allianz Capital Partners GmbH (Germany) (40% of the shares each) and Deutsche Seereederei GmbH (Germany) (20% of the shares). The company was subsequently transformed into a private limited company and now trades under the name Scandlines GmbH, uniting the companies Scandlines Deutschland GmbH and Scandlines Danmark A/S. With Deutsche Seereederei GmbH selling its shares in Scandlines GmbH in 2010, 3i and Allianz Capital Partners held 50% of the shares each. During 2012 Stena Line took over the Travemünde - Ventspils, Travemünde - Liepaja and Nynäshamn - Ventspils routes, took full control of the joint routes - Rostock - Trelleborg and Sassnitz - Trelleborg services and took over the vessels used. The freight-only route between Rostock and Hanko passed to SOL. The Helsingborg - Helsingør service remains jointly operated and continues to be branded Scandlines. In November 2013 3i Group purchased Allianz Capital Partners' share and now control 100% of the company.

MANAGEMENT CEO Søren Poulsgaard Jensen, CCO Morten Haure-Petersen, Business Development Volker Schiemann.

ADDRESS Am Bahnhof 3a, 18119 Rostock, Germany.

TELEPHONE Administration & Reservations*Denmark* +45 33 15 15 15, *Germany* +49 (0)381-77 88 77 66.

FAX Administration *Germany* +49 (0)381-29 22 05 71.

INTERNET Email info@scandlines.com Website www.scandlines.com *(Danish, German, English),*

ROUTES OPERATED Rødby (Lolland, Denmark) - Puttgarden (Germany) (45 mins; *DEUTSCHLAND, HOLGER DANSKE, PRINS RICHARD, PRINSESSE BENEDIKTE, SCHLESWIG-HOLSTEIN (HOLGER DANSKE specially for dangerous goods);* half-hourly train/vehicle ferry + additional road freight-only sailings), Gedser (Falster, Denmark) - Rostock (Germany) (2 hours; *KRONPRINS FREDERIK, PRINS JOACHIM;* every 2 hours.

1	DEUTSCHLAND	15187t	97	18.5k	142.0m	1200P	364C	30Lr	BA2	DE	9151541
2F	HOLGER DANSKE	2779t	76	14.9k	86.8m	12P	-	12L	BA	DK	7432202
3	KRONPRINS FREDERIK	16071t	81	20.5k	152.0m	1082P	210C	46T	BA	DK	7803205
4	PRINS JOACHIM	16071t	80	21.0k	152.0m	922P	210c	46Lr	BA	DK	7803190
5	PRINS RICHARD	14822t	97	18.5k	142.0m	1100P	364C	36Lr	BA2	DK	9144419
6	PRINSESSE BENEDIKTE	14822t	97	18.5k	142.0m	1100P	364C	36Lr	BA2	DK	9144421
7	SCHLESWIG-HOLSTEIN	15187t	97	18.5k	142.0m	1200P	364C	30Lr	BA2	DE	9151539

DEUTSCHLAND Train/vehicle ferry built by Van der Giessen-de Noord, Krimpen aan den IJssel, Rotterdam, The Netherlands for *DFO* for the Puttgarden - Rødby service. During Winter 2003/04 a new hoistable deck was added for cars by Neptun Yard Rostock, (Germany).

HOLGER DANSKE Built by Aalborg Værft A/S, Aalborg, Denmark as a train/vehicle ferry for *DSB* for the Helsingør - Helsingborg service. In 1991 transferred to the Kalundborg - Samsø route (no rail facilities). In 1997 transferred to subsidiary *SFDS A/S*. Withdrawn at the end of November 1998 when the service passed to *Samsø Linien*. In 1999 began operating between Rødby and Puttgarden as a road-freight-only vessel, carrying, among others, loads which cannot be conveyed on passenger vessels.

KRONPRINS FREDERIK Train/vehicle ferry built by Nakskov Skibsværft A/S, Nakskov, Denmark for *DSB* for the Nyborg - Korsør service. Withdrawn in 1997. After conversion to a car/lorry ferry, she was transferred to the Gedser - Rostock route (no rail facilities).

PRINS JOACHIM Train/vehicle ferry, built by Nakskov Skibsværft A/S, Nakskov, Denmark for *DSB* for the Nyborg - Korsør service. Withdrawn in 1997 and laid up. During Winter 2000/2001 modified in the same way as KRONPRINS FREDERIK and transferred to the Gedser - Rostock route.

PRINS RICHARD, PRINSESSE BENEDIKTE Train/vehicle ferries, built by Ørskov Christensen Staalskibsværft A/S, Frederikshavn, Denmark for *Scandlines A/S* for the Rødby - Puttgarden service. During Winter 2003/04 a new hoistable deck was added for cars by Neptun Yard Rostock, (Germany).

SCHLESWIG-HOLSTEIN Train/vehicle ferry built by Van der Giessen-de Noord, Krimpen aan den IJssel, Rotterdam, The Netherlands for *DFO* for the Puttgarden - Rødby service. During Winter 2003/04 a new hoistable deck was added for cars by Neptun Yard Rostock, (Germany).

Under Construction

8	BERLIN	24000t	14	20.5k	169.0m	1500P	480C	96L	BA2	DK	9587855
9	COPENHAGEN	24000t	14	20.5k	169.0m	1500P	480C	96L	BA2	DK	9587867

BERLIN, COPENHAGEN Partly built by Volkswerft Stralsund, Stralsund, Germany for *Scandlines* to operate on the Gedser - Rostock route. The propulsion system allows for adaption to LNG. Originally due to enter service in Spring 2012, the construction of these vessels was seriously delayed. It was then found that the vessels did not meet the specification and the order was cancelled. The BERLIN

Kronprins Frederik (*John Bryant*)

Berlin (*Peter Therkildsen*)

was 90% finished and had undertaken sea trials; the COPENHAGEN had been launched and was 50% finished. In March 2014 *Scandlines* purchased the two vessels and they were towed to Blohm + Voss Shipyards, Hamburg and then to Fayard Shipyard, Odense to be completed and modified to make them suitable for the Gedser - Rostock route. The BERLIN is expected to enter service in September 2015 and the COPENHAGEN in December.

SCANDLINES HELSINGØR - HELSINGBORG

THE COMPANY *Scandlines Helsingør - Helsingborg* is a Swedish private sector company owned by First State Investments, a subsidiary of Commonwealth Bank of Australia. Previously a joint venture between *Scandlines* and *Stena Line*, it was acquired by First State Investments in January 2015. Although now a separate company, it currently operates as part of the *Scandlines* network.

TELEPHONE *Reservations* + 45 33 151515.

INTERNET Email info@scandlines.com **Website** www.scandlines.com *(Danish, German, English)*.

ROUTES OPERATED Helsingør (Sealand, Denmark) - Helsingborg (Sweden) (25 mins; *AURORA AF HELSINGBORG, MERCANDIA IV, MERCANDIA VIII, HAMLET, TYCHO BRAHE*; every 20 mins)

1	AURORA AF HELSINGBORG	10918t	92	14.0k	111.2m	1250P	225C	25Lr	BA	SE	9007128
2	HAMLET	10067t	97	13.5k	111.2m	1000P	244C	34L	BA	DK	9150030
3	MERCANDIA IV	4296t	89	13.0k	95.0m	420P	170C	18L	BA	DK	8611685
4	MERCANDIA VIII	4296t	87	13.0k	95.0m	420P	170C	18L	BA	DK	8611623
5	TYCHO BRAHE	11148t	91	14.5k	111.2m	1250P	240C	35Lr	BA	DK	9007116

AURORA AF HELSINGBORG Train/vehicle ferry built by Langsten Verft A/S, Tomrefjord, Norway for *SweFerry* for *ScandLines* joint *DSB/SweFerry* service between Helsingør and Helsingborg.

HAMLET Road vehicle ferry built by Finnyards, Rauma, Finland for *Scandlines* (50% owned by *Scandlines AG* and 50% owned by *Scandlines AB* of Sweden) for the Helsingør - Helsingborg service. Sister vessel of the TYCHO BRAHE but without rail tracks.

MERCANDIA IV Built as the SUPERFLEX NOVEMBER by North East Shipbuilders Ltd, Sunderland, UK for *Vognmandsruten* of Denmark. In 1989 sold to *Mercandia* and renamed the MERCANDIA IV. In 1990 she began operating on their *Kattegatbroen* Juelsminde - Kalundborg service. In 1996 she was transferred to their *Sundbroen* Helsingør - Helsingborg service. In 1997 the service and vessel were leased to *HH-Ferries*. In 1999 she was purchased by *HH-Ferries*. She has been equipped to carry dangerous cargo. Now owned by *Scandlines Helsingør - Helsingborg*.

MERCANDIA VIII Built as the SUPERFLEX BRAVO by North East Shipbuilders Ltd, Sunderland, UK for *Vognmandsruten* of Denmark and used on their services between Nyborg and Korsør and Copenhagen (Tuborg Havn) and Landskrona (Sweden). In 1991 she was chartered to *Scarlett Line* to operate on the Copenhagen and Landskrona route. In 1993 she was renamed the SVEA SCARLETT but later in the year the service ceased and she was laid up. In 1996 she was purchased by *Mercandia*, renamed the MERCANDIA VIII and placed on their *Sundbroen* Helsingør - Helsingborg service. In 1997 the service and vessel were leased to *HH-Ferries*. In 1999 she was purchased by *HH-Ferries*. Now owned by *Scandlines Helsingør - Helsingborg*. Now reserve vessel. Between April and July 2015 she operated between Puttgarden and Rødby for *Scandlines*, following damage sustained by the PRINSESSE BENEDIKTE at Gdansk during a refit.

TYCHO BRAHE Train/vehicle ferry, built by Tangen Verft A/S, Tomrefjord, Norway for *DSB* for the Helsingør - Helsingborg service.

SMYRIL LINE

THE COMPANY Smyril Line is a Faroe Islands company.

MANAGEMENT Adm. Director Mr. Rúni Vang Poulsen, Accounting and Department Manager, Ms Nina Djurhuus.

ADDRESS Yviri við Strond 1, PO Box 370, 110 Tórshavn, Faroe Islands.

TELEPHONE Administration & Reservations +298-345900.

FAX +298-345901.

INTERNET Email office@smyrilline.com Website www.smyrilline.com (English, French, Dutch German) www.smyrilline.fo (Danish, Faroese, Icelandic)

ROUTES OPERATED Winter/Early Spring Tórshavn (Faroes) - Hirtshals (Denmark) (36 hrs; NORRÖNA; 1 per week), Spring/Early Summer/Autumn Tórshavn - Hirtshals (36 hrs; NORRÖNA; 1 per week), Tórshavn - Seyðisfjördur (Iceland) (19 hrs; NORRÖNA; 1 per week), Summer Tórshavn - Hirtshals (Denmark) (30 hrs; NORRÖNA; 2 per week), Tórshavn - Seyðisfjördur (Iceland) (19 hrs; NORRÖNA; 2 per week).

1	NORRÖNA	35966t	03	21.0k	164.0m	1482P	800C	134T	BA	FO	9227390

NORRÖNA Built by Flender Werft, Lübeck, Germany for Smyril Line, to replace the existing NORRÖNA. Originally due to enter service in Summer 2002, start of building was delayed by financing difficulties. She was to have been built at Flensburger Schiffbau-Gesellschaft, Flensburg, Germany, but delays in arranging finance led to change of shipyard.

ST. PETER LINE

THE COMPANY St. Peter Line is a Russian owned, EU registered private sector company.

MANAGEMENT CEO Andrey Mushkarev.

ADDRESS Ostrovskogo sq. 7, St. Petersburg, 191025 Russia.

TELEPHONE Russia +7 812 386-11-47, Finland +358 (0)9 6187 2070.

INTERNET Email sales@stpeterline.com Website www.stpeterline.ru (Russian, English, Estonian, Finnish, Swedish)

ROUTES OPERATED Helsinki (Finland) - St Petersburg (Russia) (12 hours 30 mins; PRINCESS MARIA; 3/4 per week), St Petersburg - Helsinki - Stockholm - Tallinn - St Petersburg; SPL PRINCESS ANASTASIA; 1/2 per week).

1	PRINCESS MARIA	34093t	81	20.0k	168.1m	1638P	360C	54T	A	MT	7911533
2	SPL PRINCESS ANASTASIA	37583t	86	22.0k	177.0m	2500P	380C	42L	BA	MT	8414582

PRINCESS MARIA Built as the FINLANDIA by Oy Wärtsilä Ab, Turku, Finland for EFFOA of Finland for Silja Line services between Helsinki and Stockholm. In 1990 she was sold to DFDS, renamed the QUEEN OF SCANDINAVIA and introduced onto the Copenhagen - Helsingborg - Oslo service. In 2000 rebuilt at Gdynia. In 2001 transferred to the Newcastle - IJmuiden route. In May 2007 moved to the Newcastle - Norway route. This service ended at the end of August 2008 and she was laid up. In 2009 used for ten weeks as an accommodation vessel at Oskarshamn and in December in Copenhagen. In April 2010 time chartered to Inflot Cruise and Ferry Ltd of Russia for three years for use by St. Peter Line and renamed the PRINCESS MARIA.

SPL PRINCESS ANASTASIA Built as the OLYMPIA by Oy Wärtsilä Ab, Turku, Finland for Rederi AB Slite of Sweden for Viking Line service between Stockholm and Helsinki. In 1993 she was chartered to P&O European Ferries to inaugurate a new service between Portsmouth and Bilbao. Renamed the PRIDE OF BILBAO. During the summer period she also operated, at weekends, a round trip between Portsmouth and Cherbourg. In 1994 she was purchased by the Irish Continental Group and re-registered in the

Norröna *(Smyril Line)*

Princess Maria *(Miles Cowsill)*

Bahamas. In 2002 her charter was extended for a further five years and again for a further three years from October 2007. The Cherbourg service ended at the end of 2004. In September 2010 redelivered to *Irish Continental Group*. In October 2010 renamed the BILBAO. In November 2010 chartered to *St. Peter Line*, in February 2011 renamed the SPL PRINCESS ANASTASIA and in April 2011 inaugurated a new Stockholm - St Petersburg service. In February 2011 purchased by an associated company of *St. Peter Line*. During January and February 2014 she served as a floating hotel at the Winter Olympics in Sochi, Russia.

STENA LINE

THE COMPANY *Stena Line Scandinavia AB* is a Swedish private sector company. During 2012, the operations of subsidiary *Scandlines AB* of Sweden were absorbed and some of the Baltic operations and vessels of *Scandlines GmbH* of Germany were taken over.

MANAGEMENT CEO Carl-Johan Hagman, **Communication Director** Joakim Kenndal.

ADDRESS 405 19 Gothenburg, Sweden (*Visitors' address* Danmarksterminalen, Masthuggskajen, Gothenburg, Sweden).

TELEPHONE Administration + 46 (0)31-85 80 00, Reservations + 46 (0)770-57 57 00.

INTERNET Email info@stenaline.com Website www.stenaline.com (*Czech, Danish, Dutch, English, French, German, Latvian, Lithuanian, Norwegian, Polish, Russian, Swedish*)

ROUTES OPERATED *Stena Line branded routes* Conventional Ferries Gothenburg (Sweden) - Frederikshavn (Denmark) (3 hrs 15 mins; STENA DANICA, STENA JUTLANDICA; up to 6 per day), Gothenburg - Kiel (Germany) (14 hrs; STENA GERMANICA, STENA SCANDINAVICA; 1 per day), Frederikshavn - Oslo (Norway) (8 hrs 45 mins; STENA SAGA; 1 per day), Varberg (Sweden) - Grenaa (Denmark) (4 hrs; STENA NAUTICA; 2 per day), Karlskrona (Sweden) - Gdynia (Poland) (10 hrs 30 mins; STENA BALTICA, STENA SPIRIT, STENA VISION; 2/3 per day), Rostock (Germany) - Trelleborg (Sweden) (5 hrs 45 mins (7 hrs night); MECKLENBURG-VORPOMMERN, SKÅNE; 3 per day)), Sassnitz (Germany) - Trelleborg (3 hrs 45 mins; SASSNITZ, TRELLEBORG; 4-5 per day), Travemünde (Germany) - Ventspils (Latvia) (25 hrs; STENA FLAVIA; 2 per week), Travemünde (Germany) - Liepaja (Latvia) (28 hrs 30 mins; ASK, STENA FLAVIA, URD; 5 per week), Nynäshamn (Sweden) - Ventspils (Latvia) (12 hrs; SCOTTISH VIKING, STENA FLAVIA; 6 per week). Freight Ferry Gothenburg - Frederikshavn (Train Ferry) (3 hrs 45 mins; STENA SCANRAIL; 2 per day).

#	Name										
1	ASK	13144t	82	18.0k	171.0m	186P	-	104T	AS	DK	7826867
2	MECKLENBURG-VORPOMMERN	36185t	96	22.0k	199.9m	600P	445C	230Tr	A2	DE	9131797
3	SASSNITZ	21154t	89	18.5k	171.5m	875P	314C	50Tr	BA2	DE	8705383
4	SCOTTISH VIKING	26500t	09	24.0k	186.5m	800P	185C	120L	A	IT	9435454
5	SKÅNE	42705t	98	21.0k	200.2m	600P	520C	240Tr	AS2	SE	9133915
6	STENA BALTICA	22542t	07	23.0k	167.0m	160P	-	140L	BA2	UK	9364978
7»•	STENA CARISMA	8631t	97	40.0k	88.0m	900P	210C	-	A	SE	9127760
8	STENA DANICA	28727t	83	19.5k	154.9m	2274P	555C	120T	BAS2	SE	7907245
9	STENA FLAVIA	26904t	08	24.0k	186.5m	852P	185C	120L	A	UK	9417919
10	STENA GERMANICA	44372t	01	22.0k	240.1m	900P	-	250L	BA	SE	9145176
11	STENA JUTLANDICA	29691t	96	21.5k	183.7m	1500P	550C	156T	BAS2	SE	9125944
12	STENA NAUTICA	19504t	86	19.4k	134.0m	700P	330C	70T	BA2	SE	8317954
13	STENA SAGA	33750t	81	22.0k	166.1m	2000P	510C	76T	BA	SE	7911545
14	STENA SCANDINAVICA	55050t	03	22.0k	240.1m	900P	-	260L	BA	SE	9235517
15	STENA SCANRAIL	7504t	73	16.5k	142.4m	65P	-	64Tr	A	SE	7305772
16	STENA SPIRIT	39169t	88	20.0k	175.4m	2400P	550C	120T	BAS2	BS	7907661
17	STENA VISION	39178t	87	20.0k	175.4m	2400P	550C	120T	BAS2	SE	7907659
18	TRELLEBORG	20028t	82	21.0k	170.2m	900P	200C	90Tr	A2	SE	7925297
19	URD	13144t	81	17.5k	171.0m	186P	-	104T	AS	DK	7826855

Stena Danica *(Miles Cowsill)*

ASK Built as the LUCKY RIDER by Nuovi Cantieri Apuania S.P.A., Marina De Carrara, Italy, a ro-ro freight ferry, for *Delpa Maritime* of Greece. In 1985 she was acquired by *Stena Line* and renamed the STENA DRIVER. Later that year she was acquired by *Sealink British Ferries* and renamed the SEAFREIGHT FREEWAY to operate freight-only services between Dover and Dunkerque. In 1988 she was sold to *SOMAT* of Bulgaria for use on *Medlink* services in the Mediterranean and renamed the SERDICA. In 1990 she was sold and renamed the NORTHERN HUNTER. In 1991 she was sold to *Blæsbjerg* of Denmark, renamed the ARKA MARINE and chartered to *DSB*. She was then converted into a ro-pax vessel, renamed the ASK and introduced onto the Århus - Kalundborg service. Purchased by *Scandlines A/S* of Denmark in 1997. In 1999 she was, after some modification, transferred to *Scandlines Euroseabridge* and placed on the Travemünde - Klaipéda route. In 2000 she was transferred to the Rostock - Liepaja route. Lengthened by 20m in 2001 and, in late 2001, chartered to *Nordö Link* to operate between Travemünde and Malmö. In late 2002 replaced by the FINNARROW and returned to *Scandlines*. She was transferred to the Rostock - Trelleborg route whilst the MECKLENBURG-VORPOMMERN was being rebuilt. She was then transferred to the Kiel - Klaipéda route. In 2003 chartered to *Scandlines AB* to operate on the Trelleborg - Travemünde route. In April 2005 the charter ended and she returned to *Scandlines AG*. Initially she was due to replace the FELLOW on the Nynäshamn – Ventspils route during her annual refit. In Autumn 2005 moved to the Rostock - Ventspils route. In January 2009 moved to the Nynäshamn – Ventspils route. In January 2011 moved to the Travemünde - Liepaja route. In May 2011 laid up. In November introduced as second vessel. In September 2012 sold to *Stena Line*. In Autumn 2015 to move to the Gothenburg - Frederikshavn freight service.

MECKLENBURG-VORPOMMERN Train/vehicle ferry built by Schichau Seebeckwerft, Bremerhaven, Germany for *DFO* for the Rostock - Trelleborg service. During Winter 2002/03 modified to increase freight capacity and reduce passenger capacity. In September 2012 sold to *Stena Line*.

SASSNITZ Train/vehicle ferry built by Danyard A/S, Frederikshavn, Denmark for *Deutsche Reichsbahn*. In 1993 ownership transferred to *DFO*. Used on the Sassnitz - Trelleborg service. In September 2012 sold to *Stena Line*.

SCOTTISH VIKING Built by CN Visentini, Porto Viro, Italy for *Epic Shipping* of the UK and chartered to *Norfolkline*. Operated between Zeebrugge and Rosyth until December 2010. In January 2010 chartered to *Scandlines* and placed on the Nynäshamn - Ventspils service. In September 2012 charter transferred to *Stena Line*.

SKÅNE Train/vehicle ferry built by Astilleros Españoles, Cadiz, Spain for an American trust and chartered to *Scandlines*. She is used on the Trelleborg - Rostock service.

STENA BALTICA Built as the COTENTIN by STX Finland, Helsinki, Finland for *Brittany Ferries*. Used on freight service from Poole to Cherbourg and Santander. In March 2013 replaced by the BARFLEUR (operating to Cherbourg only). During summer 2013 operated twice weekly from Poole to Bilbao and Santander. In October 2013 sold to *Stena RoRo* and renamed the STENA BALTICA. In November 2013 chartered to *Stena Line* and replaced the STENA ALEGRA on the Karlskrona - Gdynia route.

STENA CARISMA Westamarin HSS 900 craft built at Kristiansand, Norway for *Stena Line* for the Gothenburg - Frederikshavn service. Work on a sister vessel, approximately 30% completed, was ceased. Not due to operate during 2014.

STENA DANICA Built by Chantiers du Nord et de la Méditerranée, Dunkerque, France for *Stena Line* for the Gothenburg - Frederikshavn service.

STENA FLAVIA Built by CN Visentini, Porto Viro, Italy for *Epic Shipping* of the UK. Launched as the WATLING STREET. On delivery, chartered to *ISCOMAR* of Spain and renamed the PILAR DEL MAR. In 2009 laid up until February 2010 when she was chartered to *Acciona Trasmediterranea* of Spain and operated between Barcelona and Tangiers. Later that month, chartered to *T-Link* and resumed the name WATLING STREET. In May 2011 chartered to *Scandlines* and placed on the Travemünde - Ventspils service. In April 2012, sold to *Stena RoRo*; she continued to be chartered to *Scandlines*. In September 2012 charter transferred to *Stena Line*. In April 2013 renamed the STENA FLAVIA. Now .operates one weekly roundtrip from Nynäshamn to Liepaja, two roundtrips to Nynäshamn to Ventspils and once weekly Ventspils - Travemünde.

Sassnitz *(John Bryant)*

Stena Nautica *(Matthew Punter)*

Mecklenburg Vorpommern *(Frank Lose)*

Stena Jutlandica *(Miles Cowsill)*

Stena Germanica (*Stena Line*)

Stena Carisma (*Miles Cowsill*)

STENA GERMANICA Ro-pax ferry built as the STENA HOLLANDICA by Astilleros Españoles, Cadiz, Spain for *Stena RoRo* and chartered to *Stena Line BV* to operate between Hook of Holland and Harwich. In 2007 lengthened by 50m at Lloyd Werft, Bremerhaven and passenger capacity increased to 900. Between May and August 2010 refurbished at Gdansk and had an 100 additional cabins added. At the end of August entered service on the Gothenburg - Kiel route, renamed the STENA GERMANICA III. In September, after the previous STENA GERMANICA had been renamed the STENA VISION, she was renamed the STENA GERMANICA.

STENA JUTLANDICA Train/vehicle 'ro-pax' vessel built by Van der Giessen-de Noord, Krimpen aan den IJssel, Rotterdam, The Netherlands for *Stena Line* to operate between Gothenburg and Frederikshavn. She was launched as the STENA JUTLANDICA III and renamed on entry into service.

STENA NAUTICA Built as the NIELS KLIM by Nakskov Skibsværft A/S, Nakskov, Denmark for *DSB (Danish State Railways)* for their service between Århus (Jutland) and Kalundborg (Sealand). In 1990 she was purchased by *Stena Rederi* of Sweden and renamed the STENA NAUTICA. In 1992 she was chartered to *B&I Line*, renamed the ISLE OF INNISFREE and introduced onto the Rosslare - Pembroke Dock service, replacing the MUNSTER (8093t, 1970). In 1993 she was transferred to the Dublin - Holyhead service. In early 1995 she was chartered to *Lion Ferry*. She was renamed the LION KING. In 1996 she was replaced by a new LION KING and renamed the STENA NAUTICA. During Summer 1996 she was chartered to *Transmediterranea* of Spain but returned to *Stena RoRo* in the autumn and remained laid up during 1997. In December 1997 she was chartered to *Stena Line* and placed on the Halmstad - Grenaa route. This route ended on 31st January 1999 and she was transferred to the Varberg - Grenaa route. During Winter 2001/02 she was rebuilt to heighten the upper vehicle deck and allow separate loading of vehicle decks; passenger capacity was reduced. On 16th February 2004 she was hit by the coaster JOANNA and holed. Returned to service at the end of May 2004 after repairs at Gothenburg and Gdansk.

STENA SAGA Built as the SILVIA REGINA by Oy Wärtsilä Ab, Turku, Finland for *Stockholms Rederi AB Svea* of Sweden. She was registered with subsidiary company *Svea Line* of Turku, Finland and was used on *Silja Line* services between Stockholm and Helsinki. In 1981 she was sold to *Johnson Line* and in 1984 sold to a Finnish Bank and chartered back. In 1990 she was purchased by *Stena RoRo* of Sweden for delivery in 1991. In 1991 she was renamed the STENA BRITANNICA and took up service on the Hook of Holland - Harwich service for Dutch subsidiary *Stena Line BV*, operating with a British crew. In 1994 she was transferred to the Oslo - Frederikshavn route and renamed the STENA SAGA. During Winter 2002/03 rebuilt to increase passenger capacity by 200.

STENA SCANDINAVICA Ro-pax vessel built by Hyundai Heavy Industries, Ulsan, South Korea, for *Stena RoRo*. Launched and delivered in January 2003 as the STENA BRITANNICA II. Chartered to *Stena Line* for use on the Hook of Holland - Harwich service, replacing the 2000-built STENA BRITANNICA, now the FINNFELLOW of *FinnLink*. In March 2003 renamed the STENA BRITANNICA. In 2007 lengthened at Lloyd Werft, Bremerhaven. In September 2010 renamed the BRITANNICA. Between October 2010 and April 2011 refurbished and had 100 additional cabins added at Gdansk. In April 2011 renamed the STENA SCANDINAVICA IV and entered service on the Gothenburg - Kiel route. In May, after the previous STENA SCANDINAVICA had been renamed the STENA SPIRIT, she was renamed the STENA SCANDINAVICA.

STENA SCANRAIL Built by Van der Giessen-de Noord, Krimpen aan den IJssel, Rotterdam, The Netherlands. Launched as the STENA SEATRADER for *Stena AB* and entered service as the SEATRADER. In 1976 she was lengthened and then demise-chartered to *Bahjah Navigation* of Cyprus and renamed the BAHJAN. In 1981 the charter ended and she was renamed the STENA SEARIDER. In 1983 chartered to *Snowdrop Shipping* of Cyprus and renamed the SEARIDER. The charter ended the following year and she resumed the name STENA SEARIDER. Later in 1984 she was renamed the TRUCKER and in 1985 again reverted to the name STENA SEARIDER. In 1987 she was converted to a train ferry to operate between Gothenburg and Frederikshavn, chartered to *Stena Line* and renamed the STENA SCANRAIL. To be withdrawn in Autumn 2015.

STENA SPIRIT Built as the STENA SCANDINAVICA by Stocznia i Komuni Paryski, Gdynia, Poland for *Stena Line* for the Gothenburg - Kiel service (launched as the STENA GERMANICA and names swapped with sister vessel before delivery). There were originally intended to be four vessels. Only two were delivered to *Stena Line*. The third (due to be called the STENA POLONICA) was sold by the

Ask (*John Bryant*)

SyltExpress (*Matthew Punter*)

builders as an unfinished hull to *Fred. Olsen Lines* of Norway and then resold to *ANEK* of Greece who had her completed at Perama and delivered as EL VENIZELOS for service between Greece and Italy. The fourth hull (due to be called the STENA BALTICA) was sold to *A Lelakis* of Greece and was to be rebuilt as a cruise ship to be called REGENT SKY; however, the project was never completed. The hull was broken up in 2004. During the summer period on some days, the vessel arriving in Gothenburg overnight from Kiel operates a round trip to Frederikshavn before departing for Kiel the following evening. During Winter 1998/99 she was modified to increase freight capacity and reduce the number of cabins. In April 2011 replaced by the former STENA BRITANNICA (renamed the STENA SCANDINAVICA IV) and entered CityVarvet in Gothenburg for refurbishment. In June 2011 she was renamed the STENA SPIRIT and, in July 2011, transferred to the Karlskrona - Gydnia route.

STENA VISION Built as the STENA GERMANICA by Stocznia im Lenina, Gdansk, Poland for *Stena Line* for the Gothenburg - Kiel service. During the summer period on some days, the vessel arriving in Gothenburg overnight from Kiel operates a round trip to Frederikshavn before departing for Kiel the following evening. During Winter 1998/99 modified to increase freight capacity and reduce the number of cabins. In August 2010 replaced by the former STENA HOLLANDICA (renamed the STENA GERMANICA III initially) and entered CityVarvet in Gothenburg for refurbishment. In September she was renamed the STENA VISION and, in November, transferred to the Karlskrona - Gydnia route.

TRELLEBORG Train/vehicle ferry built by Öresundsvarvet AB, Landskrona, Sweden for *Svelast* of Sweden (an SJ subsidiary). In 1990 ownership transferred to *SweFerry*. She is used on the Trelleborg - Sassnitz service.

URD Built as the EASY RIDER by Nouvi Cantieri Aquania SpA, Venice, Italy, a ro-ro freight ferry, for *Delpa Maritime* of Greece and used on Mediterranean services. In 1985 she was acquired by *Sealink British Ferries* and renamed the SEAFREIGHT HIGHWAY to operate a freight-only service between Dover and Dunkerque. In 1988 she was sold to *SOMAT* of Bulgaria for use on *Medlink* services in the Mediterranean and renamed the BOYANA. In 1990 she was sold to *Blæsbjerg* of Denmark, renamed the AKTIV MARINE and chartered to *DSB*. In 1991 she was converted into a ro-pax vessel, renamed the URD and introduced onto the Århus - Kalundborg service. Purchased by *Scandlines* in 1997. Withdrawn at the end of May 1999 and, after modification, transferred to the *Balticum Seaways* (later *Scandlines Balticum Seaways*) Århus - Aabenraa - Klaipėda route. In 2001 lengthened and moved to the Rostock - Liepaja route. In Autumn 2005 this route became Rostock - Ventspils. Withdrawn from Rostock - Ventspils in November 2009. Vessel inaugurated new service Travemünde - Ventspils in January 2010. Replaced by the WATLING STREET in May 2011 and moved to the Travemünde - Liepaja route. In October 2012 sold to *Sol Dru A/S* (a subsidiary of *Swedish Orient Line*) and chartered to *Stena Line*. In August 2013 sold to *Stena Line*.

STRANDFARASKIP LANDSINS

THE COMPANY *Strandfaraskip Landsins* is owned by the Faroe Islands Government.

ADDRESS Sjógøta 5, Postboks 30, 810 Tvøroyri, Faroe Islands.

TELEPHONE Administration & Reservations + 298 34 30 00.

FAX Administration & Reservations + 298 34 30 01.

INTERNET Email fyrisitingssl.fo Website www.ssl.fo *(Faroese)*

ROUTES OPERATED Passenger and Car Ferries Tórshavn (Streymoy) - Tvøroyri (Suduroy) (1 hr 50 mins; *SMYRIL*; up to 2 per day), Klaksvík - Syòradali (20 min; *SAM*; up to 6 per day), Skopun – Gamlarætt (30 mins; *TEISTIN*; up to 9 per day). Passenger-only Ferries Sørvágur - Mykines (1 hr 15 mins; *SILJA STAR/FROYUR (chartered ships)*; up to 3 per day), Hvannasund - Svínoy (40 mins) - Kirkja (20 mins) - Hatlarvik (10 mins) - Svínoy (30 mins; *RITAN*; up to 4 per day), Sandur - Skúvoy (35 mins; *SILDBERIN*; up to 5 per day), Tórshavn - Nólsoy (25 mins; *TERNAN*; up to 5 per day.

1p	RITAN	81t	71	10.5k	22.1m	125P	0C	0L	-	F0	
2	SAM	217t	75	9.7k	30.2m	115P	17C	-	A	F0	7602168
3p	SILDBERIN	34t	79	7.5k	11.2m	30P	0C	0L	-	F0	
4	SMYRIL	12670t	05	21.0k	135.0m	976P	200C	32L	A	F0	9275218

5p	SÚLAN	11t	87	-	12.0m	40P	0C	0L	-	FO	
6	TEISTIN	1260t	01	11.0k	45.0m	288P	33C	2L	BA	FO	9226102
7	TERNAN	927t	80	12.0k	39.7m	319P	0C	0L	BA	FO	7947154

RITAN Built by Monnickenda, Volendam, The Netherlands. Used on the Hvannasund – Svínoy-Kirkja- Hattarvik service.

SAM Built by Blaalid Slip & Mek Verksted, Raudeberg, Norway. Used on the Klaksvik - Syòradali route and the Leirvik - Syòradali route.

SILDBERIN Built at Tvøroyri, Faroe Islands. Used on the Sandur - Skúvoy route.

SMYRIL Built by IZAR, San Fernando, Spain for *Strandfaraskip Landsins*. Operates on the Tórshavn – Tvøroyri service.

SÚLAN Built by Faaborg Værft A/S, Faaborg, Denmark. Used on the Sørvágur - Mykines service.

TEISTIN Built by P/F Skipasmidjan a Skala, Skala, Faroe Islands for *Strandfaraskip Landsins*. Used on the Skopun – Gamlarætt service.

TERNAN Built by Tórshavnar Skipasmidja P/f, Tórshavn, Faroe Islands for *Strandfaraskip Landsins*. Used on the Tórshavn – Nólsoy service.

SYLTFÄHRE

THE COMPANY Syltfähre (*Syltfærge* in Danish) is the trading name of *Römö-Sylt Linie GmbH & Co. KG*, a German private sector company, a subsidiary of *FRS (Förde Reederei Seetouristik)* of Flensburg.

MANAGEMENT Managing Director Birte Dettmers, CEO Christian Baumberger, Götz Becker, Jan Kruse.

ADDRESS *Germany* Hafenstraße, 25992 List, Germany, *Denmark* Kilebryggen, 6792 Rømø, Denmark.

TELEPHONE Administration + 49 (0)461 864 0, Reservations + 49 (0)461 864 601.

INTERNET Email info@rsl.de Website www.syltfaehre.de *(Danish, English, German)*

ROUTE OPERATED List auf Sylt (Sylt, Germany) - Havneby (Rømø, Denmark) (approx. 40 mins; SYLTEXPRESS; variable - approx two-hourly). Note: The island of Rømø is linked to the Danish mainland by a toll-free road causeway; the island of Sylt is linked to the German mainland by a rail-only causeway on which cars are conveyed on shuttle wagons.

| 1 | SYLTEXPRESS | 3650t | 05 | 16.0k | 88.2m | 600P | 80C | 10L | BA | CY | 9321823 |

SYLTEXPRESS Built by Fiskerstrand Verft A/S, Aalesund, Norway for *Römö-Sylt Linie*.

TALLINK/SILJA LINE

THE COMPANY AS *Tallink Grupp* is an Estonian private sector company. *Tallink Silja Oy* is a Finnish subsidiary, *Tallink Silja AB* is a Swedish subsidiary.

MANAGEMENT AS *Tallink Grupp:* Chairman of Management Board Enn Pant, *Tallink Silja Oy* Managing Director Margus Schults, *Tallink Silja AB* Managing Director Kadri Land.

ADDRESSES AS *Tallink Grupp* Sadama 5/7, Tallinn 10111, Estonia, *Tallink Silja Oy* P.O. Box 100, 00181 Helsinki, Finland, *Tallink Silja AB* Box 27295, 10253 Stockholm, Sweden.

TELEPHONE AS *Tallink Grupp* + 372 (0)640 9800, *Tallink Silja Oy* Administration + 358 (0)9 18041, Reservations + 358 (0)600 15700, *Tallink Silja AB* Administration + 46 (0)8 6663300, Reservations + 46 (0)8 222140.

FAX AS *Tallink Grupp* Administration + 372 (0)640 9810, *Tallink Silja Oy* Administration + 358 (0)9 1804262, *Tallink Silja AB* Administration + 46 (0) 8 6638149.

INTERNETEmail info@tallink.ee Websites www.tallinksilja.com *(English, Danish, Estonian, Finnish, German, Latvia, Norwegian, Swedish, Russian)*, www.tallink.com (corporate site)

ROUTES OPERATED Tallink branded services *Passenger Ferries* Helsinki - Tallinn: *Shuttle* (2 hrs; *STAR, SUPERSTAR*; 5 per day), *Cruise Ferry* (3 hrs 30 mins; *BALTIC QUEEN*; 1 per day), Stockholm - Mariehamn (Åland) - Tallinn (14 hrs; *ROMANTIKA, VICTORIA I*; daily), Stockholm - Riga (Latvia) (16 hrs; *ISABELLE*; alternate days), *Freight-only Ferries* Kapellskär - Paldiski (9 hrs - 11 hrs; *REGAL STAR*, alternate days (round trip on Sunday)), Helsinki - Tallinn (3 hrs 30 mins; *SEA WIND*; 2 per day).

Silja Line branded services Helsinki (Finland) - Mariehamn (Åland) - Stockholm (Sweden) (16 hrs; *SILJA SERENADE, SILJA SYMPHONY*; 1 per day), Turku (Finland) - Mariehamn (Åland) (day)/Långnäs (Åland) (night) - Stockholm (11 hrs; *BALTIC PRINCESS, GALAXY*; 2 per day).

1	ATLANTIC VISION	30285t	02	27.9k	203.3m	728P	695C	110L	BA2	CA	9211509
2	BALTIC PRINCESS	48300t	08	24.5k	212.0m	2800P	300C	82T	BA	FI	9354284
3	BALTIC QUEEN	48300t	09	24.5k	212.0m	2800P	300C	82T	BA	EE	9443255
4	GALAXY	48915t	06	22.0k	212.0m	2800P	300C	82T	BA	SE	9333694
5	ISABELLE	35154t	89	21.5k	170.9m	2420P	364C	30T	BA	LV	8700723
6F	REGAL STAR	15281t	00	17.5k	156.6m	100P	-	120T	A	EE	9087116
7	ROMANTIKA	40803t	02	22.0k	193.8m	2178P	300C	82T	BA	EE	9237589
8F	SEA WIND	15879t	72	17.5k	154.4m	260P	55C	88Tr	BAS	EE	7128332
9	SILJA EUROPA	59912t	93	21.5k	201.8m	3000P	400C	68T	BA	EE	8919805
10	SILJA SERENADE	58376t	90	21.0k	203.0m	2641P	450C	70T	BA	FI	8715259
11	SILJA SYMPHONY	58377t	91	21.0k	203.0m	2641P	450C	70T	BA	SE	8803769
12	STAR	36249t	07	27.5k	185.0m	1900P	450C	120L	BA	EE	9364722
13	SUPERSTAR	36000t	08	29.0k	175.0m	1800P	600C	140T	BA	EE	9365398
14	VICTORIA I	40975t	04	22.0k	193.8m	2500P	300C	823T	BA	EE	9281281

ATLANTIC VISION Built as the SUPERFAST IX by Howaldtswerke Deutsche Werft AG, Kiel, Germany for *Attica Enterprises* for use by *Superfast Ferries*. She operated between Rostock and Södertälje from January until April 2002. In May 2002 she began operating between Rosyth and Zeebrugge (with the SUPERFAST X (now the STENA SUPERFAST X)). In 2004 fitted with additional cabins and conference/seating areas. In 2005 transferred to the Rostock – Hanko (later Helsinki) route. In 2006 sold to *Tallink*. In October 2008 chartered to *Marine Atlantic* of Canada to operate on the North Sydney-Port aux Basques service and renamed the ATLANTIC VISION.

BALTIC PRINCESS Built by Aker Yards, Helsinki. A large part of the hull was built at St Nazaire, France. In August 2008 replaced the GALAXY on the Tallinn - Helsinki route. In February 2013 transferred to the Stockholm - Turku service.

BALTIC QUEEN Built by STX Europe, Rauma, Finland. Operates between Helsinki and Tallinn.

GALAXY Built by Aker Yards, Rauma, Finland to operate as a cruise ferry on the Tallinn - Helsinki route. In July 2008 transferred to the Stockholm - Turku route and rebranded as a *Silja Line* vessel.

ISABELLE Built as the ISABELLA by Brodogradevna Industrija, Split, Yugoslavia for *SF Line*. Used on the *Viking Line* Stockholm - Naantali service until 1992 when she was switched to operating 24-hour cruises from Helsinki and in 1995 she was transferred to the Stockholm - Helsinki route. During 1996 she additionally operated day cruises to Muuga in Estonia during the 'layover' period in Helsinki. In 1997 she was transferred to the Stockholm - Turku route. in January 2013 she was replaced by the VIKING GRACE. After covering the AMORELLA during her refit period she was laid up. In April 2013 sold to *Hansa Link Limited*, a subsidiary of *AS Tallink Grupp* and renamed the ISABELLE. In May placed on the Stockholm - Riga service, replacing the SILJA FESTIVAL.

REGAL STAR Partly built by Sudostroitelnyy Zavod Severnaya Verf, St Petersburg. Work started in 1993 (as a deep-sea ro-ro) but was never completed. In 1999 the vessel was purchased, taken to Palumba SpA, Naples and completed as a short-sea ro-ro with accommodation for 80 drivers. In 2000 she was delivered to *MCL* of Italy and placed on a route between Savona and Catania. In September of that year she was chartered to *Grimaldi Ferries* and operated on a route Salerno – Palermo – Valencia. In late 2003 she was sold to *Hansatee Shipping* of Estonia and, in 2004, placed on the Kapellskär – Paldiski route, replacing the KAPELLA. From February 2006 she was transferred

Romantika (*Matthew Punter*)

Baltic Queen & Galaxy (*Matthew Punter*)

to the Helsinki – Tallinn service, replacing the KAPELLA due to the hard ice conditions. She continued in this service for the summer, but the returned to the Paldiski – Kapellskär service. In June 2010 moved to the *SeaWind Line* Stockholm – Turku service for the summer seasons and returned to the Kapellskär - Paldiski route in the autumn.

ROMANTIKA Built by Aker Finnyards, Rauma, Finland for *Tallink Grupp* to operate for *Tallink* between Tallinn and Helsinki. In Spring 2006 moved to the Tallinn - Stockholm route. In May 2009 transferred to the Stockholm - Riga route. In August 2014 moved to the Stockholm - Tallinn service.

SEA WIND Train/vehicle ferry built as the SVEALAND by Helsingørs Skipsværft, Helsingør, Denmark for *Stockholms Rederi AB Svea* and used on the *Trave Line* Helsingborg (Sweden) - Copenhagen (Tuborg Havn) - Travemünde freight service. In 1981 she was sold to *TT-Saga Line* and operated between Travemünde and Malmö. In 1984 she was rebuilt to increase capacity and renamed the SAGA WIND. In 1989 she was acquired by *SeaWind Line*, renamed the SEA WIND and inaugurated a combined rail freight, trailer and lower-priced passenger service between Stockholm and Turku. This route later became freight-only. In January 2015 transferred to the Tallinn - Helsinki freight service.

SILJA EUROPA Built by Jos L Meyer, Papenburg, Germany. Ordered by *Rederi AB Slite* of Sweden for *Viking Line* service between Stockholm and Helsinki and due to be called EUROPA. In 1993, shortly before delivery was due, *Rederi AB Slite* went into liquidation and the order was cancelled. A charter agreement with her builders was then signed by *Silja Line* and she was introduced onto the Stockholm - Helsinki route as SILJA EUROPA. In early 1995 she was transferred to the Stockholm - Turku service. In January 2013 she was transferred to the Helsinki - Tallinn route. In August 2014 chartered to Australia as an accommodation vessel.

SILJA SERENADE, SILJA SYMPHONY Built by Masa-Yards Oy, Turku, Finland for *Silja Line* for the Stockholm - Helsinki service. In 1993, SILJA SERENADE was transferred to the Stockholm - Turku service but in early 1995 she was transferred back to the Helsinki route.

STAR Built by Aker Yards, Helsinki, Finland for *Tallink* to operate as a normal ferry on the Tallinn - Helsinki route.

SUPERSTAR Built by Fincantieri-Cantieri Navali Italiani SpA, Riva Trigoso, Italy to operate on the Tallinn - Helsinki route..

VICTORIA I Built by Aker Finnyards, Rauma, Finland for *Tallink*. Operates between Tallinn and Stockholm.

Under Construction

15	NEWBUILDING	49000t	17	27.0k	212m	2800P	-	-	BA	EE	-

NEWBUILDING Under construction by Meyer Turku, Turku, Finland to operate on the Tallinn - Helsinki Shuttle. She will be LNG/diesel dual powered.

AS *Tallink Grupp* also own the STENA SUPERFAST VII and STENA SUPERFAST VIII, currently on charter to *Stena Line (UK)*.

TESO

THE COMPANY *TESO* is a Dutch private company, with most shares owned by inhabitants of Texel. Its full name is *Texels Eigen Stoomboot Onderneming*.

MANAGEMENT **Managing Director** C H S de Waal.

ADDRESS Pontweg 1, 1797 SN Den Hoorn, The Netherlands.

TELEPHONE **Administration** +31 (0)222 36 96 00, **Reservations** Not applicable.

FAX **Administration** +31 (0)222 36 96 59.

INTERNET **Email** info@teso.nl **Website** www.teso.nl *(Dutch, English, German)*

ROUTE OPERATED Den Helder (The Netherlands) - Texel (Dutch Frisian Islands) (20 minutes; *DOKTER WAGEMAKER, SCHULPENGAT*; hourly).

1	DOKTER WAGEMAKER	13256t	05	15.6k	130.0m	1750P	320C	44L	BA2 NL	9294070
2	SCHULPENGAT	8311t	90	13.6k	110.4m	1750P	156C	25L	BA2 NL	8802313

DOKTER WAGEMAKER Built at Galatz, Romania (hull and superstructure) and Royal Schelde, Vlissingen (fitting out) for *TESO*.

SCHULPENGAT Built by Verolme Scheepswerf Heusden BV, Heusden, The Netherlands for *TESO*.

Under Construction

3	TEXELSTROOM	-	16	15.0k	135.4m	1750P	350C	44L	BA2 NL	-

TEXELSTROOM Under construction by LaNaval Shipyard, Sestao, Spain to replace the SCHULPENGAT.

TT-LINE

THE COMPANY *TT-Line GmbH & Co KG* is a German private sector company.

MANAGEMENT **Managing Directors** Hanns Heinrich Conzen & Jens Aurel Scharner, **Sales Manager** Dirk Lifke.

ADDRESS Zum Hafenplatz 1, 23570, Travemünde, Germany.

TELEPHONE **Administration Tel** + 49 (0)4502 801 448, **Reservations** + 49 (0)4502 801 81.

FAX **Administration & Reservations** *Travemünde* + 49 (0)4502 801 407, *Rostock* + 49 (0)381 6707980.

INTERNET **Email** info@ttline.com **Website** www.ttline.com (*English, German, Swedish*)

ROUTES OPERATED *Passenger Ferries* Travemünde (Germany) - Trelleborg (Sweden) (8 hrs 30 mins/9 hrs 30 mins; *NILS HOLGERSSON, PETER PAN*; 2 per day). *Ro-pax Ferries* Travemünde (Germany) - Trelleborg (Sweden) (7 hrs 30 mins/8 hrs 15 mins; *ROBIN HOOD*; 1 per day), Rostock (Germany) - Trelleborg (Sweden) (5 hrs 30 mins/6 hrs 30 mins/7 hrs 30 mins; *HUCKLEBERRY FINN, TOM SAWYER*; 3 per day, Swinoujscie (Poland) - Trelleborg (Sweden) (7 hrs; *NILS DACKE*; 1 per day).

1	HUCKLEBERRY FINN	26391t	88	18.0k	177.2m	400P	280C	121T	BAS2 SE	8618358
2	NILS DACKE	26796t	95	18.5k	179.7m	300P	-	157T	BA CY	9087465
3	NILS HOLGERSSON	36468t	01	18.0k	190.8m	744P	-	171T	BAS2 DE	9217230
4	PETER PAN	36468t	01	18.0k	190.8m	744P	-	171T	BAS2 SE	9217242
5	ROBIN HOOD	26790t	95	18.5k	179.7m	317P	-	157T	BA DE	9087477
6	TOM SAWYER	26478t	89	18.0k	177.2m	400P	280C	121T	BAS2 DE	8703232

HUCKLEBERRY FINN Built as the NILS DACKE by Schichau Seebeckwerft AG, Bremerhaven, Germany, as a ro-pax vessel. During Summer 1993 rebuilt to transform her into a passenger/car ferry and renamed the PETER PAN, replacing a similarly named vessel (31356t, 1986). On arrival of the new PETER PAN in Autumn 2001 she was renamed the PETER PAN IV. She was then converted back to ro-pax format, renamed the HUCKLEBERRY FINN and, in early 2002, transferred to the Rostock -Trelleborg route.

NILS DACKE, Ro-pax vessels built as the ROBIN HOOD by Finnyards, Rauma, Finland. She operated on the Travemünde - Trelleborg and Travemünde - Helsingborg routes. In December 2014 she was renamed the NILS DACKE and transferred to Cypriot registry. Moved to the Trelleborg - Swinoujscie route.

NILS HOLGERSSON, PETER PAN Built by SSW Fähr und Spezialschiffbau GmbH, Bremerhaven, Germany for the Travemünde - Trelleborg route.

TOM SAWYER Built as the ROBIN HOOD by Schichau Seebeckwerft AG, Bremerhaven, Germany, as a ro-pax vessel. During Winter 1992/93 rebuilt to transform her into a passenger/car ferry and renamed the NILS HOLGERSSON, replacing a similarly named vessel (31395t, 1987) which had been

Nils Holgersson (*FotoFlite*)

Polonia (*John Bryant*)

sold to *Brittany Ferries* and renamed the VAL DE LOIRE. In 2001 converted back to ro-pax format and renamed the TOM SAWYER. Transferred to the Rostock - Trelleborg route.

ROBIN HOOD Ro-pax vessels built as the NILS DACKE, by Finnyards, Rauma, Finland. She operated on the Travemünde - Trelleborg and Travemünde - Helsingborg routes. In January 2014, she was transferred to a new Trelleborg - Swinoujscie service and changed to Polish registry. In December 2014 she was renamed the ROBIN HOOD and transferred German Registry. Moved to the Travemünde - Trelleborg route.

UNITY LINE

THE COMPANY *Unity Line* is a Polish company owned by *Polish Steamship Company (Polsteam)*. The operator manages seven ferries on two routes: Swinoujscie – Ystad and Swinoujscie – Trelleborg. Three ships are owned by *Euroafrica Shipping* which was previously a partner in the company; the ships continue to be operationally managed by to *Unity Line*.

MANAGEMENT Chairman of the Board Jarosław Kotarski.

ADDRESS Plac Rodła 8, 70-419 Szczecin, Poland.

TELEPHONE Administration& Reservations +48 (0)91 35 95 600.

FAX Administration +48 (0)91 35 95 885.

INTERNET Email promy@unityline.pl **Website** www.unityline.pl *(Polish, Swedish)*

ROUTES OPERATED Passenger Service Swinoujscie (Poland) - Ystad (Sweden) (6 hrs 30 mins (day), 9 hrs (night); *POLONIA, SKANIA*; 2 per day). **Freight Services** Swinoujscie (Poland) - Ystad (Sweden) (8 hrs (day), 9 hrs (night); *JAN SNIADECKI, KOPERNIK*; 2 per day), Swinoujscie (Poland) - Trelleborg (Sweden) (6 hrs 30 mins (day), 9 hrs (night); *GALILEUSZ, GRYF, WOLIN*; 3 per day).

1F+	GALILEUSZ	15848t	92	17.0k	150.4m	160P	-	115L	A	CY	9019078
2F+	GRYF	18653t	90	16.0k	158.0m	180P	-	125L	BA	BS	8818300
3F+	JAN SNIADECKI	14417t	88	17.0k	155.1m	57P	-	70Lr	SA2	CY	8604711
4F+	KOPERNIK	13788t	77	18.0k	160.1m	360P	-	60Lr	SA2	CY	7527887
5	POLONIA	29875t	95	17.2k	169.9m	920P	440C	145Lr	SA2	BS	9108350
6	SKANIA	23933t	95	22.5k	173.7m	1400P	430C	140L	BA	BS	9086588
7F+	WOLIN	22874t	86	17.5k	188.9m	370P	-	110Lr	SA	BS	8420842

GALILEUSZ Built as the VIA TIRRENO by Van der Giessen-de Noord, Krimpen aan den IJssel, The Netherlands for *Viamare di Navigazione SpA* of Italy. Initially operated between Voltri and Termini Imerese. In 1998 transferred to the Genoa - Termini Imerese route and in 2001 to the Genoa - Palermo route. In 2006 sold to *Euroafrica Shipping*, renamed the GALILEUSZ and in November introduced onto the *Unity Line* Swinoujscie - Ystad service. In February 2007 transferred to the new Swinoujscie - Trelleborg route.

GRYF Built as the KAPTAN BURHANETTIN ISIM by Fosen Mekaniske Verksteder, Fevag, Norway for *Turkish Cargo Lines* of Turkey to operate between Trieste (Italy) and Derince (Turkey). In 2002 chartered to *Latlines* to operate between Lübeck and Riga (Latvia). In 2003 chartered to *VentLines* to inaugurate a new service between Travemünde and Ventspils. In 2004 sold to *Polsteam*, managed by *Unity Line* and renamed the GRYF. Entered service in 2005. In February 2007 transferred to the new Swinoujscie - Trelleborg route.

JAN SNIADECKI Built by Falkenbergs Varv AB, Falkenberg, Sweden for *Polish Ocean Lines* to operate between Swinoujscie and Ystad. Now operates for *Unity Line* on this route.

KOPERNIK Train/vehicle ferry built as the ROSTOCK by Bergens Mekaniske Verksted A/S, Bergen, Norway for *Deutsche Reichsbahn* of Germany (DDR). Used on freight services between Trelleborg and Sassnitz. In 1992 modified to increase passenger capacity in order to run in passenger service. In 1993 ownership transferred to DFO and in 1994 she opened a new service from Rostock to Trelleborg. In 1997 she was used when winds precluded the use of the new MECKLENBURG-VORPOMMERN. Following modifications to this vessel in late 1997, the ROSTOCK continued to operate to provide additional capacity until the delivery of the SKÅNE of Scandlines AB, after which she was laid up. In 1999 she was sold to SeaWind Line, renamed the STAR WIND and operated in freight-only mode between Stockholm and Turku. Initial plans to bring her passenger accommodation up to the standards required for Baltic night service were dropped. In October 2002 replaced by the SKY WIND and transferred to the Helsinki - Tallinn route. She carried a limited number of ordinary passengers on some sailings. In May 2005 returned to the Stockholm - Turku service, no longer carrying ordinary passengers, but was laid up after a few weeks. In October sold to Euro Shipping OÜ of Estonia, a company linked to Saaremaa Laevakompanii, and renamed the VIRONIA. In 2006 inaugurated a new service between Sillamäe (Estonia) and Kotka (Finland). In 2007 sold to Euroafrica Shipping, renamed the KOPERNIK and, in April 2008, placed on the Swinoujscie - Ystad route, replacing the MIKOLAJ KOPERNIK.

POLONIA Train/vehicle ferry built by Langsten Slip & Båtbyggeri A/S, Tomrefjord, Norway for Polonia Line Ltd and managed by Unity Line.

SKANIA Built as the SUPERFAST I by Schichau Seebeckwerft, Bremerhaven, Germany for Superfast Ferries of Greece. Operated between Patras and Ancona (Italy). In 1998 transferred to the Patras - Igoumenitsa (Greece) - Bari (Italy) route. In 2004 sold to a subsidiary of Grimaldi Lines, renamed the EUROSTAR ROMA and placed on the Civitavecchia (Italy) - Barcelona (Spain) service. In 2008 sold to Polsteam and renamed the SKANIA. After modifications, she was placed on the Unity Line Swinoujscie - Ystad service as second passenger vessel. In the peak summer period in 2010 operated a round trip between Ystad and Rønne for Bornholmstrafikken.

WOLIN Train/vehicle ferry built as the ÖRESUND by Moss Rosenberg Værft, Moss, Norway for Statens Järnvägar (Swedish State Railways) for the 'DanLink' service between Helsingborg and Copenhagen. Has 817 metres of rail track. Service ceased in July 2000 and vessel laid up. In 2001 sold to Sea Containers Ferries and in 2002 converted at Gdansk, Poland to a passenger ferry. She was chartered to SeaWind Line, renamed the SKY WIND and in Autumn 2002 replaced the STAR WIND on the Stockholm - Turku service. In 2007 sold to Polsteam, renamed the WOLIN and placed on the Unity Line Swinoujscie - Trelleborg service.

VIKING LINE

THE COMPANY Viking Line Abp is a Finnish company Listed on the Helsinki Stock Exchange since 1995.

MANAGEMENT President & CEO Jan Hanses, Executive Vice President/Deputy CEO and Chief Financial Officer at Viking Line Abp Andreas Remmer.

ADDRESS Norragatan 4, 22100 Mariehamn, Åland.

TELEPHONE Administration +358 (0)18 27000, Reservations +358 (0)9 1235300.

FAX Administration +358 (0)18 16944.

INTERNET Email international.sales@vikingline.com Websites www.vikingline.fi (Finnish, English, Swedish) www.vikingline.ee (Estonian) www.vikingline.de (German)

ROUTES OPERATED Stockholm (Sweden) - Mariehamn (Åland) - Helsinki (Finland) (14 hrs; GABRIELLA, MARIELLA; 1 per day), Stockholm - Mariehamn (day)/Långnäs (Åland) (night) - Turku (Finland) (9 hrs 10 mins; AMORELLA, VIKING GRACE; 2 per day), Kapellskär (Sweden) - Mariehamn (Åland) (2 hrs 15 mins; ROSELLA; up to 3 per day), Helsinki - Tallinn (2 hrs 30 mins; GABRIELLA, MARIELLA, VIKING XPRS, 3 per day), Cruises from Stockholm to Mariehamn (21 hrs - 24 hrs round trip (most 22 hrs 30 mins); VIKING CINDERELLA; 1 per day).

1	AMORELLA	34384t	88	21.5k	169.4m	2450P	450C	53T	BA	FI	8601915
2	GABRIELLA	35492t	92	21.5k	171.2m	2420P	400C	50T	BA	FI	8917601
3	MARIELLA	37799t	85	22.0k	176.9m	2500P	400C	60T	BA	FI	8320573
4	ROSELLA	16850t	80	21.3k	136.0m	1700P	340C	40T	BA	AL	7901265
5	VIKING CINDERELLA	46398t	89	21.5k	191.0m	2500P	100C	-	BA	SE	8719188
6	VIKING GRACE	57000t	13	23.0k	214.0m	2800P	556C	90L	BA	FI	9606900

Viking Grace *(Matthew Punter)*

Viking Cinderella *(Matthew Punter)*

Amorella *(Miles Cowsill)*

| 7 | VIKING XPRS | 34000t | 08 | 25.0k | 185.0m | 2500P | 250C | 60L | BA | EE | 9375654 |

AMORELLA Built by Brodogradevna Industrija, Split, Yugoslavia for *SF Line* for the Stockholm - Mariehamn - Turku service.

GABRIELLA Built as the FRANS SUELL by Brodogradiliste Industrija, Split, Croatia for *Sea-Link AB* of Sweden to operate for subsidiary company *Euroway AB*, who established a service between Lübeck, Travemünde and Malmö. In 1994 this service ceased and she was chartered to *Silja Line*, renamed the SILJA SCANDINAVIA and transferred to the Stockholm - Turku service. In 1997 she was sold to *Viking Line* to operate between Stockholm and Helsinki. She was renamed the GABRIELLA. In 2014, a daytime sailing during summer from Helsinki to Tallinn was introduced.

MARIELLA Built by Oy Wärtsilä Ab, Turku, Finland for *SF Line*. Used on the Stockholm - Helsinki service. During 1996 additionally operated short cruises to Muuga in Estonia during the 'layover' period in Helsinki. In 2014, a daytime sailing during summer from Helsinki to Tallinn was introduced.

ROSELLA Built by Oy Wärtsilä Ab, Turku, Finland for *SF Line*. Used mainly on the Stockholm - Turku and Kapellskär - Naantali services until 1997. From 1997 operated 21 to 24-hour cruises from Stockholm to Mariehamn under the marketing name 'The Dancing Queen', except in the peak summer period when she operated between Kapellskär and Turku. In Autumn 2003 transferred to a new twice-daily Helsinki - Tallinn ferry service. In May 2008 placed on the Mariehamn - Kapellskär route under the Swedish flag. In 2011 she was extensively rebuilt at Balti Laevaremondi Tehas in Tallinn, Estonia. Cabin capacity was lowered from 1184 to 418 and the restaurant and shop areas were increased. In January 2014 placed under the Finnish flag.

VIKING CINDERELLA Built as the CINDERELLA by Wärtsilä Marine Ab, Turku, Finland for *SF Line*. Until 1993 provided additional capacity between Stockholm and Helsinki and undertook weekend cruises from Helsinki. In 1993 she replaced the OLYMPIA (a sister vessel of the MARIELLA) as the main Stockholm - Helsinki vessel after the OLYMPIA had been chartered to *P&O European Ferries* and renamed the PRIDE OF BILBAO. In 1995 switched to operating 20-hour cruises from Helsinki to Estonia in the off peak and the Stockholm - Mariehamn - Turku service during the peak summer period (end of May to end of August). From 1997 she remained cruising throughout the year. In Autumn 2003 she was transferred to the Swedish flag, renamed the VIKING CINDERELLA and transferred to Stockholm - Mariehamn cruises. She operates these cruises all year round.

VIKING GRACE Built by STX Europe, Turku, Finland. She operates between Stockholm and Turku. She is powered by LNG. Entered service in January 2013.

VIKING XPRS Built by Aker Yards, Helsinki to operate between Helsinki and Tallinn. In January 2014 placed under the Estonian flag.

WAGENBORG PASSAGIERSDIENSTEN

THE COMPANY *Wagenborg Passagiersdiensten BV* is a Dutch private sector company.

MANAGEMENT **Managing Director** G van Langen.

ADDRESS Postbus 70, 9163 ZM Nes, Ameland, The Netherlands.

TELEPHONE Administration & Reservations *International* +31 85 4011008, *Netherlands* 0900 9238.

FAX Administration & Reservations +31 (0)519 542905.

INTERNET Email info@wpd.nl Website www.wpd.nl *(Dutch, English, German)*

ROUTES OPERATED *Car Ferries* Holwerd (The Netherlands) - Ameland (Frisian Islands) (45 minutes; *OERD, SIER*; up to 14 per day), Lauwersoog (The Netherlands) - Schiermonnikoog (Frisian Islands) (45 minutes; *MONNIK, ROTTUM*; up to 6 per day).

1	MONNIK	1121t	85	12.2k	58.0m	1000P	46C	9L	BA	NL	8408961
2	OERD	2286t	03	11.2k	73.2m	1200P	72C	22L	BA	NL	9269673
3	ROTTUM	1121t	85	12.2k	58.0m	1000P	46C	9L	BA	NL	8408959

4	SIER		2286t	95	11.2k	73.2m	1200P	72C	22L	BA	NL	9075761

MONNIK Built by Scheepswerf Hoogezand, Hoogezand, The Netherlands for *Wagenborg Passagiersdiensten BV* as the OERD. In 2003, on delivery of the new OERD, she was renamed the MONNIK. Used on the Lauwersoog - Schiermonnikoog route.

OERD Built by Scheepswerf Bijlsma Lemmer, Lemmer, The Netherlands for *Wagenborg Passagiersdiensten BV.* Used on the Ameland - Holwerd route.

ROTTUM Built as the SIER by Scheepswerf Hoogezand, Hoogezand, The Netherlands for *Wagenborg Passagiersdiensten BV* and used on the Holwerd - Ameland route. In 1995 renamed the ROTTUM and transferred to the Lauwersoog - Schiermonnikoog route.

SIER Built by Shipyard Bijlsma, Wartena, The Netherlands for *Wagenborg Passagiersdiensten BV.* Used on the Ameland - Holwerd route.

WASALINE

THE COMPANY *Wasaline* is the trading name of *NLC Ferry Oy Ab,* a Finnish company, jointly owned by the cities of Vaasa and Umeå.

MANAGEMENT Chief Executive

ADDRESS *Finland* Skeppsredaregatan 3, 65170 Vasa, Finland *Sweden* Blå Vägen 4, 91322 Holmsund, Sweden.

TELEPHONE Administration & Reservations *Finland* + 358 (0)207 716 810, *Sweden* + 46 (0)90 185 200.

FAX Administration & Reservations

INTERNET *Email* info@wasaline.com *Website* www.wasaline.com *(English, Finnish, Swedish)*

ROUTE OPERATED Vaasa (Finland) - Umeå (Sweden) (4 hrs; *WASA EXPRESS*; 1/2 per day).

1	WASA EXPRESS	17053t	81	17.0k	140.8m	1100P	450C	84T	BAS2 FI	8000226

WASA EXPRESS Built by Oy Wärtsilä AB, Helsinki, Finland as the TRAVEMÜNDE for *Gedser-Travemünde Ruten* of Denmark for their service between Gedser (Denmark) and Travemünde (Germany). In 1986 the company's trading name was changed to *GT Linien* and in 1987, following the takeover by *Sea-Link AB* of Sweden, it was further changed to *GT Link.* The vessel's name was changed to the TRAVEMÜNDE LINK. In 1988 she was purchased by *Rederi AB Gotland* of Sweden, although remaining in service with *GT Link.* Later in 1988 she was chartered to *Sally Ferries* and entered service in December on the Ramsgate - Dunkerque service. She was renamed the SALLY STAR. In 1997 she was transferred to *Silja Line,* to operate between Vaasa and Umeå during the summer period, and operated under the marketing name WASA EXPRESS (although not renamed). She returned to *Rederi AB Gotland* in Autumn 1997, was renamed the THJELVAR and entered service with *Destination Gotland* in January 1998. Withdrawn and laid up in December 2003. In 2004 chartered to *Color Line* to inaugurate a new service between Larvik and Hirtshals. Renamed the COLOR TRAVELLER. Operated in reduced passenger mode on this service but in summer peak period operated between Frederikshavn and Larvik in full passenger mode. In December 2006 returned to *Rederi AB Gotland.* In 2007 renamed the THJELVAR, chartered to *Scandlines* and placed on the Gedser - Rostock route. Renamed the ROSTOCK. In Autumn 2008 withdrawn and laid up. In June 2009 sub-chartered to *Comarit* of Morocco for two months. In September she resumed the name THJELVAR. In August 2008 she was chartered to *Fred. Olsen SA* of Spain, renamed the BETANCURIA and placed on the Las Palmas - Puerto del Rosario - Arrecife service. In September 2012 laid up. In October 2012 purchased by *NLC Ferry Oy Ab* and, in November, renamed the WASA EXPRESS. Entered service in January 2013.

Viking Grace (*Matthew Punter*)

SECTION 7 - OTHER VESSELS

The following passenger vessels are, at the time of going to print, not operating and are owned by companies which do not currently operate services or are used on freight -only services. They are therefore available for possible re-deployment, either in the area covered by this book or elsewhere. Passenger vessels operating freight-only services outside the scope of this book are also included here. Exceptionally we have included two freight-only vessels possibly to be chartered to an operator serving the UK. Withdrawn vessels not yet disposed of and owned by operating companies are shown under the appropriate company and marked '•'.

Rederi AB Gotland

1	GUTE	7616t	79	15.0k	138.8m	88P	-	60T	BA	SE	7802794

GUTE Built as the GUTE by Falkenbergs Varv AB, Falkenberg, Sweden for *Rederi AB Gotland* of Sweden. Used on service between Gotland and the Swedish mainland. In 1988 chartered to *Brambles Shipping* of Australia and used between Port Melbourne (Victoria) and Burnie (Tasmania). In 1992 she was renamed the SALLY SUN and chartered to *Sally Ferries*, operating between Ramsgate and Dunkerque. In 1994 she inaugurated a Ramsgate - Vlissingen service, which was later changed to Dartford - Vlissingen. In 1995 she was chartered to *SeaWind Line*, renamed the SEAWIND II and operated between Stockholm and Turku. In 1997 she was chartered to *Nordic Trucker Line* for the Oxelösund - St Petersburg service and in 1998 she returned to *SeaWind Line*. In 1998, after *Rederi AB Gotland*-owned *Destination Gotland* regained the franchise to operate to Gotland, she was renamed the GUTE and resumed her summer role of providing summer freight back-up to the passenger vessels, but with a number of short charters during the winter. In Autumn 2002 chartered to *Amber Lines* for the Karlshamn - Liepaja service. In February 2003 chartered to *NATO* for the Iraq crisis. Returned to *Destination Gotland* in Summer 2003. In Autumn 2003 chartered to *Scandlines Amber Lines* to operate between Karlshamn and Liepaja. In 2004 lengthened by 20.3m by Nauta Shiprepair, Gdynia, Poland. In Autumn 2004 chartered to *Riga Sea Line* to inaugurate a freight service between Riga and Nynäshamn. In Autumn 2005 the service ended and the vessel was laid up. In January 2006 chartered to *Lisco* and placed on the Klaipéda - Karlshamn route, also undertaking two trips from Klaipéda to Baltiysk. In May 2006 chartered to *SeaWind Line*. In March 2007 chartered to *Baltic Scandinavian Line*. Charter ended September 2007. Apart from a trip to Cameroon, conveying Swedish UN Troops for Chad, she remained laid up until October 2008 when she was chartered to *Baltic Scandinavian Line* to operate between Härnösand and Kaskinen. In 2009 this service closed and she was laid up. At the end of March 2015 she was chartered to *Færgen* to operate between Køge and Rønne covering for the HAMMERODDE. She returned to layup in May.

Sea Containers

1»	THE PRINCESS ANNE	-	69	50.0k	56.4m	360P	55C	-	BA	UK	-
2»	THE PRINCESS MARGARET	-	68	50.0k	56.4m	360P	55C	-	BA	UK	-

THE PRINCESS ANNE, THE PRINCESS MARGARET British Hovercraft Corporation SRN4 type hovercraft built at Cowes, UK for *Seaspeed*. Built to Mark I specification. In 1978/1979 respectively lengthened to Mark III specification. They underwent complete refurbishment at the beginning of 1999. Withdrawn in 2000 and laid up at the Hovercraft Museum at Lee-on-Solent.

8 - SISTERS - A LIST OF SISTER (OR NEAR SISTER) VESSELS IN THIS BOOK

The following vessels are sisters or near sisters. This refers to 'as built' condition; some ships will subsequently have been modified and become different from their sister vessels.

AMORELLA (Viking Line), ISABELLE (Tallink Silja Line), GABRIELLA (Viking Line), CROWN OF SCANDINAVIA (DFDS Seaways).
ARGYLE, BUTE (Caledonian MacBrayne).
ASK, URD (Stena Line).
ATLANTIC VISION (Tallink), STENA SUPERFAST VII, STENA SUPERFAST VIII, STENA SUPERFAST X (Stena Line).
AURORA AF HELSINGBORG, HAMLET (Stena Line), TYCHO BRAHE (Scandlines).
BALTIC QUEEN, BALTIC PRINCESS, GALAXY (Tallink Silja Line).
BASTØ I, BASTØ II (Bastø Fosen).
BEN-MY-CHREE (Isle of Man Steam Packet Company), COMMODORE CLIPPER (Condor Ferries), HAMMERODDE (Bornholmstrafikken) (Near sisters).
BERGENSFJORD, STAVANGERFJORD (Fjord Line).
BERLIN, COPENHAGEN (Scandlines).
BERLIOZ, RODIN (MyFerryLink).
CANNA (Rathlin Island Ferry Ltd), CLEW BAY QUEEN (Clare Island Ferry Company), COLL (Arranmore Island Ferries), EIGG (Caledonian MacBrayne), MORVERN (Arranmore Fast Ferries), RAASAY (Caledonian MacBrayne), RHUM (Arranmore Island Ferries).
CARRIGALOE, GLENBROOK (Cross River Ferries).
COLOR FANTASY, COLOR MAGIC (Color Line).
COLOR VIKING (Color Line), STENA NAUTICA (Stena Line).
COTE D'ALBATRE, SEVEN SISTERS (DFDS Seaways).
DAGALIEN, DAGGRI (Shetland Islands Council).
DELFT SEAWAYS, DOVER SEAWAYS, DUNKERQUE SEAWAYS (DFDS Seaways).
DEUTSCHLAND, SCHLESWIG-HOLSTEIN (Scandlines).
EARL SIGURD, EARL THORFINN (Orkney Ferries).
ECKERÖ (Eckerö Linjen), POVL ANKER (Bornholmstrafikken).
ERNEST BEVIN, JAMES NEWMAN, JOHN BURNS (Woolwich Free Ferry).
EPSILON (Irish Ferries), ETRETAT (Brittany Ferries), SCOTTISH VIKING, STENA HORIZON, STENA LAGAN, STENA MERSEY, STENA FLAVIA (Stena Line).
EUROPEAN CAUSEWAY, EUROPEAN HIGHLANDER (P&O Ferries).
FENJA, MENJA (Færgen).
FINNCLIPPER, FINNEAGLE, FINNFELLOW (Finnlines), STENA GERMANICA (Stena Line).
FINNLADY, FINNMAID, FINNSTAR, NORDLINK (Finnlines).
FINNPARTNER, FINNTRADER (Finnlines).
FRISIA I, FRISIA V (Reederei Norden-Frisia).
GOTLAND, VISBY (Destination Gotland).
HALLAIG, LOCHINVAR (Caledonian MacBrayne)
HARILAID, KÖRGELAID (Saaremaa Laevakompanii).
HIIUMA, MUHUMAA, SAAREMAA (Saaremaa Laevakompanii).
HJALTLAND, HROSSEY (NorthLink Ferries).
HUCKLEBERRY FINN, TOM SAWYER (TT-Line).
KAUNAS SEAWAYS (DFDS Seaways), VILNIUS SEAWAYS (DFDS Seaways).
KING SEAWAYS, PRINCESS SEAWAYS (DFDS Seaways).
KONG HARALD, NORDLYS, RICHARD WITH (Hurtigruten).
KRONPRINS FREDERIK, PRINS JOACHIM (Scandlines).
LANGELAND, LOLLAND (Færgen).
LIVERPOOL SEAWAYS (DFDS Seaways), STENA FERONIA (Stena Ro-Ro).
LOCH DUNVEGAN, LOCH FYNE (Caledonian MacBrayne).
LOCH LINNHE, LOCH RANZA, LOCH RIDDON, LOCH STRIVEN (Caledonian MacBrayne).
LYNHER II, PLYM II, TAMAR II (Torpoint Ferries).
MARIELLA (Viking Line), PRINCESS ANASTASIA (St. Peter Line).

Stena Britannica (Rob de Visser)

Freesia Seaways (Rob de Visser)

MERCANDIA IV, MERCANDIA VIII (Stena Line).
MIDNATSOL, TROLLFJORD (Hurtigruten).
MIDSLAND, WESTFALEN (Rederij Doeksen).
MONNIK, ROTTUM (Wagenborg).
MÜNSTERLAND, OSTFRIESLAND (AG Ems).
NILS DACKE, ROBIN HOOD (TT-Line).
NILS HOLGERSSON, PETER PAN (TT-Line).
NORBANK, NORBAY (P&O Ferries).
NORDKAPP, NORDNORGE, POLARLYS (Hurtigruten).
OERD, SIER (Wagenborg).
OILEAN NA H-OIGE, SANCTA MARIA (Bere Island Ferries).
PRIDE OF BRUGES, PRIDE OF YORK (P&O Ferries).
PRIDE OF CANTERBURY, PRIDE OF KENT (P&O Ferries).
PRIDE OF HULL, PRIDE OF ROTTERDAM (P&O Ferries).
PRINCESS MARIA (St. Peter Line), STENA SAGA (Stena Line).
PRINS RICHARD, PRINSESSE BENEDIKTE (Scandlines).
RED EAGLE, RED FALCON, RED OSPREY (Red Funnel Ferries).
ROMANTIKA, VICTORIA I (Tallink Silja Line).
SILJA SERENADE, SILJA SYMPHONY (Tallink Silja Line).
SOUND OF SCARBA, SOUND OF SHUNA (Western Ferries).
SOUND OF SEIL, SOUND OF SOAY (Western Ferries).
SPIRIT OF BRITAIN, SPIRIT OF FRANCE (P&O Ferries).
ST CECILIA, ST FAITH (Wightlink).
STENA ADVENTURER, STENA SCANDINAVICA (Stena Line).
STENA BRITANNICA, STENA HOLLANDICA (Stena Line).
STENA SPIRIT, STENA VISION (Stena Line).
SUPERSPEED 1, SUPERSPEED 2 (Color Line).
WIGHT LIGHT, WIGHT SKY, WIGHT SUN (Wightlink).

Fast Ferries

FJORD CAT (Fjord Line), MAX MOLS (Mols-Linien).
KATEXPRESS 1, KATEXPRESS 2 (Mols-Linien).
RED JET 1, RED JET 2 (Red Funnel Ferries).
WIGHT RYDER I, WIGHT RYDER II (Wightlink).

Freight Ferries

ADELINE, WILHELMINE (CLdN/Cobelfret Ferries),
AEGEAN BREEZE, ARABIAN BREEZE, ASIAN BREEZE, BALTIC BREEZE (UECC).
AMANDINE, OPALINE (CLdN/Cobelfret Ferries).
ANVIL POINT, EDDYSTONE (Foreland Shipping), FINNMERCHANT (Finnlines), HARTLAND POINT,
HURST POINT(Foreland Shipping), WILLIAMSBORG (CLdN/Cobelfret Ferries).
ARROW (Isle of Man Steam Packet), CLIPPER RANGER (Seatruck Ferries), HELLIAR, HILDASAY
(NorthLink Ferries).
AUTO BALTIC, AUTO BANK, AUTO BAY (UECC).
AUTOPREMIER, AUTOPRESTIGE, AUTOPRIDE, AUTOPROGRESS (UECC).
AUTORACER, AUTORUNNER (UECC).
AUTOSKY, AUTOSTAR, AUTOSUN (UECC).
BEGONIA SEAWAYS, FICARIA SEAWAYS, FREESIA SEAWAYS (DFDS Seaways).
BOTNIA SEAWAYS, FINLANDIA SEAWAYS (DFDS Seaways), FINNHAWK, FINNKRAFT (Finnlines).
BRITANNIA SEAWAYS, SELANDIA SEAWAYS, SUECIA SEAWAYS (DFDS Seaways).
CARRIER (Transfennica), SC CONNECTOR (Sea-Cargo), TRADER (Transfennica).
CAPUCINE, SEVERINE (Stena Line).
CELANDINE, CELESTINE, CLEMENTINE, MELUSINE, VALENTINE, VICTORINE (CLdN/Cobelfret
Ferries).
CLIPPER PENNANT (Seatruck Ferries), CLIPPER POINT (DFDS Seaways), SEATRUCK PACE,
SEATRUCK PANORAMA (Seatruck Ferries).

SECTION 8 – SISTERS

Norstream *(J.J.Jager)*

Stena Transporter *(J.J.Jager)*

CORONA SEAWAYS *(DFDS Seaways)*, FINNBREEZE, FINNMILL, FINNPULP, FINNSEA, FINNSKY, FINNSUN, FINNTIDE, FINNWAVE *(Finnlines)*, FIONIA SEAWAYS, HAFNIA SEAWAYS, JUTLANDIA SEAWAYS *(DFDS Seaways)*.
CYMBELINE, UNDINE *(CLdN/Cobelfret Ferries)*.
FRIEDRICH RUSS, PAULINE RUSS, SEAGARD *(Transfennica)*.
GENCA, KRAFTCA, PLYCA, PULPCA, TIMCA, TRICA *(Transfennica)*.
MAGNOLIA SEAWAYS, PETUNIA SEAWAYS, PRIMULA SEAWAYS *(DFDS Seaways)*.
MAZARINE, PALATINE, PEREGRINE, VESPERTINE *(CLdN/Cobelfret Ferries)*.
NORSKY, NORSTREAM *(P&O Ferries)*.
OBBOLA, ORTVIKEN, ÖSTRAND *(SCA Transforest)*.
PAULINE, YASMINE *(CLdN/Cobelfret Ferries)*.
SCHIEBORG, SLINGEBORG *(SOL Continent Line)*, SOMERSET *(CLdN/Cobelfret Ferries)*
SEATRUCK POWER, SEATRUCK PROGRESS *(Seatruck Ferries)*, STENA PERFORMER, STENA PRECISION *(Stena Line)*.
STENA FORERUNNER *(Transfennica)*, STENA FORETELLER *(Mann Lines)*.
STENA TRANSIT, STENA TRANSPORTER *(Stena Line)*.

SECTION 9 - CHANGES SINCE FERRIES 2015-BRITISH ISLES AND NORTHERN EUROPE

DISPOSALS

The following vessels, listed in *Ferries 2015 - British Isles and Northern Europe* have been disposed of - either to other companies listed in this book or others. Company names are as used in that publication.

BALTIC BRIGHT *(Sea-Cargo)* In May 2015 charter ended. Chartered to *UPM-Kymmene* for paper transport in the Baltic.

CAROLINE RUSS *(Transfennica)* In late 2014 charter ended.

CLEMENTINE *(DFSD Seaways)* In November 20914 the charter ended and she returned to CLdN/Cobelfret Ferries service.

CONDOR EXPRESS *(Condor Ferries)* In April 2014 sold to *Seajets* of Greece and renamed the CHAMPION JET 2.

CONDOR VITESSE *(Condor Ferries)* In February 2014 sold to *Seajets* of Greece and renamed the CHAMPION JET 1.

DELTA SPIRIT LODGE *(Tallink/Silja Line)* Never formally renamed and official name remained SILJA FESTIVAL. In May 2015 sold to *Medinvest SPA* of Italy to be used by *Corsica Ferries*. Renamed the MEGA ADREA.

DIEPPE SEAWAYS *(DFDS Seaways France)* In December 2014 charter ended. In February 2015 renamed the STENA SUPERFAST X and placed on the Holyhead - Dublin service.

ESTRADEN *(Mann Lines)* In January 2015 chartered to *P&O Ferries* to operate between Rotterdam and Middlesbrough.

EUROFERRY BRINDISI *(Finnlines)* In October 2014 sold to the *Grimaldi Group* of Italy. In December sold to *Polferries* and renamed the MAZOVIA.

FINNHANSA *(Finnlines)* In October 2014 sold to the *Grimaldi Group* of Italy. Renamed the EUROFERRY EGNAZIA.

FINNSAILOR *(Finnlines)* In January 2015 time chartered to *Navirail*. In February bareboat chartered by them and renamed the SAILOR.

FLANDRIA SEAWAYS *(DFDS Seaways)* In April 2015 sold to *Transportacion Maritima de California* of Mexico and renamed the SAN JORGE.

FOYLE RAMBLER (*Lough Foyle Ferry Company*) In summer 2014 sold to *Waterford Castle Hotel* and renamed the MARY FITZGERALD.

GIRL GRAY (*Arranmore Fast Ferries*) In 2013 sold to *Steve Driscoll* of Liverpool as a fishing charter vessel.

HATCHE (*CLdN/Cobelfret Ferries*) In January 2015 sold to *Alternative Tasimacilik AS* of Turkey.

HYTHE HOTSPUR (*White Horse Fast Ferries*) In August 2014 withdrawn.

LIVERPOOL SEAWAYS (*Navirail*) In January 2015 returned to *DFDS Seaways*.

LONGSTONE (*CLdN/Cobelfret Ferries*) In November 2014 renamed the DORSET. In January 2015 sold to *Finnlines* and renamed the FINNMERCHANT.

MARIN MARIE (*Manche Iles Express*) In September 2014 sold to *Maritime Travel Douya* of Gabon. Renamed the AKEWA JET. Operates between Libreville and Port Gentil, Gabon.

NORMAN ASTURIAS (*LD Lines*) In September 2014 charter ended. Chartered to *Inter Shipping* of Morocco to operate between Tangiers and Algeciras.

NORMAN ATLANTIC (*LD Lines*) In September 2014 charter ended. Chartered to *Cartour & Tourist* of Italy to operate between Salerno and Messina. In December chartered to *ANEK* of Greece to operate between Patras (Greece) and Ancona (Italy). On 28th December seriously damaged by fire but may be repaired.

ODIN SYDFYEN (*Færgen*) In March 2015 replaced by the FYNSHAV and laid up. In April sold to *J&L Shipping AB* of Finland to operate on the Åland Islands domestic service Längnäs - Överö - Snackö. Renamed the ODIN.

PAQIZE (*CLdN/Cobelfret Ferries*) In January 2015 sold to *Alternative Tasimacilik AS* of Turkey.

QEZBAN (*CLdN/Cobelfret Ferries*) In January 2015 sold to *Alternative Tasimacilik AS* of Turkey.

REALT NA MAIDNE (*Arranmore Fast Ferries*) In 2014 sold for further use in the Aran Islands.

REGINA BALTICA (*Tallink*) In April 2015 sold to *Regina Holding SIA* of Latvia.

SATURN (*Caledonian MacBrayne*) In February 2015 sold to *Pentland Ferries*. Renamed the ORCADIA.

SC ABERDEEN (*Sea-Cargo*) In May 2014 sold to *Just Mariiam Shipping* of the USA. Renamed the ABERDEEN.

SCANDINAVIA (*Polferries*) In May 2015 sold to *Ventouris Ferries* of Greece and renamed the RIGEL II.

SCHIEBORG, SLINGEBORG (*CLdN/Cobelfret Ferries*) In November 2014 the agreement with the Stora Enso group ended and the vessels ceased to be operated as part of the *CLdN/Cobelfret Ferries* network. From December 2014 chartered to *SOL Continent Line*.

SIRENA SEAWAYS (*DFDS Seaways*) In April 2015 chartered to *Brittany Ferries* and renamed the BAIE DE SEINE. Entered service in May 2015.

ST. HELEN (*Wightlink*) In March 2015 withdrawn from service.

STENA FERONIA (*Stena RoRo*) In March 2015 sold to *Strait Shipping* of New Zealand and renamed the STRAIT FERONIA.

STENA FORECASTER (*Transfennica*) In January 2015 charter terminated.

STENA FORETELLER (*Transfennica*) In January 2015 charter terminated. Chartered to *Mann Lines*.

STENA NORDICA (*Stena Line*) In March 2015 chartered to *DFDS Seaways* and renamed the MALO SEAWAYS. Operates between Dover and Calais.

VÄSTERVIK (*Gotlandsbåten*) This vessel did not enter service.

WILHELMINE (*P&O Ferries*) In November 2014 the charter ended and she returned to *CLdN/Cobelfret Ferries* service.

Norman Atlantic *(Kevin Mitchell)*

Regina Baltica *(Miles Cowsill)*

SECTION 9 – RECENT CHANGES

Dieppe Seaways *(J.J. Jager)*

Condor Express *(George Holland)*

Stena Nordica *(Gordon Hislip)*

St Helen *(Andrew Cooke)*

SECTION 9 – RECENT CHANGES

YOKER SWAN *(Arranmore Fast Ferries)* In 2014 sold to *Vincent O'Driscoll*, operator of the Baltimore - Sherkin Island Ferry, Co Cork, Irish Republic.

VESSELS RENAMED

The following vessels have been renamed since the publication of *Ferries 2015 - British Isles and Northern Europe* without change of operator.

EXPRESS *(Sea-Cargo)* In January 2015 renamed the SC CONNECTOR.

SPAARNEBORG *(CLdN/Cobelfret Ferries)* In November 2014 the agreement with the Stora Enso group ended and the vessel ceased to be operated as part of the *CLdN/Cobelfret Ferries* network. In January 2015 purchased by *CLdN/Cobelfret Ferries* and renamed the SOMERSET.

COMPANY CHANGES

DFDS Seaways France This is no longer listed separately from the rest of *DFDS Seaways* UK operations following the sale of *Louis Dreyfus Armateurs'* 18% holding to DFDS.

Gotlandsbåten This operator did not begin operations as planned. They may start in 2016 with a different ship.

LD Lines This operator has ceased trading.

Tuule Laevad This operator is now listed as *Saaremaa Laevakompanii*

LATE NEWS

DFDS/MyFerryLink On 7th June DFDS announced that it has submitted a binding offer to Eurotunnel for the charter or purchase of the ferries RODIN and BERLIOZ with an effective date of 2ndJuly 2015. MyFerryLink would cease operations after that date. Eurotunnel announced that it intended to retain the NORD PAS-DE-CALAIS to convey traffic which could not be conveyed through the Channel Tunnel, but it would not be operated by the SCOP, which was later placed in judicial administration. It is anticipated that the BERLIOZ and RODIN will join the DFDS Seaways fleet At the time of going to press no further information is available.

Saaremaa Laevakompanii The MUHUMAA & SAAREMAA will be renamed the GRETE & ANNE-MARIE respectively when moved to the new Elb-Link route in Germany. At the time of going to press no start date has been announced.

FERRIES ILLUSTRATED

AMORELLA	200	CLEW BAY QUEEN	107
ANGLIA SEAWAYS	62	COLOR MAGIC	151
ARMORIQUE	47	COMMODORE CLIPPER	49
ARROW	69	CONDOR EXPRESS	214
ASK	189	CONDOR LIBERATION	2, 26, 49
AUTORUNNER	127	CORRAN	100
BAIE DE SEINE	37	CORUISK	53
BALTIC QUEEN	193	DAGGRI	84
BALTIVIA	171	DIEPPE SEAWAYS	214
BARFLEUR	47	DUCHESS M	138
BERGENSFJORD	165	ECKERÖ	145, 161
BERLIN	178	EPSILON	17, 65
BRAMBLE BUSH BAY	132	EUROPEAN HIGHLANDER	79
CALAIS SEAWAYS	62	FINLAGGAN	50
CARRIER	127	FINLANDIA	143, 159
CLANSMAN	41	FINNHAWK	117

Seven Sisters *(Matthew Punter)*

Other books from Ferry Publications

Folkestone for the Continent 1843-2001

This new book covers the entire history of the Kentish port of Folkestone from its inception in the early years of the nineteenth century until its closure in 2001. Although the history of the port will for ever be linked with Boulogne, other services were operated to Flushing, Ostend, Dunkirk and Calais and are also covered. The book is enhanced with a complete fleet list, traffic statistics and maps of the port at different stages of its development. Price £21.50 plus p&p

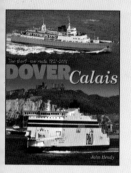

Dover-Calais

This will be an updated version of the Dover-Calais 2009 edition. Written by John Hendy, it covers the history of the most famous ferry crossing in the world but looks in detail at the development and expansion of the ferry operations and the new tonnage which has been introduced since the opening of the tunnel. The bookl includes DFDS and MyFerryLink operations. The title will be richly illustrated in colour and black and white. Now due to published early 2015. Published Autumn 2015. Price £18.95 plus p&p.

TT Line

Since the introduction of the first Nils Holgersson in 1962, this German ferry has been both an innovative and reliable player in the southern Baltic ferry market. Their core Travemunde Trelleborg route has seen no less than six different generations of ferries so far. TT-Line is also known for Olau Line and for a service between Rostock. In 2012 TT-Line celebrated its 50th anniversary. This book captures the fascinating history of TT-Line, their routes and their ships. Price £16.95 plus p&p.

Order online from
www.ferrypubs.co.uk
By telephone on
+ 44 (0)1624 898445
By post from
PO Box 33, Ramsey, Isle of Man IM99 4LP
Please telephone or email for current postage costs.

The Ostend Ferry

This title traces the history of Ostend links with the UK. The publication covers the history of RMT and later the Dover Ostende Line. It also covers the history of the Ostend services to Folkestone Harwich, Ramsgate, Margate and also the other ports from Kent, Essex, and northern England. Also included are the local excursions from Ostend. Wealth of unpublished photos. Price £22.00 plus p&p.

The SeaFrance Years

SeaFrance came into being on New Years Day 1996 after splitting with former partners Stena Line. Although a late starter in the operation of vehicle ferries across the Channel, the fleet that eventually developed was a fine collection of purpose-built ships embodying the best examples of French design and technical advancement that frequently eclipsed their British contemporaries. This book traces the post-war development of French participation in the English Channel, also briefly looking at the Dieppe-Newhaven and Dunkirk-Dover operations which played such an important part in cross-Channel communications. Price £18.00 plus p&p.

Silja Line

Silja Line and Tallink are two of the world's best known ferry companies. This book gathers together for the first time in English their entire histories, from humble beginnings with small steamers to the leisure-oriented cruise ferries of today. Partial bilingual text in Finnish. Price £22.00 plus p&p.

Irish Ferries

In 1973, a newcomer to the Irish ferry scene began sailings between Rosslare and Le Havre. This company would grow from a single ship operator to become Irish Ferries. Today the company is the market leader on the Irish Sea to the UK and France. Price £19.75 plus p&p.